OFFSHORE
High

OFFSHORE

High

Grand Prix Yacht Racing | Big Business | Epic Love Story

STEVE & DORIS COLGATE
And Offshore Sailing School

BY HERB MᶜCORMICK

Design and composition by Claire MacMaster

barefoot art graphic design

Printed by Printworks Global Ltd., London & Hong Kong

First Edition

ISBN: 978-0-998556-59-8

Dedications

For Sailors of All Stripes, On All Seas
(And Those Yet to Be)

For Bernadette Brennan Bernon, our North Star

And Steve and Doris wish to dedicate this book to each other
and to all those friends, clients and employees (past and present)
who supported and continue to support our efforts
to promote the sailing lifestyle.

Contents

Yank & 16 dead in yacht storm; search goes on

Plymouth, England (AP)—Storm-battered survivors of the world's worst yacht-racing disaster straggled into ports along England's southwestern coast yesterday. The death toll was at least 17. All American craft were reported safe.

The Royal Ocean Racing Club, sponsor of the 670-mile Fastnet yacht race from southern Ireland to the English Channel, said that 21 boats sank or were abandoned Tuesday when gale-force winds whipped up mountainous seas that tore through the 306-yacht, 19-nation fleet.

The racing club said that 13 of the victims were British, one was Dutch and one was an American, Frank H. Ferris, who lived in London. The Coast Guard at Land's End, Cornwall, said last night it had found two more bodies, bringing the known death toll to 17.

The American yacht Toscana sailed safely into windswept Plymouth harbor yesterday, the last of 12 American yachts to be accounted for.

An air-sea rescue operation continued as night fell. Twenty-four boats, with crews ranging from four to 12, were still unaccounted for as sailboats struggled one by one into ports or were towed to safety. Rescuers pulled more than 125 survivors from the wreckage of their yachts.

The Fastnet race is the final event in the five-race Admiral's Cup series, held every two years. Ships and helicopters searched the Atlantic off southwest England for bodies and survivors of yachting's worst disaster. By midday yesterday, 21 yachts worth an estimated $4.5 million were known sunk or abandoned.

A spokesman for the Royal Ocean Racing Club said the yachtsmen were warned ahead of time about possible high winds, but once the race started "it is their own responsibility to judge the weather as it occurs."

Unofficial tabulations, based on a

(Continued on page 75)

A crewman is lowered from British naval helicopter to deserted yacht to look for survivors.   AP

Former British Prime Minister Edward Heath drinks a beer after his yacht arrived in Plymouth, England.   UPI

May never sail again, some say

Plymouth, England (Special)—The storm-battered survivors of the worst yacht-racing disaster in history straggled into port yesterday and crew members filled the pubs to talk about it, some unsure they would ever take to the sea again.

The storm that lashed into the fleet of more than 300 yachts from 19 nations left at least 17 dead and destroyed 21 ships while leaving others abandoned in the tossing seas.

"The waves were taller than a three-story house," said British skipper Alan Bartlett, who lost his boat and three crew members.

Bartlett, rescued by helicopter after six hours in the ocean, witnessed the death of his crew members. "After their raft split, the men dropped into the sea and were drowned," he said. "They were my friends."

Stephen Colgate, 43, of New York, an experienced transatlantic sailor, said the waves were the worst he ever encountered. Reached by phone by the Daily News, he described the disaster. Colgate, who skippered the 50-foot Sleuth, said the trouble began when the fleet reached Fastnet Rock in a group just as the Force 10 winds (up to 70 mph) started battering the ships.

"The most frightening fact was the low visibility," he said. "You'd see another boat's light right in front of you and then it would be gone." He attributed the casualties to crews that had never experienced such

(Continued on page 75)

For Turner, a 'great accomplishment'

Plymouth, England (Special)—For Ted Turner, the ferocious storm that took the lives of at least 15 sailors and left 21 sleek yachts destroyed or abandoned only added to the thrill of his victory in the tragedy-scarred Admiral's Cup race.

"This was the greatest sailing accomplishment in a long time," Turner told reporters as he and his 19-member crew relaxed after reaching land. "We weren't really concerned with the conditions, we were concerned with winning."

'Only spray, waves and other yachts'

Turner, the owner of the Atlanta Braves and Hawks and a major television station, won the Fastnet race after adjusting for handicaps. His heavily bottomed boat, Tenacious, crossed the finish line Tuesday evening after completing the 605-mile, four-day race.

"It wasn't the worst weather I've ever known," he said, "but it was the worst while racing." Shrugging off suggestions that he ever feared for the safety of his yacht or crew, he said the only damage sustained was a bent steering wheel. "Of course, during the worst of the storm we could see only spray and waves and other yachts coming at us."

Turner, an experienced yachtsman who won the coveted America's Cup race in 1977, criticized the trend to lighter, sleeker yachts which are more prone to storm damage. Asked why he enjoyed such a difficult sport, he provided the classic answer: "For the same reason guys climb Mt. Everest," he said. "Because it's there."

A clipping from the *Daily News* summed up the unprecedented disaster that was the deadly and infamous 1979 Fastnet Race.

Preface
Plymouth, England
1979

TED TURNER was lit, again, in more ways than one, and he was letting people have it. Oh, boy. There was a time and place for everything, and for heaven's sakes, not to mention simple common decency, this was neither one. Cocktail in hand, Turner was holding court in a noisy hotel pub in Plymouth, England, on the fateful 15th day of August in 1979, and he certainly had cause for celebration. But he was also, certainly, pushing all the boundaries.

Off to the side, nursing her own drink and with plenty to occupy her already worried mind, Doris Colgate—to whom Turner, the well-known media mogul who was also a champion, world-class sailor, was clearly addressing his comments—could only shake her head. She'd seen this movie before.

Late the previous evening, Turner had crossed the finish line off Plymouth aboard his 61-foot yacht *Tenacious*, the provisional winner on handicap time of what would come to be known as the deadliest, most destructive yacht race of all time, the '79 Fastnet; the race was so named for the prominent rock off the coast of Ireland that was the primary feature of the racecourse, which all the boats had to round before returning to the English Channel and the finish line. Four days earlier, a massive fleet of 303 yachts had set forth from Cowes to begin the biennial 605-nautical-mile contest, which descended into utter and complete chaos on the third day when a powerful gale—with 70-knot gusts and 40-foot seas, well beyond the sporty but manageable conditions that had been forecast—ripped across the Irish Sea.

Among the yachts getting creamed in the maelstrom was a 54-foot, U.S.-flagged vessel named *Sleuth*, skippered by a vastly experienced New York sailor and sailing instructor—one who'd raced across the Atlantic on multiple occasions, not to mention competing in the Olympics and for the America's Cup, among countless other races and regattas—named Stephen Colgate.

He was also Doris's husband, Steve, with whom, a little over a decade earlier, she'd fallen head over heels in love at her very first sight.

The 1979 Fastnet would become legendary…for all the wrong reasons. It would spawn several documentaries; numerous post-mortem investigations delving into the seaworthiness and structural integrity of the competing vessels; and a small library of sailing books, including John Rousmaniere's definitive report, *Fastnet Force 10* (the name refers to the prodigious number on the Beaufort scale, an empirical measurement that relates wind speed to observed conditions at sea; one never wants to be boating, or for that matter anywhere but solid terra firma, in Force 10 conditions).

Turner had set foot on sweet, dry land the night before, where he was met by a waiting press corps thirsty for a first-person, first-hand update from a scene that was quickly becoming tragic. Rumors were swirling, unsubstantiated ones. It was clear that many boats had been dismasted or toppled, and that a huge, unprecedented rescue effort was underway (it would ultimately become the largest peace-time rescue operation ever, spanning 8,000 square miles and 4,000 people, in navy vessels, lifeboats, commercial craft and helicopters). But how many boats had come to grief? Furthermore, it was also being reported that there were fatalities, perhaps plenty of them. Had five sailors perished? Ten? Twenty? Nobody had a clue. The only sure thing known at the time was that the storm was still raging. And sailors were still dying.

Into all this uncertainty stepped Turner, with the opportunity to provide both insight and empathy. He chose not to. Instead, when asked by a British reporter about the brutal conditions, he wisecracked, "If it wasn't for these waves and weather (off the south coast of England), you'd all be speaking Spanish right now." (The inference was that the powerful Spanish Armada in the 1500s would've crossed the English Channel and conquered the British Isles centuries earlier, had it not been deterred by a savage storm. Turner never graduated from his alma mater, Brown University—though he did captain the sailing team—but he apparently attended some history classes.) And the only "bitter disappointment" he expressed in those first moments ashore was the remote possibility that some other, smaller boat might squeak ahead of *Tenacious* on corrected time and deny him victory. Winning. Turner made it abundantly clear it was his only concern.

As for the dead and missing? Crickets. As in, silence.

He doubled down when he saw Doris, who happened to be accompanied by Steve's mother, Nina, on a road trip along the southern shores of England that had taken a decided turn for the worse. (Even in the best of circumstances, which these obviously weren't, it would've been a strange journey; Steve's relationship with his mom was, well, "complicated.") Apart from his own, Turner wasn't interested in anybody's feelings.

This became clear when he spied Doris sitting alongside Pat Nye, the wife of another Fastnet skipper sailing under the Stars & Stripes, Dick Nye aboard *Carina* (Steve had also logged plenty of miles aboard *Carina* back on his home waters of Long Island Sound and also in the prestigious, international Admiral's Cup series, and knew the extremely well-sailed and seaworthy boat well). Turner acknowledged the two anxious wives and basically said, loudly, that it was extremely unlikely anybody would see *Sleuth* or *Carina*—or their husbands—ever again.

Yikes.

This whole Fastnet race was an anomaly in the Colgate's marriage, as it had become very rare indeed for the couple to be separated, even briefly. Actually, Doris had sailed plenty of hard miles and races on *Sleuth*, and the sole reason she wasn't alongside Steve at this very moment was because she'd made the decision to have her mother-in-law join her in England for the festivities, and to drive her from Cowes to Plymouth, for the start and finish, respectively.

However, it wasn't just their shared love of sailing that fused them, or even their rock-solid matrimonial bonds. No, Doris and Steve's partnership extended well beyond shared recreational pursuits and their deeply committed relationship. For they were in business together, a business called Offshore Sailing School.

Quite simply, before everything else happened, it's how they met.

Steve had started it in New York City in the mid-1960s, after college and a stint in the service, almost as a whim; he was already one hell of a sailor and it wasn't like he had something else he wanted to do. Doris had discovered Offshore—and sailing and Steve, all at once—as a diversion from a stifling job and a shaky marriage. Once Steve and Doris were together, they found in their work a nearly perfect complimentary balance, a yin and yang to their own best talents and aspirations. Steve turned out to be a natural teacher, with deep knowledge of his subject and an almost intuitive understanding of how to share it. Doris soon learned she had the soul of a burgeoning entrepreneur, and the workaday world at Offshore was also a portal to empowering women and spreading her wings into other fulfilling ventures.

In the final days of the 1970s, having run Offshore together for a decade, they'd built the business into something strong and lasting. Even so, there was no possible way they could've had any notion of what obstacles and adventures lay ahead, personally and professionally, in the ensuing decades to come.

Back on the racecourse, in just about every important metric, Steve Colgate was the antithesis of Ted Turner (though Steve had plenty of experience racing against him, and had deep respect for Turner's gifts as a sailor). Some people find their creative passion in painting, or writing, or music. Steve found his in racing sailboats, a craft that he honed with the same care, devotion and determination as any accomplished Broadway actor. Steve sailed for neither fame or money or notoriety, but for the pure challenges the sport presented him, in all its nuances and competitiveness.

He prided himself on being an amateur competitor, a Corinthian yachtsman, not a professional. When he started racing, there were no such things as pro sailors; the closest applicable comparison was a hired boat captain. These days, there's a clear professional class of sailors who compete for big paychecks. But when, for example, Steve sailed in the Olympics in 1968, anyone paid to play their sport was automatically disqualified. Steve was every bit as good as any "pro," but it was a point of pride that he always played for free.

Furthermore, unlike with Turner, there was no spit or bombast in Steve. In fact, one of his attributes that he was most proud of was remaining calm and cool under pressure: There was no screaming or hollering or histrionics on the boats Steve sailed. Which was another way that he was separated from Turner. Over the years of his own prodigious sailing career, Steve had come to the conclusion that skippers who yell in the heat of competition rarely did well. Turner was a rare exception.

Beyond the competitive sailing arena, there was one other big difference between the pair: Turner was a very wealthy man. And while Steve had been born into a noted and successful American family, and enjoyed a rather privileged upbringing, he was now very much a member of the working class. When he started his business, he did have a trust fund, but it was actually kind of an inside joke: a whopping $62 a month. In fact, when he'd launched Offshore back in the mid-1960s, he slept in a tiny spare room in the school's offices of its East Side-walkup. He couldn't afford two separate rents.

Two years prior to the Fastnet fiasco, the Colgates had endured their first unpleasant Turner encounter, this time together, shortly after the nicknamed "Mouth of the South" had won the 1977 running of the America's Cup aboard *Courageous*, in which he was ably assisted by a prodigal young tactician named Gary Jobson (Turner had stumbled into the winner's press conference completely wrecked on the bottle of Aquavit that he was still swigging).

A few weeks later, Steve and Doris ran smack dab into Turner and his young protégé, Jobson, at a reception for the Cup defenders at the regal Manhattan headquarters of the New York Yacht Club on West 44th Street. Turner had taken it upon himself to mentor the 20-something Jobson, and provide some career advice, and when he saw the couple he just couldn't help himself. "The Colgates!" he blared. "Jobson here is going to start a sailing school and run you guys out of business!" (Many years after, Jobson said that Turner was just being his usual "wise ass" and the last thing he ever intended to do was launch a sailing school: "Oh my god, you'd have to buy all these boats, and the insurance, and you're stuck in one place…I wanted to keep moving and sailing." Plus, he concluded, "That's hard work!")

But Steve and Doris had a difficult time letting it slide. When it came to what they were building at Offshore, it was personal, as they took their business very, very seriously. And now, yet again, here in England, Turner was back at it.

But there in the pub, unfortunately, for all his unnerving bluster and nonsense, even Doris realized Turner had actually raised a couple of very pertinent questions. For instance: How were *Sleuth* and her crew faring in the tempest?

And then, of course, there was the far more pointed one, for which Doris was pining for the answer: Where the hell was Steve?

Even legendary ocean racers have to start somewhere.
Steve was curious about the relationship between wind and sails at an early age.

1

World's Fair
The Sphere and the Obelisk

THE FAMOUS THEME of the 1939 New York World's Fair was "The World of Tomorrow," and it truly was a wondrous glimpse into the future. Divided into seven separate geographic or thematic zones, the 1,200-acre fairgrounds consisted of a remarkable array of pavilions and displays created by the leading architects of the day, all of whom had been encouraged to push the innovation envelope when it came to the building designs and construction materials.

In the Community Interest Zone, the "Electrified Farm" was actually a working farm that showcased the amazing possibilities of electricity, which was becoming more widespread in everyday society. In the Transportation Zone, the centerpiece was the Futurama exhibit in the massive General Motors Pavilion, a 36,000-square-foot building that transported fair visitors over a huge diorama of a fictional America 20 years down the road.

Something called "television" was first introduced to the public at large in the RCA Pavilion, which broadcast President Franklin D. Roosevelt's opening-ceremony speech not only at the Fair but on some 200 sets scattered through the city. At the pavilion itself, stunned fairgoers could see themselves on TV. But RCA also displayed one set in a transparent case, so folks could see the internal components, visual proof that it wasn't a trick or illusion.

Even so, the most extraordinary, iconic edifices at the 1939 World's Fair were a set of towering, monumental structures called the Trylon and Perisphere, designed by noted architects Wallace Harrison and J. Andre Foulihoux; together, they constituted what was known as the Fair's Theme Center, and served as its iconic cornerstone. The Trylon was a towering spire connected by, at the time, the world's longest escalator, to the Perisphere, a giant orb measuring 180 feet in diameter. It housed yet another diorama, this one called "Democracity," a utopian city of the future.

Steve, aloft in Central Park. The boy loved to climb trees.

The modernistic assemblies left a huge, lasting impression on three-year-old Stephen Colgate, who'd come to the Fair with his father, Gib, his mother, Nina, and his older brother, Gil, soon after its opening in the summer of 1939. Together, they made their way up the long circular staircase to the very peak of the 610-foot Trylon, with its commanding views of the entire spectacle. Decades later, he'd recall that trip to "the sphere and the obelisk," as he called it, with clarity. It was, after all, his very first recorded memory.

THE COLGATES HAD not traveled far to the Fair, located in Flushing Meadows in the borough of Queens, from their home on the Upper East Side of Manhattan at 885 Park Avenue, a distance as the crow flies of a dozen or so miles. But on many fronts, the Colgate residence was another world away.

Steve, the middle child of three kids, came into existence on June 25, 1935. Brother Gil arrived in 1931, and younger sister Cornelia, or Nita, in 1938. He was actually born right around the corner from his home, at Lenox Hill Hospital, so named for the tony neighborhood where it was located. Looking back, he'd deadpan, "Talk about your silver spoons."

Indeed, that's because the Colgates of Park Avenue were the descendants of one of early America's great success stories, a devout Baptist—and soap and candle maker, who peddled his wares door-to-door—called William Colgate, whose family emigrated from England in the 1700s. William founded a company in the early 1800s that would ultimately become known as the Colgate-Palmolive Company. Eventually, as his business took off, he and his children became seriously involved with a small Baptist school in upstate New York that would ultimately be named after them: Colgate University.

So, yes, those Colgates.

For Steve, as he grew older, his family's rich history would serve as a complicated, double-edged sword. On the one hand, there's no question that his early and defining years were ones of privilege, comfort and opportunity, with the added benefit of a truly elite education at some of the East Coast's best schools. But later, when he set forth on his own, everyone assumed that because he was a "Colgate," he was also rolling with dough. Which, by the time he reached his early 20s, he most decidedly was not.

At Yale, Gib (front left) competed on the boxing squad.

The primary reason that Steve and his siblings did not inherit a fabulous fortune of their own, they would come to realize, was because of their father, who by many accounts, squandered his. In countless ways, Gilbert "Gib" Colgate, Jr., was a true renaissance man (in his later years, he was a founder of Planned Parenthood) and a terrific sportsman (something that he did, in fact, pass down to son Steve, a very solid all-around athlete). A big-game hunter (he took down tigers, elephants and elk, and their skins, tusks and heads adorned his homes), skier and champion sailboat racer, feats of derring-do came naturally to Steve's dad. For heaven's sake, he was even an Olympic medalist, having earned a bronze at the 1936 Winter Games in the Bavarian Alps in what was then known as "bobsleighing": he was the driver of the two-man American sled, something he picked up on his frequent vacations to Lake Placid.

Certainly, Gib was very talented at many things. But business, alas, was apparently not one of them.

"Daddy was not savvy about dealing with people," said his daughter and Steve's younger sister, Nita. "But he was really good at sports. He played polo in the 1920s and all sorts of things after that. I truly wished that America was like England (at the time), where if you were rich enough not to work, that was fine. You could just do your sports. He was wonderful at that. But when it came to being part of a business, and dealing with people, and negotiations, he wasn't good at all."

Gilbert Colgate Jr., Steve's dad, circa 1925, while serving on the Colgate Company board before the merger with Palmolive-Peet. An all-around athlete, he also medaled in the 1936 Olympic Games at the helm of the two-man "bobsleigh." Steve's mother, Nina, keenly takes in the action (far left, across track).

In fairness, a huge reason Gib Colgate did not possess generational wealth—and to be clear, he was still rich by nearly anyone's standards for much of his life—was a disastrous decision he made near the outset of his career, but one that was motivated by a sense of honor, out of brotherly loyalty.

The company William Colgate founded had several iterations on its way to becoming a corporate behemoth. By the end of the 1800s, William's son, Samuel, was in charge when they introduced Colgate Toothpaste, in jars. Shortly after the turn of the century, they'd repackaged and reengineered the stuff and began mass-producing it in tubes. In 1928, the toothpaste giant merged with the equally colossus Palmolive-Peet soap manufacturer and became the Colgate-Palmolive-Peet Company (it wasn't until 1953 that Peet was dropped from the name).

One of Samuel's six sons, Gilbert, eventually became a partner in the firm (and also ran the perfume division), and had five children of his own: three girls and two boys, Gil Jr., or Gib (Steve's dad), and Robert (Steve's Uncle Bob).

Gilbert Colgate, Steve's grandfather.

When they turned 21, each kid was gifted with a million dollars, tax free, the equivalent of over $12 million today. Gib received his in 1921, soon after his graduation from Yale, which both he and his brother attended, and proceeded to take a grand trip around the world. Ostensibly, his visit to China included a mission to investigate possible Colgate Company business interests. But he also made a side journey to Burma to hunt elephants. Their feet were hollowed out, lined with metal and turned into wastebaskets, which Steve remembers scattered around their houses.

By the late 1920s, around the time of the Palmolive merger, both brothers were still engaged in the longtime family business, with Uncle Bob running one of its division, and Gib on its board of directors, which was undergoing rapid changes. Which is when Uncle Bob got unceremoniously canned. (Uncle Bob was a known tippler, sometimes to excess.) In protest, Gib sold all his company stock, a not-insignificant amount, the value of which over time would eventually be worth a fortune on its own. (The timing was horrendous. On October 29, 1929—"Black Tuesday"—the stock market crashed, leading to the Great Depression.)

Steve said, "If he'd kept it…" His voice trailed off. The inference of riches beyond imagination was clear. "But he was a moral man. He had principles."

Those principles were manifested in the most elemental way possible. No product bearing a Colgate-Palmolive label was ever permitted in the Colgate household again.

BY THE START of World War II, Steve's family had decamped from their grand Park Avenue apartment to a spacious new home on Lloyd Neck, off Huntington Bay, on the North Shore of Long Island. The sprawling, single-level house, designed by the renowned New York architect Merrill Prentice, had a huge living room with 14-foot ceilings and was adorned with a large, lovely painting of Atlantic-class sloops, the timeless Starling Burgess-design that Steve's dad raced often and well. The home was actually built several years earlier, in 1935, and had originally served as a weekend retreat from the city. But once the war started, the decision was made to move to Long Island full time so the children could attend public elementary school in the nearby town of Lloyd Harbor.

"The three of us kids had duties for which we received stars on a chart under the date," Steve would later write in a series of what he called "vignettes" about some of the defining moments of his life. "Every day we had to make our bed, clean our room and sweep the large porch overlooking a lawn that extended to a bluff above our beach

On Lloyd Neck, on the north shore of Long Island, the Colgates lived
in a sprawling home designed by well-known New York architect Merrill Prentice.

at the edge of Long Island Sound. If we did our duties, we received the princely sum of 25 cents a week."

There was plenty of other help around the place as well. "There were a lot of cooks and maids," said Steve's sister, Nita. "There was a butler, and five people working as residential servants. My brother Gil had his own nanny. Mummy could handle two children, but she wouldn't accept taking care of a third."

The move to Long Island, however, was not predicated on the children's education alone. After dumping his Colgate-Palmolive stock, Gib had given Wall Street a whirl and, as Nita was later told, uncharacteristically did quite well with his new investments. Once the war began, he took some of those earnings and started a factory in Amityville, on Long Island's southern shores, to make aircraft parts for the war effort.

This proved to again be disastrous.

The story Steve later got, which was woven into the ever-growing quilt of family lore, was that Gib refused to pay the standard bribes to the parts inspectors. Whatever the actual circumstances, there was an irrefutable result: the business failed. In 1944, the Colgates returned to Manhattan.

The third-grade class photo at the Lloyd Harbor School;
Steve is seated, third from left.

Steve had attended the Lloyd Harbor School for three years, for grades 1-3.

In the spring of '44, in impeccable penmanship on one of his final third-grade assignments, the rather worldly 9-year-old penned this note to his mom:

Dear Mother,

This is to let you know all about our plans for our trip to the Museum on Thursday of this week.

We are planning to take the 9:52 train and to return on the 4:38 from New York which gets here at 5:45. Mrs. Lincoln will bring me home to her house.

I will need to have $1.50 for expenses. If I want to buy anything I must have more as the $1.50 covers my train fare, subway fare and lunch.

With love,

Stephen

Clearly, young Steve had no qualms about navigating the Big Apple. The boy was a native New Yorker.

Upon returning there, the Colgates moved into a new apartment at 55 East 86th Street, a fine but somewhat less-grand address than their former digs on Park Avenue.

Steve was enrolled in the prestigious Buckley School on East 74th Street, an upwardly mobile institution so named for founder B. Lord Buckley, who preached the attributes of a classical curriculum. Steve ran track, mostly cross-country—he'd come to realize he was graced with a high motor and plenty of endurance—and enjoyed his classes, but one thing always amazed him.

Steve, with mother Nina and sister Nita, during his time at Manhattan's prestigious Buckley School.

"I used to walk to school," he wrote. "Looking back on that time, it's hard to imagine how in 1944 to 1948 the son of a multi-millionaire could walk about 14 blocks to school alone and not be kidnapped or harassed. The closest I came to any problems was at a bus stop one time. I think the fare was 15 cents and a boy about my age, but bigger and tougher-looking, asked me for a dime. I gave it to him and he handed it back, saying, 'I was just seeing if I could get it.' Those were such civil and innocent times."

On their 15th floor apartment, the Colgates were one floor above the residence of one Max Wylie, a novelist and advertising executive whose brother, Philip, was the author of the popular science-fiction work *When Worlds Collide* as well as *Generation of Vipers*, a rather scathing non-fiction indictment of American society.

"Max's only daughter was Janice and her bedroom was right below mine," Steve wrote. "I had fun lowering a little basket with messages to her, though I haven't the foggiest what they were, since this was before puberty, so I'm sure they were benign." Alas, poor Janice Wylie would not be long for the world; just a few years later, along with her roommate, she was brutally slain in her Upper East Side apartment in a horrible crime that came to be known as the "Career Girls Murders." Her sad fate was neither civil nor innocent.

In addition to the Wylies, the Colgates also had a truly famous neighbor in their building, the noted English Shakespearian actor Basil Rathbone, who was renowned for his many portrayals of Sherlock Holmes in a long string of films, and who became fast friends with Steve's dad. So much so that, when Rathbone approached him about investing in a new play about Holmes written by his wife, Ouida (Steve liked Basil—"a gentleman"—but had few nice things to say about his haughty missus), he was all in. Rathbone's production opened in Boston, the plan being to stage a limited run there before bringing it triumphantly to Broadway. But the reviews were soul-crushing; it didn't last a week in Beantown, and perhaps inevitably, everyone took a bath.

In those pre-television times, Steve had a brush with show business himself. He loved listening to *The Adventures of Sam Spade* on the radio, which was sponsored by Wildroot Cream Oil, basically an elixir to plaster your hair to your scalp. "The program introduction talked about how Sam Spade's adventures will make your hair 'stand on end.' So, I wrote the company and suggested they create a ditty to the effect that Sam Spade will make your hair stand on end and Wildroot will smooth it down again," he recalled. "Weeks later, I received a 50-page legal document, which I showed to my father asking what this was all about. He said, 'They want to use your idea and not pay you for it.' I ignored it…and about a month later, the ditty was on the air."

It was also during the Buckley years that Steve began "inventing" things, some of which saw the light of day, but mostly hypothetical gadgets and tools and beneficial improvements to society that he'd sketch out in his spare time or when riding the subway. One of his earliest, "The Snow Plow of Tomorrow," was colorfully illustrated and described thusly: "The snow is picked up and put into a trough that loads into the inside of the truck. It is hot in there so the snow melts and goes out the back."

The habit, begun in his youth, carried forth for many years, into adulthood. Steve later kept a brown, pocket-sized spiral notebook with him at all times, and jotted fresh ideas down incessantly, almost daily: new, improved traffic patterns through toll-booths; a better method of sign language; aerodynamic kids' sleds, shaped like sports cars; more efficient token stations at train stations; conveyer belts down the middle of Florida piers for easy loading and unloading of gear and groceries onto pleasure craft; and on and on, page after page. Nothing was too pedestrian for a thorough examination in Steve's fertile mind.

The boy that couldn't stop thinking turned into that very same man.

OF COURSE, all of that—the war, the business drama, school—was still all ahead of young Steve Colgate and his family as they surveyed the World's Fair from the apex of the Trylon. As they prepared to descend, suddenly brother Gil grabbed a cushion near

Steve always enjoyed inventing things, even as a boy.
Later in life, he was awarded a patent for a "jib-magazine"
for quick headsail changes, a precursor to the head-stay foil.

the chute leading down a long tunnel back to sea level and promptly disappeared.

Steve glanced down the tunnel, then up to his mother. "I'm not doing that," he said.

"Neither am I," she replied. "Let's walk down."

The response was remarkable for one reason, and one reason only. It was the first and probably last time that Steve ever said no to an adventure.

Steve's mother, Nina, striking her favorite pose.

2

Setting Sail
The Sea Beckons

IT'S FITTING, given that sailing would become Steve Colgate's vocation and avocation, his raison d'etre, and even how he met his wife, Doris, that his parents' very first date would revolve around a sailboat. Before the many trips, occasionally trying marriage, three children, several lavish homes, and seemingly endless ups and downs—in other words, before every bloody thing else—Gilbert "Gib" Colgate, Jr. and Cornelia "Nina" King went for a sail.

They were, at first blush, an unusual pairing, linked by their deep ties to the gilded circle of Manhattan society, if little else. After all, Gib had both feet planted in the real world—not to mention money and connections—and was beginning to navigate through it. Poor Nina, alas, was still trying to find her way.

It was 1929 when they first met: Nina was 21, Gib eight years older (and embroiled in the Colgate-Palmolive controversy surrounding his brother Bob's dismissal from the company). What nobody could possibly have known at that point was how truly harrowing and unsettling Nina's early life had been. For she had been raised by a woman—her mother, Cornelia Haven Peabody, was better known as "Sunny," which may have been the most ironic nickname ever—whose eccentricities, peripatetic lifestyle and genuinely risqué behavior were not exactly a blueprint for responsible parenthood. The Jazz Age and the Roaring Twenties produced no end of high-spirited socialites like Zelda Fitzgerald and Doris Duke, women who put indelible marks on the cultural zeitgeist, and may have been a tad crazy. But none of them had anything on Steve's grandmother, Sunny Peabody.

The Peabody family was, as they say, "Old Money." Originally from New England, members of the clan eventually settled in Manhattan, and at the tender age of 17, Sunny married a young man from another prominent New York family, Thomas White King, having waited a year until his graduation from Yale. (Steve's sister, Nita, a family historian, described King as "a proper person.")

Nina was the lone offspring from what was a tumultuous union that lasted six years and concluded, as Nita said, in "a scandalous divorce." There were charges and countercharges, all played out in the newspapers; King's alcoholism was reportedly a factor, but hardly the only one. It was many years before Nina learned the actual reason behind her parents' parting; she'd been told her father died, and never saw him again. That's because soon after the legal proceedings were finalized, Sunny took her two-year-old daughter and fled to England. The entire fiasco was an undisputed mess.

But Sunny was just getting started.

She remarried, had a second child, a boy, and they all moved to South Africa until just before the outset of World War I, when they returned to England. At six, Nina's formal education began, in a pair of Catholic convents, the first in London and later in another one down the south coast. These became her most stable homes for the next eight years.

Then Sunny was on the move again, this time to France—with Nina, her stepbrother, and a third child, another boy—after deserting her second husband. "Her behavior became even more scandalous," said Nita. "She didn't send Mummy to school, she said it was too expensive." Nina did return to the states for a year and attended the Rosemary Hall prep school in Connecticut for the ninth grade, but at that juncture her schooling ceased once and for all, something she always regretted. She was then sent back to Europe, where she lived until she was 19, when Sunny passed away. In her own special way, she'd packed a lot of punch (and punches) into her 42 years.

"Grandmother was feckless," Nita said. "She (created) a dysfunctional family. Quite grim for the kids. After she died, Mummy came back to Manhattan where she lived with her grandfather, and tried to fit into a society she'd never been a part of. She'd been raised almost entirely in Europe."

Two years later, Nina caught perhaps the first real break of her life, when she met Steve's dashing dad, Gib.

It was all very happenstance. Nina had been invited out to Long Island's Cold Spring Harbor for a weekend at a friend's house; he happened to be a close mutual pal of Gib, who was racing his long, lean, full-keeled Atlantic-class sloop, *Nichevo* (Russian for "All's Okay"), as he did most Saturdays. Gib needed crew for the day,

Gib Colgate at the helm of his Atlantic-class sloop, *Nichevo*, around 1935,
with his close friends the Hoppins' handling crewing duties.

and his buddy volunteered Nina, who weighed 105 pounds soaking wet and knew absolutely nothing about sailing. But she had other attributes, important ones.

"She was charming, pretty, very delightful and very considerate," said Nita. "Daddy was interested in her and asked her on another date, to the 21 Club, which was then a speakeasy." They had more fun. A romance blossomed. They realized they had a future as a couple.

In essence, then, Steve Colgate's very existence, at least peripherally, could be attributed to sailing.

Steve returned the favor by devoting his life to sailing.

Steve (on left), around the time he first got into sailing, with his best friend, Jim Righter, and Jim's brother.

IT'S SAFE to say that Steve's yacht-racing career began, quite literally, at the bottom: like, in the bilge. There was no way to go but up.

He was nine-years-old when he was offered his first "ride" on a racing sailboat, yet another Atlantic-class sloop, this one owned by Harry Platt, a family friend who just happened to be the president of Tiffany & Company (it's impossible to recount the tale of Steve's youth without a fair amount of name dropping). The Atlantics were wooden boats with open cockpits parked on moorings off the Cold Spring Harbor Beach Club all week while the club members worked in the city. Then, on the weekends, they came to race.

"Those wood boats just sat there in the sun with their topsides drying out and shrinking," Steve wrote. "When they raced on Saturday and the topsides went into the water when heeling, the water flowed in with a vengeance. A light kid was needed to sit in the bilge to leeward and bucket the water out as fast as it came in. I fit the bill and that's how I got started in sailing."

The human-bilge-pump routine might have driven a different kid straight back to the beach and his friends, permanently. But not Steve. "My bailing job didn't turn me off," he said. "It was good fun."

The spark was lit.

The Atlantics were good boats on which to learn—they raced in one-design fleets and all went about the same speed, so your tactics had to be sharp to do well (Steve's dad was very adept, and had a case full of trophies to prove it). By the time he was a teenager, Steve had emerged from the wet bilge and graduated to the fresh air of the foredeck. One of his earliest fond memories is sailing across Long Island Sound to Fairfield, Connecticut, for the Atlantic-class Championships, hosted by the Pequot Yacht Club. There, he rubbed shoulders with yet another famous yachting enthusiast.

"The local sailors put up the visiting sailors and I had the honor of staying with the novelist John Hersey, who won the Pulitzer Prize for *A Bell for Adano* and became a professor at Yale," Steve wrote. "John showed me his gazebo where he wrote and when I commented on the lack of a typewriter—the modern computer of the time—he told me that he wrote everything in longhand. It felt better and could be more easily corrected. John also introduced me to mint juleps, which he made in stainless cups he kept in a freezer. What a pleasant way to end a hot day of sailboat racing."

It's important to note that Steve's formative sailing years were quite unlike those of junior sailors in more recent times, when kids began racing dinghies like Optimists in yacht-club programs at an early age, with coaches and chase boats, and regularly travelled to regattas at distant venues. In fact, he never helmed a boat in competition until he was 14 and his dad rented him a Lightning, a 19-foot centerboard sloop, for the summer.

"I enjoyed it and won a racing series," he wrote, though it was ultimately memorable for a different reason. "I asked my sister, Nita, to crew for me one time…and that's how long that (partnership) lasted. We were doublehanding, though the Lightning is usually raced by a crew of three. Rounding a leeward mark, I called for the centerboard to be lowered all the way. Somehow Nita's fingers got caught and she was in pain. I was singularly unsympathetic as I needed her weight on the windward rail going upwind, and we both were tiny. Funny—she never sailed with me again."

But the real reason Steve loved it all wasn't for the competition: it was for the sheer joy of it. When he was a little older, he'd hop on a Lightning with some friends and sail up to the harbor on Lloyd Neck called "Sand City," and he and his mates would throw the anchor over the side and quaff a few beers. They'd then sail the length of Cold Spring Harbor back home after the sun went down, right up to a mooring. "What fun," he wrote. "Nothing untoward happened, but alone and away from parents helped develop independence."

It wasn't all fun and games, however. There were lessons in seamanship and safety at sea as well. Serious ones. Like the time he rescued a pair of kids from what could have been a catastrophe on Long Island Sound.

Bombing around on a midweek September day with his pal, Johnny Trask, on his dad's Atlantic, the boys had the waters almost all to themselves, with the exception of a charter fishing boat. Well, almost to themselves.

"We spotted something in the distance that looked like a floating log and the flapping wings of some birds," Steve wrote. "I suggested we sail over and take a look. It turned out to be a Lightning class sailboat with two young kids in the water—maybe 12 or 13 years old—which was getting cold late in the season. They were too weak and light to right the boat and bail it out. They had been at a regatta in Connecticut the day before and were sailing home to Long Island. They had set a spinnaker to gain some speed and then did a 'no-no'—they cleated the spinnaker sheet to have a sandwich and a gust of wind caused the boat to capsize."

Steve and Johnny got the kids aboard and realized they had hypothermia, so they stashed them in the Atlantic's little cuddy-cabin wrapped in spinnakers. They'd pulled the extremely lucky youngsters from the drink in the nick of time. Steve sailed over to the fishing boat and got them to call the Coast Guard to tow the Lightning back, then sailed his capsized passengers safely to shore.

Steve's good-Samaritan deed would pay dividends some 15 years later, when he advertised for a model maker to craft a scale model of a Soling for teaching purposes at his sailing school. He almost immediately got a phone call from a New York lawyer whose hobby was making models. When Steve asked the price, he was told $100. "How can you do that so cheaply?" he wondered. The reply stunned him: "I owe you one. Remember those two kids you saved on Long Island Sound. Well, I was one of them."

Besides the heroics, around the same time, he learned something else about sailing that would stand him well in the future: you could make a little coin from it.

In his later teens, he earned some spending money taking care of a handful of boats at the Seawanhaka Yacht Club on Oyster Bay. His favorite, by far, was a meticulous wood yacht called *Gray Lady*, built at the renowned German boatyard, Abeking & Rasmussen. Steve was in awe of the joiner work and craftsmanship, and was invited along for many a race and cruise, which he thoroughly enjoyed. But what he remembers most about the *Gray Lady* days are the aromas: the wonderful smell of

The meticulous *Gray Lady* gave Steve his first real taste of "proper yachting,"
an experience he thoroughly enjoyed.

Two generations of Colgates: Steve treats his dad to a breezy sail aboard *Gray Lady*.

the mahogany and, after a deep sleep on one of the cozy berths in the main saloon, waking up to the smell of frying bacon and percolating coffee. It was all heaven on earth, or better yet, at sea.

By the time he was 19, Steve was a very competent sailor who certainly had acquired some solid skills, but he knew nothing, really, about bluewater ocean sailing, his experiences being limited to the rather confined waters of Long Island Sound.

That was about to change. In a big way.

LIKE SO many occurrences in Steve's life, kismet played a prominent role. Which is how, at the age of 19 in 1955, he found himself in Cuba, aboard the 72-foot yawl *Mare Nostrum* (Spanish for "My Sea"), preparing to sail in a 4,200-nautical mile transatlantic race from Havana to San Sebastian, Spain. As he wandered the decks familiarizing himself with the boat, he had no idea that he was about to undergo a defining, life-changing experience.

After all, just four short days earlier, he'd been back in Connecticut at a coming-out party for a young debutante in Greenwich. But fate works in mysterious ways.

That Sunday, Steve's mom, Nina, had been playing golf with a friend whose cousin was Woody Pirie, a scion of a wealthy Chicago department-store clan. The well-known Florida yachtsman was a former Star-class World Champion and owned a fast cruising boat called *Hoot Man* that regularly cleaned up at the highly competitive Southern Ocean Racing Conference. Pirie had signed on as a watch captain aboard *Mare Nostrum* for the upcoming Transat contest, which started a scant week later, and was having trouble rounding up English-speaking crew for his watch.

"Do you think he'd like to ask Steve?" Nina wondered to her friend.

A call was placed to Woody. "Yes, I would," he replied. Woody had one stipulation: "I want Indians. I don't want chiefs."

When Steve's dad, Gib, put the idea on the table, he added, "Think about it. It can be dangerous. The sea isn't a lady."

"I thought about it for two seconds," Steve said later. "And said, 'I'm going.'"

Last-minute airline tickets for Havana were hastily purchased. In the relative wink of an eye, Steve was in Cuba, preparing to go to sea. As if it was surely meant to be.

Mare Nostrum's owner was a Spanish millionaire named Enrique Urrutia, who Steve remembers as a "fairly pudgy guy in his thirties, a really nice fellow." But Enrique was a keen sailor, and Steve was very happy to be aboard. Decades later, he'd still remember the thrill of motoring out to the starting line "amidst all sorts of spectator boats with horns blaring." He was a long way from Cold Spring Harbor.

But Steve quickly found out Woody wasn't joking about wanting "Indians." Steve was allowed nowhere near the helm, which was Woody's domain. Instead, his primary duty was laying down on the foredeck, to reduce windage, with his eyes peeled on the jib luff (telltales were yet to be invented), and calling the trim: whether to steer up or down, or ease or sheet the sail.

It was somewhat tedious work. Until it got scary.

Mare Nostrum was off Cape Hatteras on the proverbial "dark and stormy" night and Steve was in his usual position on the bow, which was pitching and tossing in the rising seas. At one stage the boat plunged deep into the sea and Steve found himself completely underwater—these were the days before safety harnesses and jack lines—and damn near floated away. "The hell with this," he thought, and started to make his way aft, when there was another commotion; his shipmates were trying to reef the

The accomplished Florida yachtsman Woody Pirie, a Star-class
world champ and the owner of a quick racer/cruiser called
Hoot Man, was Steve's ticket to his first Transatlantic race.

mainsail when the maneuver went sideways and the winch spun out of control, with its whirling handle chipping the bone of the sailor trying to tame it.

But that was nothing compared to a short time later, when another "all-hands-on-deck" situation arose, this time when a spinnaker flailed out of control and got stuck under the yacht, on its keel, effectively stopping it. The resulting pressure on the mizzen staysail took down the mizzen mast about two-thirds of the way up the spar.

"It was a mess like I had never seen before," Steve said. "Pandemonium. I thought, 'Oh my god, what's happening, how can we survive this chaos?' But we got it together. And Enrique said, 'Oh that mast was too tall, with too much sail, anyway.' It was actually refreshing, something I learned from: Don't worry about what happens, we'll just take care of it. Things will always get better."

Aboard *Mare Nostrum*, Steve was relegated to the foredeck.
When the mainsail winch failed, a firm lashing served as a jury-rig.

And by the time *Mare Nostrum* was in mid-Atlantic, in a groove, Steve had another revelation: "I was good at it. I didn't get seasick. I was willing to do anything and everything on the boat, whatever was necessary. I felt this was something I could be very good at."

Mare Nostrum went on to win the race, nipping its main rival, another 72-footer called *Ticonderoga*, a classic L. Francis Herreshoff-design owned by the rental-car magnate John Hertz, by over a day. *Ti* was quick, but *Mare Nostrum* was better sailed.

And to the victors went the spoils.

Woody and Enrique had taken a shine to Steve, and invited him to a lunch hosted by Spain's dictator, Generalissimo Francisco Franco, aboard his private yacht. Steve knew of his sadistic reputation, yet found him "small and friendly," then noticed the high-powered harpoon mounted on the bow for his favorite sport, harpooning whales. And as it happened, Juan Carlos, the future king, was also there; he took a liking to Woody's daughter, and Steve met a local gal, and the four of them hit the nightclubs of San Sebastian. That was before he went to Pamplona for the running of the bulls, drinking red wine out of leather Bota bags.

"I just remember thinking, 'What's not to like about this ocean-racing life?'" he said.

The victors! The crew of *Mare Nostrum* dockside in Spain after knocking off *Ticonderoga* in the 1955 Transatlantic race from Cuba. Steve is kneeling at left, Woody Pirie is center, and owner Enrique Urrutia is in white at the upper right.

The magical summer continued when Enrique pulled him aside and said, "Now that you've sailed the longest race in the world, how would you like to join us for the *best* race in the world?" Which is how Steve crewed in his first Fastnet, the classic, English, biennial 605-nautical-mile race from Cowes, around Fastnet Rock off the coast of Ireland, and back to Plymouth.

By now, *Mare Nostrum*'s 16-man crew was an efficient, well-honed machine, and they proved it by setting a new race record, and in the process, after a voyage of three days, 23 hours and 48 minutes, becoming the first boat in the history of the event to knock it off in under four days.

There would be another half-dozen transatlantic races in Steve's future, and almost 30 years later, he'd again sail on a record-breaking Fastnet Race yacht, a state-of-the-art Maxi he couldn't have conjured in his wildest dreams in 1955. But that first crossing, and Fastnet, on *Mare Nostrum* were special. What he learned, what he saw—and most importantly, what he felt—set the table for the countless nautical adventures yet to come.

Steve said, "Everyone had a job, everyone knew we had each other's backs, everyone was there for the challenge, and the communal and personal rewards of being able to say, 'I did it! We did it! Together!'

"Thus I found my niche. I loved the sea, the communing with nature, the competition… And I was good at it. Those first races changed the direction of my life. Forever."

And little did he know, but he was just getting going.

The graduate: Steve puts St. Paul's School behind him, 1953.

3

Growing Up
The Preppie, the Yalie, the Wild Blue Yonder

THE LIST of alumni from St. Paul's School, the prestigious, highly selective prep school in Concord, New Hampshire, is long and distinguished. It includes publisher William Randolph Hearst; politicians John Kerry, the U.S. senator, and John Lindsay, the mayor of New York; Pulitzer Prize-winning historian Samuel Eliot Morison and *Doonesbury* cartoonist Garry Trudeau, who also won a Pulitzer; Robert Mueller, the former FBI director and Special Counsel in the 2019 investigation of Russian interference in the election; and a whole parcel of Vanderbilts, including Cornelius Vanderbilt III, who served as commodore of the New York Yacht Club and won the America's Cup aboard his massive sloop *Reliance* in 1903.

Add to that roster of high achievement a distinguished member of the illustrious National Sailing Hall of Fame: Steve Colgate.

After his elementary school years at Buckley School in Manhattan, Steve was feeling quite chuffed about his acceptance to "SPS," as it is known to insiders. That bubble was unceremoniously burst when he discovered, to his mild chagrin, "It turns out I'd been enrolled there since birth. Yes, they had me signed up pretty early."

Steve's gold-plated education continued at two bastions of American private education: SPS and, later, Yale University, in New Haven, Connecticut, which his father, brother, uncle and many other close relatives had attended. He was a good student and did well in school; afterwards, a stint in the United States Air Force rounded out his leafy formal studies with a good, hard dose of real-world pragmatism, not to mention some equally enlightening follies. But throughout those formidable years of maturing and growing up, there was another consistent thread that tied together all the lessons and, in defining his character, proved

Steve on his steed, the inappropriately named "Old Buck," at the Sunlight Ranch. Road trip: Nita, Steve and Gil on the family vacation to Wyoming, 1948.

every bit as enlightening and essential—not to mention sheer fun—as any degree or promotion he ever earned—Travel.

The Colgates were always enthusiastic travelers and Steve remembers his trips with far more detail than anything he ever picked up in a classroom. In 1948, his parents corralled their three kids for a grand, summer-long, cross-country road trip. "We stopped along the way," Steve wrote. "Hotels like Holiday Inns were few and far between. Our greatest pleasure was reading the Burma Shave signs we passed. These were wonderful rhymes with about two lines on each sign posted about 100-yards apart. Brother Gil became a great poet in my mind, and though he wouldn't admit it, I bet Burma Shave was his initial inspiration."

Their ultimate destination was the Sunlight Ranch, a dude ranch near Cody, Wyoming. "We drove through some desert-like areas and, since water was scarce and cafes few, we had canvas water bags strapped to the two front fenders of our Chrysler," Steve recalled. "The canvas was designed to seep water, so evaporation kept the bulk of the water cool. I thought this was amazing."

The entire experience was idyllic. Steve spent his days fishing for trout, hunting gophers with his trusty 22-caliber rifle, and riding a docile horse that for some reason was called "Old Buck," though bucking was the last thing on the steed's mellow mind. "That was one beautiful summer vacation," said Steve.

There were also fairly regular sojourns to Bermuda, where Steve's mother, Nina, had close friends. Steve would eventually sail *twenty-one* Newport Bermuda Races, but he fell in love with the island outpost when he was a kid. Riding bikes all over the isle, flying kites with local kids: It was all very good. The one close call came when he was playing with bows and arrows and slipped on a hill just when a friend had fired one off: "It whizzed just over my shoulder next to my head. I lead a charmed life."

But Steve's first real taste of true adventure, even before the epic transatlantic race on *Mare Nostrum*, was a bicycle trip to Europe with several classmates—and a college-aged chaperone named Dick Pierson—on one of his summer breaks from SPS. It all began with a very different sort of transatlantic crossing, on an Italian Home Lines ocean liner from New York to Barcelona, Spain. "I remember on a rough night taking a girl my age up to the bow of the ship and we ducked behind the bulwarks as the waves crashed over it," he said. "Then, suddenly, the whole area was lit up with searchlights and a loudspeaker said in accented English, 'Get off the fucking bow,' or words to that effect."

From Barcelona, the gang hopped a train to Southern France—they decided to skip cycling through the Pyrenees—where they purchased bikes and began their journey in earnest. "We camped out in fields and stayed in youth hostels, as cheaply as possible," Steve said. "We visited a fair one evening and as we were leaving, I got pinched on my butt. I was surprised and expressed it. Dick explained that it was a message from a nearby French whore."

Apart from that monkey business, it was all eye-opening. They rode the Maginot Line—the series of forts and barriers along the French border that was meant to deter the Germans from invading, which proved to be of minimal success—and were startled to see the difference between the post-World War II ruins in France and the quite tidy towns in Germany once they'd crossed the borderline. This was history come to life. In Dusseldorf, Dick talked his way onto a Dutch barge sailing up the Rhine River to Holland, where the boys stashed their bikes in the bow and took over the forecastle. When it was all over, they sold their bikes and hopped a four-engine Lockheed Constellation prop plane for the return flight, which took just this short of forever.

It had all been, to say the least, a formidable exercise. "We learned so much about other people," Steve said. "It was very worthwhile."

Of course, so was SPS. Though it did have its moments.

Perhaps because of her own convent-based education, and deeply held religious beliefs, Nina had secured Steve's spot in the Episcopalian-based institution, St. Paul's School, at a very tender age. And while most of his ancestors were also devoted Christians, starting with family patriarch William Colgate, Steve wasn't particularly buying any of it ("I tried and I just couldn't believe there was a God"). The daily chapel services—and twice on Sundays!—were small tortures administered far too regularly for his taste. The only part he ever really liked was evensong, the calm hymns and period of reflection at the end of the day.

Steve's own true religion, he was discovering, was in nature, the great outdoors. And luckily, SPS had plenty to offer, which he drank in deeply. "Near the soccer field was a brook in the adjoining woods," he wrote. An avowed loner, "I would sit by myself for hours contemplating the stream. The leaves changing to bright colors each fall was fascinating, but in the five falls I was there, one was amazing. A flash frost made every maple tree change from green to bright reds and yellows overnight. I was captivated."

His vigils continued in the winter, where he'd fashion a makeshift igloo on the ice of a nearby pond, and huddle there for hours, just thinking, until the cold drove him ashore.

But Steve also found solace of a different sort on another sheet of ice. At SPS, he fell in love with hockey.

It was impossible to get away from the sport; the first ice-hockey games in the United States were played there in the 1870s. He never made the varsity team (though he got better as he grew and became stronger, and went on to make the freshman team at Yale), but the intramural league was tough and competitive: each of the school's three sections had nine teams apiece, so there were 27 different squads at SPS. He'd arrived hoping to be on the ski team, but it was a very minor sport, and his days on the ice more than made up for it.

"We played on ponds," he said, "on natural ice over three-feet thick. There were nine rinks in all. And they had these big New Hampshire 'work horses' with spikes in their hooves that towed shavers to shave the ice. The spikes left these little holes in it. It was so beautiful, so natural. It was just an incredible place."

Sadly, however, one of Steve's other lasting memories of SPS is dark. Very dark. All because of an Episcopalian minister, his dorm master upon his arrival at the school,

Among other things, St. Paul's instilled in Steve a deep love of hockey,
which he went on to play as a freshman at Yale
and in a semi-pro league during his Air Force years.

who shall be referred to as Reverend H.

"Unfortunately," Steve wrote, "he liked little boys and particularly me."

Steve's first dormitory was laid out with small alcoves for each student, with a bed and a bureau situated behind a curtain on a rod, for privacy. Reverend H "wrote me love letters and every night when we all retired, he would do his rounds, slide the curtain and kiss me goodnight. I have never gotten over it and to this day can hear the squeak of the curtain hooks on the steel rod signaling his approach."

To add insult to injury, the next summer, Reverend H paid a visit to the Colgate household in New York and Steve refused to greet him, hiding in his bedroom, until forced to join everyone, and scolded for treating guests poorly. "I gave Mom all the love letters I had received from him and expected to be supported," he remembered.

"I wasn't, and it was one of my great disappointments with my parents."

It wasn't until much later, when Steve fell in love—really fell, hard and forever, for the love of his life—that he was finally able to put to rest any questions about his sexuality, and the concerns that still shamed him about why this Reverend H had chosen him. For these clarities, naturally, he was eternally grateful.

THE YALE UNIVERSITY sailing team has consistently been a powerhouse in collegiate sailing circles, and its long list of All-Americans, Olympic medalists and America's Cup veterans is a who's who of legendary sailors: Briggs Cunningham, Stan Honey, J.J. Fetter, Peter Isler, Steve Benjamin, Jonathan McKee…the list goes on and on.

One notable exception to that stellar gang of alumni, especially considering his long contributions to and accomplishments in the sport, is…Steve Colgate.

"I didn't even know there was a sailing team," he said, many years later. "It wasn't well-known, that's for sure."

No, for Steve, there were other games to play; after his year on the freshman hockey team (that included an unfortunate loss to St. Paul's), he continued playing intramural hockey and even gave the swim team a brief try. And there were other pressing priorities.

"After SPS—and I remember thinking how much more I could have learned there if they'd pushed me harder—Yale was a snap for me," he said. "So, I partied." And once he'd put his freshman year in New Haven behind him, he was back to one of his favorite places—the road.

It was another trip out west, this time with a couple of pals from Yale in his dad's borrowed '53 Ford, a far different excursion than the cross-country family trip years earlier.

"My father asked how much money we were taking with us," Steve wrote. "We said $200 each. He scoffed and said, 'You will be calling for money in two or three weeks.' Those were 'fighting words' and we were determined not to call and ask. By Utah, we started looking for jobs, any jobs. Nothing. We were camping by the side of the road and cooking on campfires. We got to Washington and were down to a buck apiece."

There, Steve's "charmed" existence again came into play. On the hunt for a can of soup in a small store, he made an off-handed remark to the clerk about job possibilities and learned the pea farm down the road was hiring seasonal workers for the harvest. Suddenly, he and his mates were earning $1.50 an hour and knocking off

14- to 16-hour days, complete with basic meals and a lumpy mattress in a communal bunkhouse with an eclectic group of hardscrabble survivors. It was a long way from the pleasures of Long Island…and could scarcely have been better. A couple weeks later, they'd recouped their original grubstake of $200 and carried on.

There was one adventure after another. They rigged up an "aquaplane" they towed behind the car and went tearing down the roads adjacent to the many irrigation canals to see who could go fastest. They came upon a Boeing factory, snuck in, and climbed into the prototypes for the B-52s going into production. In Glacier National Park, they made friends with the many European kids who'd obtained summer jobs there. They even scored another gig picking cherries, though they were paid by the bucket and the ripened fruit was so delicious, they ate most of their potential earnings.

"After this wonderful trip," Steve said, "we returned home and were able to tell our parents that we came back with $207 each—a single-digit profit of about seven bucks. Success!"

While Steve didn't sail competitively during his Yale years, he did manage some yachting. During one spring break, he and some mates chartered a boat in the Bahamas and had a grand time of it. Over another break he ventured to Charleston, South Carolina, to help his brother Gil outfit an old wood boat he'd purchased. Later on, that summer, he helped bring it north up the Intracoastal Waterway, and had an unexpected triumph regarding his ever-expanding boat-handling skills.

Brother Gil's old yawl, *Mandela*, aboard which Steve wowed a dockside crowd in a tight docking maneuver on the Intracoastal Waterway.

"One evening under power, we needed to dock the boat at a marina for the night," he wrote. "We passed one that had a long dock parallel to the waterway with only one empty space left. There was about 50-feet between two large commercial boats; our boat was about 40 feet. I went past the marina down-current in about two knots of current and found enough space to turn around and head back into it. When opposite the space, I throttled back so we were just stemming the current and motionless over the bottom.

"As often happens, a group of spectators came out to see a boat attempt to dock (in such a tight spot), including a man and his young son. I turned the bow of the boat about five degrees from dead into the current and started to crab sideways. We moved sideways right into the slip and tied up. The man turned to his boy and said, 'Son, that's the way to park a boat.' For a young college kid, wow, was I proud!"

But it was a decision Steve made midway through his time at Yale that radically changed the trajectory of his life for the next several years. With the Korean War in full swing, he realized he wanted to be in control of his own military duty, and that given a choice, he'd prefer to be an officer, not an enlisted man. He tried to get into Yale's Naval ROTC program but flunked the eye test. Ironically, that wasn't an issue for the Air Force ROTC. In he went.

Perhaps somewhat belatedly, it occurred to him that he should probably find out if he liked flying, so he signed up for flight lessons at the New Haven Municipal Airport. Thanks to his sailing experience—years later, after he'd started his Offshore Sailing School, he discovered pilots pick up the sport quickly and easily—he was a natural, and after the minimum requirement of eight hours of training, he was flying solo.

However, a couple of incidents

Flyboy: Steve attended an Air Force ROTC summer camp in 1956 following his junior year at Yale.

gave him pause about a career in the sky. The most startling came on a day he was practicing in a single-engine Piper Cub as the breeze built and built. "As I approached to land, the wind kept me high up, like a glider," he wrote. "There was an Eastern Airlines passenger aircraft waiting for me so they could take off. I figured if I took the time to go around again and let them take off, the wind was increasing so much I might have trouble controlling my plane. I had been taught how to burn off altitude by side slipping, so I did it from about 300 feet. I wound up landing in the middle of a field rather than the end of the runway… I taxied to the hangar and never piloted an aircraft again."

At that juncture, having concluded he might not survive the five-year commitment he'd need to make to become an Air Force pilot, he opted instead for the two-year active-duty obligation if he remained on the ground.

He still got some Air Force flight time, including one memorable spin during an ROTC summer camp at Wright-Patterson Air Force Base in Columbus, Ohio.

"Part of the indoctrination was a ride in a T-33 training jet," he wrote. "The pilot was in the forward seat and the passenger right behind him, with dual controls. The pilot was known to be a hotshot and had committed himself to getting every ROTC guy airsick. I was the fifth person to ride with him and he had a 100-percent score so far. I knew from sailing that if you want to avoid seasickness, it is best to steer and look at the horizon. By steering you can feel the direction of the boat even though there is a time lag.

"So, I held lightly onto the backseat stick control of the T-33 and had a split-second advance warning of any maneuver that the pilot initiated," he continued. "He put the plane through the ringer. He did a low-altitude pass (about 10 feet off the runway) over the field and pulled up vertically. He claimed to have pulled six G's… and we didn't have G suits on. My vision went pink as the blood drained from my head. Then he flew straight down from about 10,000 feet at about 350 knots. He was playing 'chicken' with me and I was about to cave and suggest it was time to pull up. When he did, I guessed we had maybe 1,000 feet left at the bottom of the plunge. Anyway, sailing saved the experience for me. I didn't get sick."

That was Steve's first wild Air Force ride. It wouldn't be his last.

ON JUNE 25, 1958, Steve sat down with pen and paper and, in neat longhand, began composing a letter. "Dear Mom & Dad," it began. It was his 23rd birthday and, having just that morning reported to duty at Langley Air Force Base adjacent to Newport News, Virginia, he'd received one hell of a present.

"I'd better write now because it looks like I'll be mighty busy," he continued. "They've made me Supply Officer for the 498th Bomb Sq. I'm taking the place of a Captain who's leaving in a few days. They were in desperate straits with no substitute and by dogging the Commander they got me—poor guys. Usually they send you to supply school, or (start you off as) an assistant supply officer, but not for me. They also usually give a newcomer about three days to get acclimated, processed, etc., but I have to start work tomorrow at 7:15. They figure I'll just have to sink or swim."

It had actually been a little over a year since Steve's graduation from Yale; the Air Force had left him in limbo until a posting opened up. He'd spent that time working for a company called H.A. Callahan in Mamaroneck, New York, a small operation that nonetheless marked his initial foray into the marine industry.

"Mr. Callahan was a promoter of a product called 'Chilled Varnish,'" he recalled. "I thought it was a gimmick. You put a can of this varnish in a bucket of ice and used it cold. It would spread out evenly on a warm surface. I don't think he had a special varnish that he bought wholesale from a paint company, just a (novel) way of applying it. He took out full-page ads in *Yachting* magazine and sold a ton of it."

A few years later, *Yachting* would play a very influential role in his life. But first he had to knock off his military commitment. To that point, his travels had been fairly widespread for a young man, and totally enjoyable and educational. Now, thanks to the Air Force, he was about to get a much larger taste of the big, wide world.

It started quickly. Three days after assuming the role of supply honcho for the B-57 squadron, he'd signed off on several million dollars-worth of planes, engines, gear

You're in the Air Force now: Second Lieutenant Stephen Colgate, supply officer, 498th Bombing Squadron, Incirlik Air Base, Turkey, 1958.

Prior to reporting for the Air Force in '58, Steve (far left) knocked off a Class B victory in that year's Newport Bermuda Race aboard *Touche* with fellow crewmen Bob Van Nostrand, Jim Feglia, Larry Gleason, *Touche*'s designer Bill Tripp, Frank Lawson, Alan Smiles and owner Jack Potter.

and what not. He was astonished, and secretly worried that if the stuff went missing, he'd have to personally pony up for it. A long week later, the Middle East exploded. The 1958 "Lebanon crisis" was yet another dust-up in the region's endless history of religious and political uprisings, and President Dwight Eisenhower responded by mobilizing a huge force of personnel that ultimately occupied Beirut. In support of that operation, Second Lieutenant Colgate was immediately transported to the Incirlik Air Base in Turkey, outside the city of Adana, where he spent the next hundred days living in a tent until the situation was stabilized. (It was hard to believe, but roughly one month earlier he'd been driving Jack Potter's sloop *Touche* through the Gulf Stream en route to a class victory in that year's edition of the Newport Bermuda Race.)

Later, Steve would write about his early Air Force days in a report entitled "Morale at Adana." In it, he sounded literate, level-headed, righteous, indignant...and plain-old pissed off, with prejudice.

"The most important aspect of good morale is pride," he began. "There must be a pride in the outfit, a pride in the job being done, and a pride and respect of its leaders. With this trait, no discomfort is too great to be endured, no job too difficult to handle.

"This pride," he construed, "did not exist at Adana."

It took another eight pages to get things well and truly off his chest. The problems there were manifold. To begin, everyone who arrived was immediately placed under the umbrella of the 498th squadron, losing whatever organizational identity they'd arrived with, much to their chagrin. Many of his fellow airmen let their beards grow out, and were a scruffy lot compared to the squared-away, clean-cut Army outfits that passed through. The "leaders," such as they were, were largely career officers who felt their time in Adana was short, so didn't bother with the simplest tasks, like ordering the building of clean latrines, which were just filthy. On and on it went.

"The lack of pride in the outfit, in the job being done, and in its leaders was not inherent," he concluded. "It was a by-product of disillusionment caused by unrealistic indoctrination."

From those jolly days in Turkey, Steve said, "They sent me to Amarillo, Texas, to supply school, to learn what I'd already been doing for three months. Typical service." His time in Texas was punctuated by another strange occurrence; each day after school, he'd lace up his skates to practice or play semi-pro hockey with the local team, followed by massive dinners at his favorite Amarillo home-style restaurant, which served giant platters of tasty grub to all the base's hungry young servicemen.

"At the end of the supply course, I was asked where I would most like to be 'permanently' stationed," he wrote. "The most popular selection at that time was Germany, so I put that down. Of course, I was sent halfway around the world in the opposite direction—to Tokyo!"

To say that Steve enjoyed his detachment to Japan would be to traffic in understatement. "It couldn't have been better," he said.

The gig at Fuchu Air Base, just outside Tokyo, was super sweet in infinite ways, and more than made up for his miserable deployment to Turkey. The Air Force had generously shipped overseas his blue '53 Ford, so he had wheels, though it was simple enough to hop a train anywhere he wished to go. He'd take off with some pals and play tourist for long weekends, downing sake and beer in the bar car all along the way.

His duties also presented plenty of opportunities to see many sights: "One of my tasks as the supply office for the weather headquarters at the base was to visit weather detachments throughout the Far East… I made a trip to Eniwetok Atoll where the Bimini atomic tests were coordinated. What a miserable piece of sand with relics of World War II on the beaches. But the swimming was exotic…

"I made another trip to Cheju Do, South Korea, a little island off the southern coast that housed North Korean prisoners during the Korean War. The duck and pheasant hunting was incredible. After inspection trips, our team would bring back about 30 of each per person…

"Another trip was to Iwo Jima and again, I inspected (the outpost) in record time and walked up to the top of Mount Suribachi and the monument there for the iconic photograph of the raising of the American flag. There was a plaque of the beautifully selected words of Admiral Nimitz, which I remember to this day: 'Among the Americans who served on Iwo Jima, uncommon valor was a common virtue…'"

Steve often says he's lived a blessed existence, which was probably the case in an incident near the end of his deployment. He wrote, "I palled around with another 2nd Lieutenant and one time we took two Japanese girls to dinner in Shinjuku and later had after-dinner drinks in a second-floor club. A Japanese (fellow) who was covered with tattoos on a solid blue background pulled up a chair to our table. The tattoos were a sign that he was a member of one of the violent gangs that made Shinjuku a dangerous place for U.S. servicemen.

"The girls were white as sheets and he kept reaching into his kimono for something. We were smiling and trying to make small talk in our limited Japanese. Then the jukebox played a song I had learned called 'Kuroi Hanabira.' I knew all the words (and still do) and sang them. The gang guy's threatening visage turned 180-percent and he became a friend, my *tomodachi*. Upon confirmation that we were *tomodachis*, I asked what was in his kimono. He spread it apart showing a long knife in a sheath. A close call: one of many in my lifetime."

All good things, of course, do come to an end, and on April 2, 1960, Steve was honorably discharged; he'd signed up for two years, but a "reduction-in-force" ended his service days after 22 months. Another milestone chapter in his life was closed.

And so, with his official departure from the Air Force, Steve's dalliance with the "wild blue yonder" was well and truly finished. From that moment forward, his life would be all about the sea.

The award-winning scientist Dr. Bernard Horecker,
also known as Doris's dad, circa 1945.

4

Girlhood
Life with the Doctor and Duck

OVER THE COURSE of his long, distinguished career, biochemist, enzymologist and molecular biologist Bernard Leonard Horecker was nothing less than a rock star in his chosen fields of science, health and academia. After completing undergraduate and graduate studies at the University of Chicago, he moved east during the Second World War to take a position at the National Institutes of Health in Bethesda, Maryland, where he recorded some of his major accomplishments.

After developing a method to determine the carbon-monoxide hemoglobin content of the blood of Navy pilots returning from combat missions, he was approached by future Nobel Prize-winner Arthur Kornberg to collaborate on a series of enzyme studies that proved to be groundbreaking. Though Dr. Horecker would ultimately receive practically every award available in the disciplines of biochemistry and microbiology, unlike Kornberg, he never did win the Nobel for science, a slight he would never quite get over in his 96 long years.

Married to the former Frances Lillian Goldstein, Bernie, as he was best known to his friends and colleagues, also was a family man, and helped raise three daughters (a pair of sons tragically died soon after birth). The youngest was Linda, who would go on to become an artist, teacher and cruising sailor, among other pursuits. The middle girl was Marilyn, another artist who was destined for three rocky, tumultuous marriages, and who also earned a small fortune with her second husband, Harvey Diamond, after they co-authored a somewhat controversial book in the mid-1980s called *Fit for Life* ("Gimmick," dismissed one critic), which sold over a million copies and launched a whole cottage industry of guides to diet and health.

Doris with her mother, the former Frances Lillian Goldstein.

The eldest daughter, born in Washington, D.C. in May of 1941, was named Doris. Nobody could have possibly predicted the life of travel, enterprise and adventure awaiting her.

Doris remembers the day her father came home singing "It's sedoheptulose!" It happened to be the sugar he'd discovered that day at work, a monosaccharide found in various fruits and vegetables that plays a vital role in reducing low-level inflammation in humans. Let's just say Bernie was not exactly your typical dad.

The original Horecker household in Bethesda, on North Lane in the heart of the city—just a block away from the movie theatre on Wisconsin Avenue—was a bustling place. Bernie tended to a mighty garden, his passion, and built a big patio and barbecue with flagstones out back. It was a very lively place. From an early age, Doris recalls the parade of post-doc graduate students and young scientists who gathered there on pleasant evenings, and also in his lab, "who hung on his every word."

The proud homeowners: Bernie and Frances in front of their first home on North Lane in Bethesda, Maryland, 1946.

She often accompanied him there on Sundays. He was also an accomplished pianist, and when he played Chopin's *Les Sylphides* with the windows wide open, Doris and Marilyn pretended to be "fairy wood nymphs" while swirling and dancing on the front lawn.

Like her husband, Steve, Doris has written extensively about her life and times in her own diaries and essays. At age seven, the family moved to a bigger home on Glenwood Road, which Doris remembers vividly:

"My bedroom was on the first floor and everyone else slept on the second floor… Dad continued gardening and paid me five cents a bushel for picking crabgrass out of his manicured lawn. I was learning how to make a living, painfully. He also decided he should teach me to play the piano, an upright we had in the den next to my bedroom. I am very thankful he set me on the path so long ago, but I dreaded his daily question when he got home from work: 'Did you practice today?' Several years later he acquiesced, and a professional piano teacher began to train me. The only recital I remember was when I had to play Chopin's *Nocturne* in E minor from memory in front of my parents and all the other parents and forgot where I was. Flustered, I kept repeating the previous phrase until magically I made it through to the end."

Along with her dad's status as a trusted, respected mentor, and his tendency to be a bit of a taskmaster, there is something else Doris remembers strongly from her youth:

Merry Merry! Doris with sisters Linda and Marilyn—and their beloved dachshund, Tina—in the living room of the family's Glenwood Road home, Christmas 1956.

She was a worker bee who embraced the notion of "employment" and who enjoyed making some cash of her own.

"I got my first job, collecting dirty clothes at a drive-in dry-cleaner owned by the people who lived across the street from us," she wrote. "I never wanted to stop working after that. I was paid every week and brought my pay envelope home to my mother, who put it in a bank account. When it was time for me to get a prom dress for junior high school graduation, it made me angry that she bought it from my savings. I never forgot that. But in reality, Dad didn't make much in those days and my mother made a lot of our clothes."

Along with her skills with a sewing machine, Frances was an excellent cook (something Doris evidently inherited from her), though a frugal one. Doris hated the salami omelets that appeared on the dinner table weekly because they were both nourishing and cheap. And mother and daughter did not have what one would call a warm and fuzzy relationship. They didn't talk much, nor did they take trips together, like some of Doris's friends did with their moms. By nature, Frances was a person who kept other people at arm's length, even her kids.

Perhaps because she was the oldest daughter, Doris was frequently punished, as she and her mother seemed to have a knack for rubbing each other the wrong way. "When I was 12, I felt I had the right to tell her off, I'd come of age," she remembers. "So I told her to go to hell. Which ended up in a sort of hell when my father came home with anger pouring from his ears." Bernie was not the sort to "spare the rod and spoil the child," and Doris was corporally punished for that transgression. "I deserved it, I guess," she remembers.

Still, in those days long before the Internet, though the family dynamic was indeed complicated, it was largely a wholesome childhood. Television time was limited to viewings of *Howdy Doody* and *Kukla, Fran and Ollie* (Doris dug Dolores Dragon). There were games of touch football with neighborhood kids most every evening. And there was the time the whole clan piled into a car for a cross-country adventure when Bernie landed a job teaching in California at Berkeley for the summer; the Horeckers stayed in a rented home overlooking San Francisco Bay with fruit trees in the backyard.

Doris was also a pretty young lady, and drew her fair share of attention; but not all of it was wanted or appreciated. The worst incident came in the 9th grade, when one night a troubled boy who stood behind her in chorus lit her house on fire (Doris wasn't his only victim; he torched eight other places before he was caught). Bernie tried to put it out with a lawn hose until the fire department showed up, and she went to school the next day smelling like smoke.

Her subsequent years at Walter Johnson High School in nearby Rockville were formative ones. Among other things, Doris was, how shall we put it, rather well-endowed.

She wrote, "I was allowed to join a select group of girls who called themselves the Itty Bitty Tittys, even though I had developed early and did not quite fit the mold. In fact, I was teased a lot in my early teens by boys asking, 'Can you see your feet?' I was editor of my high school paper and quite outspoken, putting into print my feelings about how the school should be run. I got caught holding a piece of paper circulating around our Latin class that one of the falsies worn by our old-maid teacher had slipped to her waist, and I ended up again in the principal's office. I started dating football players my sister Marilyn called 'meatheads.'"

It was all fairly standard coming-of-age stuff until the day Bernie came home from work and, totally out of the blue, announced to the family that he'd scored a year-long sabbatical in France at the Institut Pasteur.

It was 1957. The Horeckers of Bethesda were bound for Paris.

"MY LIFE went through its first major change." That's how Doris would come to see that magical year in Paris: embracing the fashion, learning a new language, being exposed to a different culture, taking fun trips, dating interesting boys. It all began with an ocean passage on a cruise ship called the *SS Statendam* from New York to Le Havre. Once in France, the family settled in a home in Palaiseau on the outskirts of Paris, and the three girls caught the Ligne de Sceaux train into the city each day to attend the American Community School near the edge of the big, beautiful park called the Bois de Boulogne.

If it all sounds exotic and foreign and adventurous, that's because it was.

"I learned to speak French by palling around with other teenagers in Palaiseau," Doris wrote. "In those days, everyone had a *carte de séjour* (residence permit), which meant the gendarmes could stop us and ask us to show our papers. Dad collaborated with Jacques Monod (a former Vichy resistance fighter and Nobel Prize winner) in his lab that year, and we traveled every holiday (there were many) to different countries in the Studebaker station wagon that went over to Europe with us on the ship.

Doris and mom in head-to-toe high Parisian couture
(note those red Ferragamo heels) in Paris, of course, in 1958.

"That fall we were in Munich, Germany for Octoberfest, an absolutely amazing celebration where men dressed in drag and with every 'skol!' a huge skein of lager beer had to be downed. My parents let me go off with two of Dad's students while they returned to the pension where we were staying. The sun was about to rise when I found myself pounding on the locked pension door."

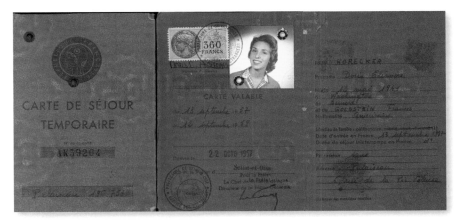

Doris's *carte de séjour*—her residence papers—for the magical year abroad in France.

The American Community School prom, with Doris seated beside her boyfriend, in the white jacket, in 1958.

The only real downside was the school part. A straight-A student back in Bethesda, at the American School—where her fellow students weren't suburban Maryland kids but the sons and daughters of diplomats and executives in the European branches of big American corporations—she got her first C. "The teachers were tougher than any I ever had and the lessons a lot harder," she said.

On the other hand, once the school day was done, the good times rolled. Her American Community School boyfriend, whose father was a bigshot at Esso (now Exxon), had a three-wheeled enclosed Messerschmitt for tooling around Paris (she often dragged her bewildered sister Linda, seven years her junior, along with her on dates). It was all a very fancy world, one she was completely unfamiliar with and had never before experienced, but she became very caught up in it.

And then there were the clothes: "Mom and I became fashionistas, shopping on the Champs-Élysées, in Le Bon Marché and other stores that made me giddy." But the goods they purchased were simply the icing on the cake for those excursions with Frances. They were easily the best, most enjoyable times Doris ever had with her mother.

Ultimately, the year passed very, very quickly. Which became problematic. Because Doris hadn't wanted to come to Paris in the first place. And now she didn't want to leave.

Back across the Atlantic they went, once again on the *SS Statendam*, "to a world," she said, "I would soon be happy to leave behind."

"It was horrible for her," recalled Linda. "She was so sophisticated compared to the other kids in high school. She was wearing French clothes; my mother had taken her to Galleries Lafayette and the other beautiful, historic department stores. The dollar was so strong that we'd been wealthy there. She was (now) fashionable and sophisticated, and she got back to the suburbs of D.C. and it was hard for her."

Doris not only thought differently. "I looked a lot different, too," she wrote. "I wore make-up and stylish clothes. I tried out for a high school musical called *Damn Yankees* and got the part. I wasn't a good athlete but (somehow) became captain of the girl's field hockey team, and named it *The Merdes*. When the team's schedule was announced on the PA system one morning I was called to the principal's office, where the French teacher stood scowling. *Merde* means 'shit' in French. I thought it was cute, she did not."

Somehow, in fits and starts, she made it through her senior year of high school. So, what next? The notion of further education was mostly unappealing (though she'd been a cheerleader, and thought the hijinks at the University of Maryland might be a giggle); she was ready for a job, to get on with life already. Her parents thought differently; the daughter of Dr. Bernard Horecker would not be denied the opportunity to attend college. They even decided where she'd go, to a somewhat alternative option called Antioch College in Yellow Springs, Ohio, a town its students jokingly called

The thespian: Back in Maryland, Doris (number 57!) performs
in her high-school adaptation of the Broadway musical, *Damn Yankees.*

"Yellow Gulch."

And so, Doris said, "I boarded a train to my next destiny."

ANTIOCH COLLEGE was lovably weird, quirky and open-minded, a far cry from Bethesda…or even Paris for that matter. It was also where she fell in love. Sort of.

"In those days Antioch was known as 'the Little Red Schoolhouse' because of its very liberal leanings," she wrote, "and it was full of high achievers we might today call 'nerds.' Going to class was not required, you just had to pass. And guys were allowed in the women's dorm, all someone had to do was holler 'Man on!' So, I got in real trouble because self-discipline was difficult for me. I was a rebel, I didn't think I had to go to class, and I ended up on probation. All the while I was training to follow in my father's footsteps, to be a microbiologist, too, because I was the oldest 'son.'"

The best part of the Antioch educational experience, Doris came to realize, was leaving it: to a series of work-study programs at other institutions. The highlight of those courses was a semester at the University of Michigan, where she spent her days in a biology lab staring through microscopes and counting amoeba, and her off-hours in a rooming house for graduate students where she collected efts, or salamanders, in the backyard, stashed them in a glass aquarium and fed them worms. "The other women thought I was nuts," she confessed.

In Ann Arbor, she found herself surrounded by ambitious, motivated individuals, "especially a Black woman—the term African-American did not exist at that time— that I palled around with. She was brilliant, number one in her law class, able to study a book and knit at the same time. Remember, this was 1959, when women were not supposed to achieve." Her friend left a lasting impression. "Achievement," Doris realized, was a quality that was becoming important to her.

Of course, she was also forging her own identity on other levels. She was, perhaps incongruously, staking her claim as a hipster.

"I wrote a lot of poetry and became a beatnik," she wrote. So were many of her friends, who liked getting blasted on Cokes laced with aspirin, which Doris wanted no part of, but hung with them anyway. (Kids those days…) "I ended up burning—sadly in retrospect—my book of poems in a crazy ceremony. I regret that. The first lines from a poem I wrote about the elms in Ann Arbor that were all dying from Dutch Elm Disease comes to mind often: *The elms their massive branches reach, across the darkened sky, and kiss the moon with flirting leaves, uttering but a sigh.* That's all I can remember. But I have continued to write poetry throughout my life."

Her freshman year truly came to a fork in the road, however, when she met an Antioch junior named Dick Buchanan, who was known as "Duck" for his rather elaborate "duck-ass" hairdo, which seemed to take hours to artfully arrange. Among other attributes, Duck had a sweet navy-blue Austin Healey he'd gotten for Christmas—his mother was the successful editor of *Parents* magazine—with the keys stashed under the tree.

Many years later, Doris remembered, "He was tall, dark black hair, very well-educated, kind of a bon vivant sort of guy. He talked a good game, held forth in any social situations." Duck almost immediately asked Doris to marry him. And mainly because her mother told her not to, she said "yes."

They got hitched in New York on a rainy summer day in 1960, after meeting with a rabbi who wore a tie with "see no evil, hear no evil, speak no evil" monkeys emblazoned upon it. ("Perhaps an omen," Doris later wryly observed.) Returning to Yellow Gulch, they moved into a large apartment (with an enclosed garage for the Austin Healey) with "a big TV with no guts we called our 'sculpture,' and we ate on the floor around a large table with no legs, because we'd removed them. I was still definitely a beatnik."

And a married one at that. But for how long?

NEW YORK, New York: the city so nice they named it twice. Doris's parents had already moved there. Bernie had taken a position as dean of the Albert Einstein School of Medicine and would later move on to become the dean of microbiology at New York University.

Upon Duck's graduation from Antioch, the Ohio beatniks followed suit, and both also enrolled at NYU, Doris for her continued undergraduate studies in science, and her husband for his graduate work in psychology. But Doris, frankly, had had enough. She still craved getting out into the working world, and now she had to, to support herself and Duck. First she started skipping class. Then, unceremoniously, her school days ceased altogether.

An ace typist, she landed her first real gig as a receptionist for a psychiatrist named Dr. Impostato, whose elaborate three-story office, with a luxurious penthouse apartment on the corner of 5th Avenue and 10th St., was a short walk away from her own new place in Greenwich Village.

"Our patients were almost all first-generation Italians and immigrant grandparents who wanted to go home to die in their homeland," Doris wrote. "It was an all-cash business: I went to the bank every day with wads of $20 and $100 bills. I saw people get strobe therapy (sodium pentothal enhanced by strobe lights as they went into a twilight zone and started to talk). One afternoon, one of those patients, who was supposed to be 'under'—a strong young guy—suddenly appeared at the top of the stairs where that treatment room was located, with a large swivel chair in his hands, aiming it at me."

Working with depressed people was…depressing. Nobody seemed to get better. It wasn't long before she sought and found a new job, as a supervisor in the research department at an ad agency in midtown-Manhattan called Geyer, Morey, Ballard. But that job proved knotty as well, as the research "results" teetered on the unethical. Within a year, she answered a help-wanted ad in *The New York Times* for a secretary at a "sports magazine." It would be yet another turning point.

To add to her angst, her marriage was cratering, her husband spending every night at "the library" while she whiled away her time alone with her little dog, Cleo.

It was now readily apparent: Duck was not going to float.

But as it turned out, there was someone else out there awaiting her in the Big City.

Many of Steve's best offshore-racing memories were made
aboard Clayton Ewing's yawl, *Dyna*, including a Class A win
in the 1960 Newport Bermuda Race.

5

Real Sailing, Real Job
A Sailing School Called Offshore

THREE MONTHS SHY of his Air Force discharge, in early February of 1960, Steve sat down at his typewriter, pecked out a long letter, and addressed the envelope to Mr. and Mrs. Hendon Chubb of New York City. Mrs. Chubb was, in fact, his sister Nita, already a couple of years into marriage at the ripe old age of 20; her husband, Hendon, was an offspring from the family that had founded Chubb Insurance, which started as a rather modest marine-underwriting service focused on ships and cargo in the 1800s, long before becoming the global power-house it is today. In his letter, Steve thanked the couple for their recent Christmas present and recounted his various Air Force adventures roaming far and wide in the Far East before getting down to the business at hand: his immediate future. He had some exciting news to share.

"I have something else in the fire before I give up traveling," he wrote (without a trace of irony…the last thing Steve was going to give up was traveling). "I'm going on a boat called the *Dyna* with Woody Pirie, my friend from the race to Spain (on *Mare Nostrum*), on the Newport Bermuda Race on the 18th of June. Then on the 30th of June we start on a race to Sweden from Bermuda. So, my summer will be spent in Europe again. This time Scandinavia, of which I've heard so much but never had the pleasure. The *Dyna* is a very fast boat and we have a good chance of winning both races."

At 24 years of age, with his schooling and service commitment now in the figurative rear-view mirror, Steve's priorities were crystal clear, his focus razor sharp: he had every intention of sailing his ass off, on every good boat that was available and in every competitive race to which he was invited, for as long as possible. And over the next four years, he would certainly accomplish that goal.

What's notable about this period in his life—actually, what's amazing about his entire sailing career—is that unlike so many sailors, he wasn't limited to (or interested in) just one racing discipline, inshore or offshore. So many sailors become specialists, and rack up their victories and achievements in either dinghies or ocean racers, but rarely both. Not Steve. From 1960 through 1964, Steve's sailing resume would include, among many other races, a long campaign in the highly technical 5.5 Metre class; the Pan American Games and the U.S. Olympic Trials; three Newport Bermuda Races; and two Transatlantic Races. When it came to yacht racing, he was a man of all seasons, for all reasons.

But, of course, that was only half the story. Now that his regular Air Force paycheck was over (not to mention all the extra bonus checks he cashed as an officer's perk for his "inspection trips" throughout the Pacific), he had to make a living.

It was actually kind of a family joke.

Steve's biggest antagonist in this arena was his "Aunt" Lou—his godmother, not an actual aunt, and a dear friend of his mom and dad. Aunt Lou's grandfather was Louis Comfort Tiffany and her son, Harry, ran the famous family business (it was Harry who'd given Steve his first crew job on his Atlantic sloop many years before). Lou told Steve she could arrange a cushy position at Tiffany's, a prospect he could not possibly have found less appealing, and she knew it.

But that just gave her more fuel for the fire. Practically every time she saw him, she let him have it: "Steve, when are you going to get a real job?"

As it happened, that would come a few years later.

In the interim, in his first gainful employment after the Air Force, he asked for and landed a spot at the A.L. Don Company, a boat-supply store on South Street in Lower Manhattan. Lee Don, the proprietor, was "a little wary" at first, said Steve, "as if the job was below me." Well, after all, we are talking about a Colgate. But Steve threw himself into his duties with his characteristic enthusiasm.

"I was basically a salesman, but really a jack of all trades," he recalled. "For instance, I biked down to South Street one Sunday because the front of the store needed a fresh coat of paint. That lasted until a cop came along and reminded me of the 'Blue Laws' back then forbidding work on Sundays. I felt the need to make a catalog of all the blocks and cleats we were selling and mailed out thousands of copies. I could take time off for sailing, but most of my racing (at first) was on weekends. Dick Nye came in often and asked me to race with *Carina* on the race around Long Island. That got me started with *Carina*. It happened that whenever I was invited to race on a boat, I was always asked back."

Dick Nye's *Carina*, aboard which Steve recorded countless miles, including here
in the 1971 Fastnet Race. Navigator Larry Huntington, with whom Steve enjoyed
a very satisfying Bermuda Race two decades later, takes a sextant sight
while Dick Nye Sr. enjoys his cigar, Chris Wick trims sails and Dick Kurts drives.
Safety harnesses had yet to be invented.

The *Carina* program spanned 50 years and a trio of boats with the same name.
Steve raced on the second *Carina*, a Philip Rhodes-designed 53-foot yawl, and in
addition to that first circuit around Long Island, competed aboard her in all the major
races on Long Island Sound: Stratford Shoals, the Vineyard Race, the Block Island
Race and many others.

But, taking a longer view at the big picture, his participation in many other
defining, international sailing events was on the very cusp of launching.

IN THE 1960s, before it became obsessed with Muhammad Ali, Super Bowls and
the Masters golf tournament, among other national stories, the great *Sports Illustrated*
magazine devoted a lot of ink to the sport of sailing. In its September 16, 1963, edition,

writer Hugh Whall previewed the upcoming, month-long U.S. National Champion-ships of the 5.5 Metre class "at Long Island's aristocratic Seawanhaka Corinthian Yacht Club" in a cover story (!) entitled "Two Texans Shoot It Out With A Pair Of 5.5s." Whall noted that the fleet would include "a Norwegian Crown Prince, a Soviet naval officer, a Leningrad mill hand and assorted Swedish, German and Swiss sailors," but his angle for the piece was "an unlikely pair of oil-rich Texas brothers, 50-year-old Albert Fay, in his red-hulled *Flame*, and 49-year-old Ernest Fay, in Yale-blue *Pride*."

Though he's not mentioned in the story, before the regatta was through, Ernie Fay would enlist the talents of a local Long Island ringer on his three-man crew: Steve Colgate.

In a journal entry, Steve wrote how it all went down:

"Ernie was one of the best sailors in the class. One day I had a call from Tony Hogan, who was crewing with Ernie in the Nationals out of Seawanhaka in Oyster Bay. Tony had told Ernie he had other obligations near the end of the regatta, but would get a good substitute. Ernie was skeptical. I told Tony that I had never sailed on a 5.5 Metre, having mainly sailed ocean races. He said, 'Don't worry. You're a good crew and it's just another sailboat. Plus, Wednesday is a lay day and you will go out and practice with Ernie before the last two races of the regatta on Thursday and Friday.'"

Steve joined the crew for the mid-week practice session and was assigned the fore-deck and spinnaker trimmer, the latter a slightly intimidating task. "The kite was over 600 square feet—a tremendous spinnaker for a 33-foot boat!" he recalled. His first race on a 5.5 was the next day and was uneventful. But it set up a final race on Friday, for all the marbles, as Ernie Fay was near the top of the fleet. Steve remembers it like it was yesterday:

"We led at the windward mark and the first reach was fairly broad. Of course, that meant a tighter reach for the second (one) after the jibe. I was agile and had good timing, but wasn't very muscular. So, at the jibe I hit it perfectly with the pole on the head stay as we left the mark. The next boat blew the jibe as did a few more after that. The rest of the 20-odd fleet decided to play it safe rather than sorry, and doused before the mark so we sailed away from the fleet and were first around the leeward mark 'by a mile.' We won the race and the regatta.

"From then on, I was Ernie's regular crew," he remembered. "Sorry, Tony. Oppor-tunity knocked and I answered."

Steve was a major player in the 5.5 Metre class, sailing in plenty of international regattas, but none were bigger than the 1968 Olympics in Mexico; he's shown here hiking out just forward of Dr. Stuart Walker.

It should probably be noted that, in Steve's long legacy of outstanding sailing moments, this one—in the heat of high-stakes competition, nailing the perfect jibe—stands out. He never forgot it.

As Whall noted, the 5.5 Metre was a developmental class, and each boat was slightly different, designed to a specific formula but with subtle variations (as opposed to a strict one-design class where all the boats are identical). Fay was not only the skipper of his *Pride*, he was also the boat's designer. And after winning the Nationals, he set his sights on something much bigger: the 1964 Olympic Games.

"The Olympics are meant to be a test of athletic prowess, and Olympic sailing shouldn't be any exception," Ernie told Whall. "In 5.5s, you expect that sort of test. Furthermore, the crews like the boats because of the challenge they offer. If they didn't, they'd be sailing in Dragons or that old man's boat, the IOD (the similar-sized International One-Design)."

Whall added his own postscript to Ernie's thoughts: "What Ernie Fay neglects to mention is that it helps to have the agility of a Nijinsky, the bravura of an Errol Flynn (the action movie star) and the endurance of Gibraltar when crewing on a 5.5." In other words, a guy like Steve was very useful.

(There was an ancillary benefit to winning the Nationals with Ernie, as his team qualified for that year's Pan American Games in Brazil. Unfortunately, as there were few 5.5s in South America, there was no 5.5 class for that event, but Steve made the U.S. national team as an alternate in the Finn, Flying Dutchman and Lightning classes. He never sailed in the games but was able to observe all the racing from a chase boat and learned all sorts of tactical tricks that he later applied to his own racing and incorporated into the racing programs when he opened his own sailing school.)

Now a member of Ernie's trusted team, and as the reigning national champs, the *Pride* crew set their sights on the Tokyo Olympics. The sailing events were to take place on Sagami Bay, a body of water Steve was familiar with, having paid a visit during his Air Force days. He was very anxious to return. In preparation, he made numerous trips to Galveston, Texas, Ernie's home waters. By the time the Olympic Trials for the '64 Games took place off Newport, Rhode Island, the *Pride* squad was a well-honed machine.

The regatta came down to the last race, a battle between *Pride* and Don McNamara's *Bingo*: winner take all, with a punched ticket to Tokyo the prize. In the early going, Ernie made an uncharacteristic tactical error and *Bingo* took the lead. On the next couple of reaching legs, there were no passing lanes, and *Pride* remained in arrears. The final race came down to the final leg. *Pride* was still behind, the Olympic dream quickly vanishing. Desperate times called for desperate measures. Then Steve remembered the 5.5 Metre crew from Louisiana, who'd regaled their fellow sailors with tales of witches and voodoo. And hexes.

"They said one of their strongest hexes was to tie a pelican feather to a competitor's backstay," said Steve. "Of course, our crew checked our boat every morning for such an omen."

With everything on the line, Steve wrote, "I thought of something. Earlier in the series, the head of *Bingo*'s jib had pulled out. It was a computer-designed jib, the first of its kind, designed by Jerry Milgram, an MIT professor. This was the same or similar jib, and as hexes were the current rage with the Louisiana crew, it was now or never.

"I sat on the weather rail, closed my eyes and repeated quietly to myself, mouthing the words, 'Hex on *Bingo*'s jib, hex on *Bingo*'s jib,' over and over. For a moment, I opened my eyes to see our third crew member looking at me as if I was crazy. I closed them again and kept up my quiet chant. Suddenly, at about four minutes from the finish line, he said, 'What's happened to *Bingo*'s jib?' The clew had pulled out. I smiled, but it was not to be. McNamara was a big, strong guy, so he handed the helm over and went forward and held on to the clew of the sail, since the jib sheets weren't attached anymore. He kept it trimmed in for the light-air reach while we gained on them foot by foot. We crossed the finish line overlapped. Another hundred yards and *Pride* would have competed in Japan."

Steve later made a joke about it: "Lesson learned: when you hex, be specific. I should have hexed the head of the jib." Still, it was a bitter pill to swallow. Little did he know at the time, but he wasn't quite finished with Olympic sailing.

SURPRISINGLY, SAILING wasn't the only game Steve was playing hard, and well, during these active days. The headline of a Long Island newspaper clipping from the early 1960's—"Colgate Cops 50-Mile Bike Grind"—summarized his other pursuit. The story continued:

"The hour was 6:46 a.m. and the day dawned with a cloak of rain and mist. Despite the weather, four hardy cyclists, the earliest to get under way, pushed hard on their pedals (to start) the annual 50-mile George Steppello Memorial handicap bicycle road race over Nassau County highways yesterday.

"The test, first in a series to score toward the U.S. all-around championship, was sponsored by the 62-year-old Century Road Club Association. One hundred and eight more bikers followed the pioneering foursome, but only 78 finished.

"Two hours, 29 minutes later, Stephen Colgate, sporting the host club's colors and in his first major race, pedaled across the finish line, the victor. The 25-year-old marine supply salesman, aided by a 20-minute allowance, outsprinted six others in the lead pack to win by two lengths. He was clocked in 2:21:00."

Perhaps unsurprisingly, the origins of this tale also go back to Japan. There, in the bar car of a train on one of his frequent jaunts (where else!?), he made the acquaintance of a professional bike racer named Namio, and they hit it off. So much so, that when Steve returned to the States, he had a skittish track bike with him—they don't have brakes—a gift from his new friend. At the time, he was living with a quintet of fellow bachelors in a large apartment called the Cambridge House near West End

Wheels man: In Japan, Steve was introduced to bike racing,
and at the Kawasaki Race Track pedaled his skittish track bike
over a 200-meter course in 14.5 seconds.

Avenue on 86th Street. It was a fast pedal over to Central Park (he quickly swapped the brakeless bike for a road bike, before he killed himself) where he joined the Century Club, which raced around its 6.25-mile perimeter every Sunday: the four-lap races pegged a neat 25 miles.

Before long, he was biking everywhere. Down to South Street for work. Out to New Haven and back, a 175-mile round-trip ride to *watch* a race. For a while, he actually toyed with the idea of trying to make the Olympic team in cycling. Then came a 50-mile race in New Jersey called the Tour of Somerville. With just a couple laps to go, he was in the lead pack with ten other riders. And then, he said, "My chain came off."

He continued, "I was too inexperienced to know that if I had just reached down and slowly turned the pedals I could have gotten the chain back on without losing too much time. But I stopped, got off the bike, got the chain back on, and by that time... So, then I said to myself, it would be stupid for me to go into bicycle racing without the great experience that all these other people had."

That pretty much confirmed what he knew already. He was a sailor, not a cyclist.

MANY YEARS after the fact, on the wall of his office, Steve hung a framed note that he penned with a simple title: "Perseverance."

It was a simple statement of fact: "On the morning of July 13, 1963, the yawl *Dyna* lost her rudder while participating in a Transatlantic Race from Newport, R.I. to England. Her location was 980 nautical miles from the Eddystone Light, the finish of the race, and 1,110 nautical miles from Southampton, England, her ultimate destination. Through experimentation and continuous close attention to the trim and selection of her sails, *Dyna*'s crew continued the race unassisted and completed the course six days later.

"During this rudderless period, she had one noon-to-noon run of 180 nautical miles. There is no known record of any sailing vessel having sailed as far or as fast after the loss of its rudder. This unprecedented accomplishment was solely the result of the collective ability, stamina and spirt of *Dyna*'s unusually capable crew. Each man contributed his full measure to successfully and speedily sail her to port."

It's one of the crowning achievements of Steve's sailing career, and as fondly recalled as the perfect jibe that won the 5.5 Metre National Championships. But this was bigger, much bigger, and not only because it was a potentially very dangerous situation. While the 5.5 Metre wars with Ernie Fay were fun and rewarding, what happened on *Dyna* was altogether different. It didn't occur in the relatively sheltered waters of Long Island Sound, but on his first love: the wild open sea.

This was Steve's third Transatlantic Race (and fourth crossing, if you count the summer lark on the ocean liner); he'd already knocked one off aboard *Dyna* almost immediately after his departure from the Air Force in 1960, a relatively tame affair compared to this one. Few sailors compete in a single transatlantic contest, but Steve would eventually record seven of them. He couldn't get enough of deep-blue water. Looking back, he tried to capture their very essence:

"Each one was a learning experience, each with its own personality. The striking thing about all of them was the peaceful isolation of being out at sea for long periods of time. Within days you get into a routine of watch systems. Nothing else but sailing at the greatest possible speed concerns you. The world could be blowing up, but your world is the boat, your crewmates and the challenges at the time. You are living completely in the present and all other concerns are banished.

"The other extraordinary takeaway," he continued, "is no matter how bad things get, you are responsible for your own fate. No matter what Mother Nature has in

The crew of *Dyna* in the 1960 Transatlantic race from Sweden to Bermuda,
with Woody Pirie on mainsheet, Lynn Williams just aft,
owner Clayton Ewing next to son Mark, and Steve just behind him.

store, you know you will handle breakdowns if they occur, and a new, beautiful day
will dawn soon."

Along with the pair of transatlantics, between 1960 and 1974, Steve would sail
seven Newport Bermuda Races aboard *Dyna*, including a first in Class A in the '60
running. She was a fantastic yacht, designed by the legendary naval architect, Olin
Stephens, and built of welded aluminum (a first for his firm, Sparkman & Stephens)
with a centerboard and shoal draft (she was conceived to race on the Great Lakes). But
Steve's favorite part of being aboard *Dyna* was sailing with her no-nonsense skipper
and owner, Clayton Ewing, for whom he harbored deep respect.

"He was a fantastic leader," Steve wrote. "He had owned and built up a paper company in Wisconsin and had sold out to Scott Paper. He had a good sense of humor, treated all the crew with a great deal of respect, was bright and confident, never lost his cool and never yelled."

Still, Steve remembered some pretty hilarious incidents aboard her. There was the time racing on Chesapeake Bay when he tried to engage a new youngster who'd come aboard as he rested in a sea berth. Steve talked and talked, but never got a reply, and wondered whether the dude was deaf or rude. It turned out he was asleep, and Steve was gazing into his opened glass eye.

Then there was the time on a Port Huron to Mackinac Island Race when the cabin was invaded off the coast of Michigan by an infestation of fat, black flies. Suddenly, a crewmember captured one of the slow-moving insects, dabbed a bead of contact cement to its butt, and affixed a torn strip of Kleenex to it. Before long, a couple-dozen wispy strips of Kleenex were hovering about the saloon. There's a comedian on every boat.

But it all got serious as a heart attack when *Dyna* dropped her rudder en route to Eddystone Light in '63.

"Clayton immediately divided the crew into two groups to be led by the respective watch captains," Steve wrote. "I was one watch captain and a man who ran an engineering company that Clayton also owned was the other watch captain. My group was assigned to figure out how to sail the boat steering with the sails alone, while the other was assigned to figure out a mechanical way of creating an ersatz rudder to steer the boat.

"Both groups worked for 48 hours on each project in 60-knot winds and then tested the results. The other watch came up with a sweep consisting of a spinnaker pole with floorboards attached and lines to genoa winches on either side of the boat. It worked so well that we could set a spinnaker when the wind moderated to about 15 knots. However, because of the drag, *Dyna* ended up sailing slower than with my system of full mainsail, winged out jib, staysail trimmed amidships and fine-tune steering using the mizzen sail. Not only was it faster, but we could steer within five degrees of course, better than when we had a rudder."

Once Steve's sail-only solution proved superior, they carried on with it until the finish line. It was a remarkable feat of seamanship, and the satisfaction among the crew when they passed Eddystone Light was palpable. Remarkably, *Dyna* still managed a

4th-place finish on both elapsed and corrected time among a fleet of 14 yachts. It had been one hell of a voyage.

Matters ashore were almost as eventful.

IN THE FALL of 1964, in perhaps the most serendipitous moment of his young life, Steve attended a cocktail party and was introduced to a man named Mike D'Agostino, an architect for J.C. Penney who just happened to own a cruising sailboat, a 38-foot yawl. More or less out of the blue, Mike asked Steve if he was interested in starting a sailing school. Each man had something of value to offer the other. "I had the sailing experience and he had the boat," said Steve.

Interesting prospects weren't exactly knocking his door down. Why the hell not?

There wasn't a ton of competition. In fact, as far as they knew, there were only two other "schools" that they were aware of: a yacht brokerage in California called Ardell that taught people how to sail the boats they sold them, and a modest outfit in Annapolis, Maryland, that was basically doing the same thing, instructing folks who purchased one of their small sailboats how to use the bloody thing.

Offshore Sailing School

Ocean Racing Sailboats
in
Small Personal Classes

A real job: the cover
of Steve's first brochure.

Steve and Mike almost immediately incorporated their two-man operation as Offshore Sailing School, Ltd. Steve has no recollection how they came up with the name, though many years later he wondered what in the world they were thinking ("Everyone uses it"). In their first year, they did pretty well teaching aboard Mike's boat that was berthed out on City Island in the Bronx, at Minneford Yacht Yard.

Then a rather sticky situation cropped up. Mike was divorcing his wife, Shirley, to whom he owed $3,600 for the time she got him out of hock for winter storage for his yawl. Steve said, "He said he would sign his stock (in the company) over to me if I came to an agreement with Shirley. She agreed to $100 a month for three years. This was a big sum for

More milestones: the June 4, 1966 issue of *Business Week* profiles
Steve and his Offshore Sailing School, another first in what would become
many decades of extremely favorable media coverage.

me to pay at the time. Two years later, Mike dropped by the office and asked if I was still paying off Shirley. I said 'yes' and he, rubbing it in, said what a shame as he had already paid off his alimony to her."

It's never fun paying off an ex, but even less so if you weren't married to them in the first place.

Along with the berth out on City Island, Offshore's "assets" included a rented office and classrooms on the fourth floor of a brownstone on East 40th Street, a space Steve shared with a marine-electronics firm run by a guy named Tom Cole, who smoked like a fiend and had yellow fingernails to prove it. Having left the bachelor pad he shared with his pals, Steve was also crashing there, on a small bed in a side room. To say that money was tight would be an understatement. Yes, he did have a small monthly trust fund of 60-odd whopping bucks a month, which did help with the rent. But he couldn't give hands-on sailing classes in the winter, and his monthly rent needed to be paid regardless, which meant he had to get creative.

To make ends meet, Steve said, "I decided to have other classroom courses. I hired a NOAA meteorologist from the weather bureau to teach a four-week course, a marine mechanic to teach an engine-maintenance course, a celestial-navigation instructor from the New York Planetarium, and I taught a Learn-to-Sail course on weekday evenings."

Almost from the outset, there was no lack of clientele, mostly professionals who'd done well in their careers, had some discretionary income, found the notion of sailing interesting, and had a thirst for knowledge. "And there wasn't anywhere else for them to go," said Steve. "The yacht club sailing programs didn't cater to adults, just kids. And if you've never been involved with yacht clubs, and now you're a doctor or lawyer who's done plenty of studying and you have some free time and money, how do you get into sailing?"

Steve had the answer. And he found he was a good, intuitive teacher. "I'd personally been in classrooms for ages," he said. "I was very lucky. I'd had a very good education. I knew how I learned. First, you needed a textbook." He worked up the first of what would become many, many sailing books with his byline on mimeographed pages. He'd been sailing for 20 years. Could he condense his own knowledge into a week-long sailing curriculum? Why, yes. Yes, he could.

In 1965, five years removed from his Air Force duty, and with thousands and thousands of sea miles also behind him, Steve was hustling, sailing at an extremely high and competitive level, and trying to make a go of it with his fledgling business. It was hard. Like real work, the kind his Aunt Lou had chided him about for years. But things were about to take a serious turn for the better. He had no clue, not yet, but it was not so long, in the big scheme of things, before he would meet someone who was going to make it all so much easier and worthwhile.

A lovely 34-foot yawl was the yacht on which Offshore Sailing School was launched.

Bob Bavier, the blueblood publisher of *Yachting* magazine—and Doris's boss—
at the helm of the 1964 America's Cup winning *Constellation*,
with the 12-Metre's legendary yacht designer Olin Stephens nestled astern.

6

Mad Men and the Sailing Instructor
A Magazine and a Love Story

WHEN DORIS BUCHANAN answered the ad in *The New York Times* in early 1967 for an open secretarial position at a Manhattan "sports magazine," she was desperate for change on multiple levels. Her early working life in the city had by no means been a disaster, but it was far from fulfilling. Her marriage, she'd come to realize, was basically on the rocks, her husband Duck a largely absentee figure in her life. And if the publication where she interviewed for her new job had been *Tennis*, or *Golf Digest*—or, for that matter, any one of the hundreds of other titles flourishing in and around New York in the lush media landscape of the mid-1960s—a Golden Age of magazines—her life and fate probably would've turned out completely differently. But the place where she landed her fresh gig wasn't about bashing around little white balls at posh country clubs.

The magazine was called *Yachting*.

The long-running, award-winning television series *Mad Men* captured the wild, anything-goes era well. The title was a clever double entendre, for the fictional Sterling Cooper advertising agency of the TV show was certainly staffed by a crazed crew of mad executives and their minions, but "Mad men" was also how the real-life protagonists referred to themselves, "Mad" being short for Madison Avenue, where most of them were actually based. Upscale magazines with tens of thousands of well-heeled readers—like *Yachting*—were coveted clients and major targets for the Mad men, who enjoyed all the trappings of the period: private car services, boozy lunches, wide-open expense accounts. Magazines like *Yachting* covered their basic operating costs by selling subscriptions, but the hard revenue, the real money to be made, was in advertising.

And make no mistake about it, *Yachting* was a real juggernaut, a bloody license to haul in reams of cash.

The gentlemen running the show there were, of course, accomplished, life-long sailors with peerless, illustrious backgrounds. Executive editor William "Bill" Robinson was a Princeton man and war hero, having commanded a sub chaser in the Pacific during World War II, then ascending through a series of New Jersey newspaper jobs before landing at *Yachting*. A prolific writer who would pen more than two dozen sailing books, Robinson's love was cruising under sail.

However, when it came to yacht racing, advertising director Robert "Bob" Bavier's resume was even more impressive. Having honed his competitive skills on Long Island Sound as a youth, he led his Williams College sailing team to back-to-back intercollegiate championships before the war. After also serving in the Navy during the war, he joined *Yachting* as an ad salesman and worked his way steadily up the ranks. In 1964, still maintaining a very full racing schedule in addition to his demanding job, he won the America's Cup as the skipper of the 12-Meter *Constellation*. Bavier was a Yankee blueblood, but he was also the real deal.

And, he was Doris's boss.

Bavier was the extremely rare magazine ad man who also contributed to the editorial product, writing plenty of articles and even a regular monthly column. Among Doris's duties was typing up the soft-spoken Bavier's letters and stories, which he mumbled into a Dictaphone with his pipe in his mouth. The nautical lexicon is rife with unique words and phrases, and sometimes Doris had no clue what Bavier was droning on about. Her very first transcription was his recounting of a New York Yacht Club cruise that stopped in Padanaram, a coastal Massachusetts village along Buzzards Bay. "Padanaram?" she repeated to herself. "Where the hell is that? How do you spell it?"

Yachting's offices were in the Hippodrome Building on West 44th Street, right across the street from the famous Algonquin Hotel and the New York Yacht Club, to which she was often dispatched to deliver documents from Bavier. As a woman in the not-yet-enlightened mid-1960s, she was not allowed in the front door, but could use a side entrance as long as it was past four p.m. Just like in the TV show *Mad Men*, New York was still fashionably sexist.

"I was hired by a woman I remember only as the wicked witch of Manhattan," Doris wrote. "She ran the company even though she was only in charge of HR. Her boyfriend supplied the paper. She promised me a raise I never got. She sent me home when I showed up in a smashing orange-knit pantsuit, the first woman to wear pants in that office. My boss and his compatriots took long two-martini lunches at the Algonquin; that was what everyone did in those days, not just at *Yachting*. But none of that mattered. Because I loved my job."

And she was damn proficient at it.

As Bill Robinson's secretary, Diane Duryea was Doris's direct counterpart as the assistant to one of *Yachting*'s top dogs. The two women became close, lifelong friends. Diane has fond memories of both the magazine and her pal.

"The people who worked at *Yachting*…were the best," she said. "They were professional, kind and always helpful. The whole atmosphere in the company was very pleasant. During the time I was there, *Yachting* carried more pages of advertising than any other magazine, in any other field. I was very proud of our publication. Doris and I got to know one another because we often had to interact with each other in our jobs. She was always very friendly and I could tell she was very good at what she did. She was self-assured and the kind of person very dedicated to her job and position."

Doris shared warm feelings about her co-workers. As she became more accustomed to the daily routine, she began to realize they were especially happy, and full of life and fun stories, on Monday mornings. Eventually, she said, "I figured it out…it was because they sailed!" She decided that she, too, needed to get in on this sailing thing.

As far as where to actually take lessons, her colleagues at the magazine were unanimous in their praise of one place in particular, which a co-worker lauded for the seemingly small attribute of having boats with clean, smooth bottoms. Offshore Sailing School ran a regular ad in *The New York Times* classified section. And it was run by a fellow with a sterling reputation not only in *Yachting*'s offices but, she learned, in all of sailing's wide circles.

Some guy called Steve Colgate.

ALMOST FROM the very first magical moment she stepped aboard a sailboat, Doris was hooked, entranced, smitten. Back in Bethesda growing up, boats of any variety were non-existent in her life; she'd been raised a complete, total landlubber. Truth be told, she was afraid—very afraid—of the water. But she was determined to conquer that fear. She decided to drag Duck along, as well. They plonked down $300 for the two of them, and signed up.

"Although I was done with my marriage, we tried one last-ditch effort to find

Doris's best friend and compatriot at *Yachting*, Diane Duryea.

something we could enjoy together and took Steve Colgate's four-weekend course at City Island, New York, with another couple," Doris wrote. "It was July, hot and muggy, with little wind. Our instructor was a handsome young man who drove a bright green Lamborghini. 'Steve Colgate,' whoever he was, was not around: he was in Newport, Rhode Island, on *American Eagle* in the America's Cup trials. When he took his shirt off, that lovely instructor had 'loving' scratch marks on his back. We all laughed at that one."

The wild young man who taught Doris to sail would not last the summer, tragically perishing in a sky-diving accident a few short weeks later. But he'd done his job well. The sensation of a well-trimmed sailboat leaning into a fresh breeze, under her command, was nothing short of addicting. Feathering a sailboat into the wind, her hand light on a tiller, gave her a sense of control she'd never experienced before. It made her feel good about herself. It did wonders for her confidence and self-esteem. It was an elixir for her soul. She did not fully realize it at the time, but her life had completely, inexplicably, unalterably changed. And there would be no going back.

"I'd caught the sailing bug," she said.

That's not to say she'd become an expert. Not yet. "After the course ended, we were

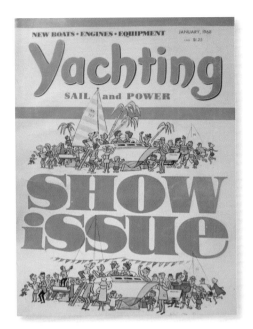

The January 1968 cover of *Yachting* magazine, in which the bylined story
from Doris Buchanan, "We Learned at School," covered her experiences
learning sailing at Offshore Sailing School.

allowed to take the boat out without the instructor," she wrote. "I was at the helm and drove that lively Soling we'd learned aboard right onto the rocks. No worries, I tried to call this Steve Colgate to apologize, but instead wrote a gee-whiz article for *Yachting* about learning to sail."

Doris's story about her lessons, the first in what would become her own long side career in sailing journalism, appeared in the January, 1968, edition of the magazine and was simply titled, "We Learned at School." It's an upbeat, fun piece that details the entire experience, including the eight hours of classroom training and 16 hours of sailing lessons; the general cluelessness at the outset of the program; a gradual realization that there's a whole lot more to the sailing game than immediately meets the eye; the steady, enjoyable accumulation of skills; and the last, wild day, caught in a thunderstorm on the final approach to the mooring (which they missed!).

"Soaked through, dead tired and ravenously hungry, we ended our course in the school's equipment house at Bob Taylor's Marina," she writes in conclusion. "And as we devoured sandwiches and beer, we joked about the mistakes and fun we all had."

Still, her education in the sport was just beginning. The next step was a week-long course—with Duck, once more, their first real vacation together—at the Jack Tar

Resort on Grand Bahama Island, where Colgate had a side gig in the winter months running "Sailing Symposium" racing programs on a fleet of six Solings with a rotating roster of guest experts, some of the giants of the sport: Buddy Melges, Bruce Kirby, Dr. Stuart Walker, Tom Blackaller, John Marshall and many others. Doris wanted to learn how to race, like so many of her *Yachting* colleagues, though she admits she was "the epitome of clueless." But there was an additional agenda, as well.

"As soon as we arrived, I put on my best bathing suit and see-through cover-up, my long blond hair flowing, and strolled down the docks on my own to finally meet the real Steve Colgate," she wrote. She hoped to say she was sorry, face to face, for banging up his boat back in City Island. "He was working on the boats. Another guy popped his head up when I asked where Steve Colgate was, and said 'He's busy.' But then Steve poked his head out of the bilge. And I fell in love."

It was January 18, 1968, a date Steve and Doris would come to see as "their real anniversary." Eventually, they'd even use it as the combination lock on their suitcases: 1/18.

However, on the day itself, let's just say the "love-at-first-sight" feeling was not immediately mutual. Doris stammered something about being the author of the story in *Yachting* about his school. "He was," she recalls, "not impressed."

Still, there was sailing to be done. Excellent sailing.

"That was a whirlwind week," wrote Doris. "I was put on a boat with a pediatric orthopedic surgeon from Winnipeg, Canada, who slapped me on the back at breakfast the morning we were to start flying spinnakers and said in his Scottish accent, 'Eat up lass, we need all the ballast we can get today!' He called the spinnaker 'the machination of the devil.' I weighed all of a hundred pounds soaking wet and had no idea what I was doing, after all I had only had that (beginner's course back in New York). The only sailing I had done since then was a couple of weekend sails on a 36-foot cruising boat with a co-worker. Having learned on a Soling, I found the cruising boat boring because it took so long for it to react when the wheel was turned. It was windy in the Bahamas. When I saw waves, I thought we were going to go aground, but I persevered."

The days, then, were very exciting. Soon, the nights became more interesting, too.

Steve was in the Bahamas with, Doris remembers, a "striking blonde" girlfriend. And she was with Duck. Both of them—his girlfriend and her husband—took inordinately long times to primp themselves for dinner, each vitally concerned with not having a single lock of hair out of place. Which gave Doris the opportunity to catch

Steve with sailmaker and Guest Expert Wally Ross at a Sailing Symposiums racing session at Jack Tar Resort, Grand Bahamas Island, in 1968.

Steve at the bar for a drink or two while they waited for their respective dates.

For Duck, forever tending to his spectacular, eponymous "duck tail," his absence at cocktail hour was basically a self-inflicted wound. His final one.

To Doris, Duck was a "big bravado guy who took over every conversation anywhere we ever went. I remember always having a cigarette and a glass in my hand because I didn't know what to do with myself. He was so domineering. I was self-conscious. He put me down."

Steve was different. Serious. Quiet. He didn't say anything unless he had something worthwhile to say. And he listened. Doris liked that. They could talk freely, have real conversations. It was all very nice and easy and sweet. Wait. Was something clicking?

Back in New York a few weeks later, Doris threw a party at her apartment to reunite with her fellow students from the Sailing Symposium; the funny doctor from Winnipeg even showed up. As did Steve. Somehow it was decided that Doris would skip out on her lunch breaks to help Steve get organized and tend to his books; *Yachting* was on West 44th and 6th, and Offshore on East 40th and 5th, so it wasn't a long hike.

Soon enough, the noontime work rendezvous became after-hours sessions, and

Teacher has to teach: Steve explaining how to unlock the secrets of a Soling at a Sailing Symposiums session in 1968.

the couple became intimate. There was only one problem, really, a seriously knotty one. Doris was still hitched.

GETTING DIVORCED in New York in 1968 was, to put it mildly, a huge hassle. You had to file papers, wait a year, yadda yadda.

It was a whole lot simpler in Mexico.

Duck may have been just as unhappy with Doris as she was with him. Yet he still did not take the news of the impending conclusion to his marriage kindly, and pushed her against a wall in anger. Talk about a "mad man." That actually made the first-class flight from New York to Juarez much easier.

The entire plane was chock full of divorcees-to-be. They all boarded the same bus to Tijuana, all stayed in the same hotel, all signed the same paperwork, which of course was in Spanish, and nobody had any real clue as to what exactly it said. Somebody even arranged for them all to see "a show," which basically turned out to be an all-women orgy. The pregnant participant isn't something Doris ever forgot. It was the first time she'd ever traveled alone, and was quite simply the most bizarre, freakiest experience of her entire life.

But then, after eight years of what was never exactly blessed matrimony, she was free. Now what?

The answer was crystal clear.

Steve. Colgate.

But he wasn't about to make it easy.

Steve had actually been perfectly okay seeing a married woman; it was a built-in excuse not to get too serious. After all, he was already spoken for, by sailing. Who needed a wife? And he was still dating the big blonde from the Bahamas. When he went to Acapulco to compete in the 1968 Olympics, she followed him down, which sent Doris into a brief tailspin: She couldn't quite decide whether to be livid or hurt. But when Steve returned to New York, he asked Doris to lunch and told her that that relationship was over. Which made her happy. Because she was crazy about him.

She remembers so many little things about their early days together. The first time he touched her, lightly holding her hand while driving out to City Island in his old, gray, dilapidated Volvo. Making love on the floor of a Soling out on a mooring, the boat's stringers jammed into her back. Ah, amore.

Steve moved into Doris's apartment, put his dopp kit on the toilet, hung his stuff up in a closet, and almost immediately told her he had no intention whatsoever of marrying her. She told him to get out. Pronto. But she let him stay.

"We came from very different backgrounds and upbringings," Doris wrote. "He'd led a charmed young life with very wealthy parents and relatives who were died-in-the-wool conservatives. I grew up in the modest D.C. suburbs in a tiny house. He grew up on the water, literally, in a rambling house his parents built for a million dollars on Lloyd Neck. The only water I saw as a youngster was Lake Michigan when visiting grandparents there. I went to public schools. He went to prep schools. We were truly a very odd couple."

What was that saying about "opposites attract?" Because the attraction was real, and getting stronger.

Doris's job at *Yachting* proved to be a real boon to the budding couple. She'd proven she could piece together solid magazine articles, and wrangled story assignments to cover races Steve was sailing in: First the Canadian Olympic Regatta Kingston, or CORK, where he sailed an International 14 with Canada's own Bruce Kirby, and later a Transatlantic Race from Marblehead to Ireland on Clayton Ewing's good old *Dyna*.

Then, in the late summer of 1969, they traveled together to Holland, Michigan, where Steve had scored a coaching job running clinics for hopeful Olympic prospects in 420 dinghies. Doris looked hot in a bikini and had no issues whatsoever flaunting it. Which wasn't sitting well with the moms of the fledgling Olympians. Nor was the fact that this very unmarried pair was shacked up in the same motel as the rest of them. The quiet murmurs were growing louder and louder, to the point where they couldn't be ignored: "Bad examples."

Doris said, "I guess he was either shamed into it, or figured the time was right, because it was there, in that motel, that Steve got down on his knees and—finally— asked me to marry him."

If Doris was on the water, she was usually adorned in a bikini.

Good man.

As to the wedding, Doris wrote, "My mother was pleased because she felt Steve was an academic (he was in the teaching business). We were married in a Presbyterian church on 76th Street in the snow, on December 17, 1969, and celebrated at Steve's sister's brownstone on 91st street on the East side. It was a rollicking party. Bob Bavier was there, and so many of our mutual friends, and our families with some of Steve's little nephews. Because I had been married before, and still had a lot of that beatnik blood in me, I was dressed in a light green sleeveless short dress with flowers in my hair and insisted the cake be something other than a traditional white wedding cake.

When Doris accompanied Steve to regattas, she was more than happy
to help out, here cleaning the bottom of a Thistle while Steve
and skipper Jim Miller egg her on.

Friends and family are still talking about the golden-hued pyramid of profiteroles, which were so solidly glued together with honey, we could barely cut through it. Twenty years later we threw ourselves an anniversary party with a traditional wedding cake that Steve loved!"

The next morning, the freshly married couple caught an Eastern Airlines flight back to the Bahamas for another season of Sailing Symposiums. Also aboard the plane were the quirky, high-pitched singer Tiny Tim and his own brand-new

The knot tied: December 17, 1969.

bride, Miss Vicki, who'd been married the same night as the Colgates, only their nuptials were carried live on *The Ed Sullivan Show.* The Tiny one was wearing the

Newlyweds: a day after getting married, the Colgates
were back on Grand Bahama Island, preparing for the sailing season.

filthy tan raincoat and carrying the sloppy brown shopping bag that accompanied
him during his performances. Doris reckoned he was heading to Freeport to sing
"Tiptoe Through the Tulips" to his adoring fans.

As for her own honeymoon, she spent it painting the bottoms and cleaning up
the Solings to be used in the Symposiums. She didn't care. It was all an adventure.
Figuratively speaking, she was tiptoeing through the tulips herself. And working long
hours next to Steve was certainly a preview of coming attractions.

Bob Bavier had written a note to Steve at the announcement of their engagement
with words Doris always remembered: "Please don't take away the best secretary I
ever had." Doris was in fact much more than a "secretary" at that point; she sold ads,
wrote stories, served as the filing clerk and mail girl. Prior to giving her actual notice
at *Yachting* in 1970, not long after her wedding, she'd asked Bavier if she could have
a bit more exposure (and pay), and requested a new title: administrative assistant. She
was told that was not the way it was done at *Yachting*. Of course, once she was gone,
Bavier hired his daughter as his...administrative assistant.

But that was behind her now. And in any event, Doris had a new job in front of
her, her greatest challenge yet. For she had not only wed a man named Steve Colgate.
As she would say time and time again in the years ahead, she'd also become married
to a business called Offshore Sailing School.

The real honeymoon: Cortina, Italy, 1971.

City Island, circa 1970.
A veritable speck of real estate in western Long Island Sound,
City Island always punched above its weight.

7

North and South

The Bronx, the Islands, the Sunshine State

CITY ISLAND has always been a New York anomaly, a tidy, tiny enclave of a few thousand souls in an old-timey Bronx neighborhood, with an easy vibe, on the outskirts of the major metropolis. For Offshore Sailing School's on-water classes, at least at its outset in the mid-1960s and early 1970s, it was also home port and base camp. In the years that would follow, Offshore's vast network of sailing programs would have operations and bases in eight "foreign" locations in the Caribbean, the Bahamas, Bermuda, Mexico and Tahiti. And then there were the 63 domestic locations in 15 states, plus the territory of Puerto Rico. And on top of that, there were more than two dozen other locales where, with an RV/camper and a Soling under tow, they'd taken their "Learn to Sail" course on the road.

But it all started on City Island.

For a spit of real estate jutting into the far western reaches of Long Island Sound—measuring a mere mile-and-a-half long by a slight half-mile wide—in terms of both cultural relevance (countless television shows and movies have been filmed there including, fittingly, Andy Garcia's *City Island* and Robert De Niro's *A Bronx Tale*) and maritime history (it's been home to countless oystermen, anglers and boatbuilders), City Island always punched way above its weight.

"When I started Offshore," Steve wrote, "we based the experiential part of the course there at Minneford Yacht Yard. City Island has wonderful history as a sailing center. Square-rigged ships would wait there for the tide to change in the East River in order to dock at South Street in Manhattan to unload their wares from all over the world. During World War II, minesweepers were built on City Island at the Nevins Boatyard. Nevins also built a number of 12-meter yachts for the America's Cup."

DAILY NEWS
NEW YORK'S PICTURE NEWSPAPER ®

New York, N.Y. 10017, Monday, July 5, 1971*

ONLY HUMAN

Offshore Off Fifth Avenue

By SIDNEY FIELDS

Except for one aberrant period when he went off keel and tried to sell baby lotions but failed, Steve Colgate has been faithful to sail boats and sailing.

He's the founder, dean and president of the Offshore Sailing School, right here on E. 54th St., off Fifth Ave. No, he doesn't do the sailing on E. 40th. That's where he gives his students 8 hours of classroom work; the other 12 hours in the 20 hour course are spent on Long Island Sound off City Island.

"We've put about a thousand people through the school in the last five years," said Steve, 35, shy, wiry, who couldn't make Naval ROTC at Yale because of his eyesight, but made the Olympics and was a lieutenant in the Air Force.

One-third of all his students were women. The youngest sailor was a 14-year-old girl. Some were over 60. Among them were a judge, a bar manager, several doctors, stenographers, lawyers, dentists, nurses and teachers, an airline stewardess, an architect, a printing pressman, a photographer and a YWCA ballet instructor.

Steve, a Yale graduate whose forebears founded Colgate University, keeps careful charts on why people come to Offshore Sailing. "To learn sailing, to perfect their sailing skills, out of a sense of excitement or curiosity, or because they're afraid of the water."

The interest is big and getting bigger. Last year Americans bought 51,000 sailboats, which brought the total registered to 627,000.

Steve began his school in 1965 with himself as the sole faculty and two Solings, the 27' Olympic class keelboats, for which he paid $2,400 each. He now has a fleet of six Solings and a seventh on order, eight teachers in New York and four instructors for three branches of the Offshore school he recently opened in Martha's Vineyard, Mass., Sturgeon Bay, Wis., and Nassau in the Bahamas. He also holds some eight symposiums in the Bahamas during the winter to teach sailboat racing.

"I get the better known sailors in America to come down and serve as coaches," Steve said.

When he first began his school he couldn't find the proper textbook for the instruction he wanted to give, so he wrote a complete one himself. He's eminently qualified. At 22 he went on a 4,200 mile race from Cuba to Spain and his boat beat the four others in the race.

He's since been in three other transatlantic races, lasting from 16 to 20 days in all kinds of wild and uncertain seas and weather. Steve was on the crew of five other races from Newport, R.I., to Bermuda, participated in the 1963 Pan-American Games, sailed in the America's Cup trials in 1967 and again in 1970, and was in the 1968 Olympics on the 5.5 meter sailboats.

"No, we didn't win," he said, "but just to get into the Olympics is a triumph."

Steve Colgate—on an even keel.

In his classrooms aspiring sailors are first taught the language of sailing, which is essential. They've got to know port from starboard, how from stern, and what to do when they hear, "Jibe ho!" or "Ready about!" They also learn to recognize different kinds of boats, how sails react to wind, wind shifts, apparent winds, all about docking, knots, balancing a boat, theory of navigation and what to do when someone falls overboard.

"Then we get out on the water and cover everything in actual practice," said Steve. "In the boat they learn their basic sailing, coastal navigation and celestial navigation."

Last winter an applicant, bearded and about 40, told Steve he was sailing on an archeological expedition to Yucatan, Mexico and wanted only the 8 hours of classroom; he'd take navigation and all that when he returned. Steve warned him that he couldn't learn enough in the classroom to make such a difficult and dangerous trip and besides, he could expect a mean northerly gale on his route. The man shrugged and said it would be okay because his partner was great on celestial navigation with his sexton and then he left. Months later the man returned, phoned Steve to tell him that when his partner first held up the sexton in the boat he said "damn! I've forgotten how!" and that gale did hit them and so did a Castro machine gun when they were blown near Cuba and they had to bail water as they fled because of the bullet holes in the boat.

"The man never did take navigation and all that," Steve said.

One of his more industrious students, a pretty blonde learned to sail so expertly on the Sound that she went on to take a racing symposium in the Bahamas and became vice-president of Offshore Sailing.

"She is also Mrs. Colgate," Steve said.

Oh, the rewards of sailing!

Reporter Sidney Fields filed a flattering piece on Offshore in the July 5, 1971 edition of the *Daily News* tabloid.

City Island's newest waterfront denizen was Offshore's newly minted vice-president, Doris Colgate, who was more than ready to put an indelible mark on the business. At *Yachting*, Doris had never risen farther up the corporate ladder than "secretary," a title that was frustrating (and inaccurate) on multiple levels. Her rapid trajectory to V.P. of Offshore was more satisfying, and very soon it would become clear the "promotion" was worthy of her talents.

Even so, in a profile of Steve and the company in the July 5, 1971, edition of the city's popular *Daily News* tabloid, reporter Sidney Fields boiled it down to the basics. He wrote, "One of his more industrious students, a pretty blonde, learned to sail so expertly on the Sound that she went on to take a racing symposium in the Bahamas and became vice-president of Offshore Sailing.

"'She is also Mrs. Colgate,' Steve said.

"Oh, the rewards of sailing!" concluded Fields.

Oh, dear.

The *Daily News* writer may have been a bit of a smart aleck, but there were real-life "wise-guys" lingering about, too. During their long tenure in City Island, Offshore moved addresses to different marinas on several occasions. Steve wrote about one search for new digs:

"There were rumors that City Island had in the past been a hotbed of organized crime. On one occasion, Doris and I were looking into moving the school to another boatyard and were told by the manager to come back on Sunday when the owner would be there to discuss an arrangement. We showed up at the appointed time and found a black, stretch limousine parked there. A window in back was lowered and a bony, beckoning hand waved us over. As we approached, the door swung open and we were ushered into the back seat. I don't remember much of the negotiations except wanting to get out of there as fast as possible."

Mr. Limo had apparently made the Colgates an offer they could, and did, refuse.

Conducting business on City Island presented other challenges, as well. Doris recalls, with some amusement, their first years there when she accompanied Steve when he taught.

"It was a very small yard at the west end of the island on the Sound side," she said. "It really was just a house with a dock. I would hang out there when Steve was out teaching, in my bikini, and the kids who lived in the house would delight in creeping up behind me and untying my top. Steve had his two Solings there, on moorings, and that's where I learned to sail."

Those original Solings had been purchased with a $5,000 loan from Steve's mother: $2,400 a pop. By the time they moved to the United Boatyard several years later, the fleet had grown to seven Solings and a Pearson 33 for cruising courses, also financed, but by Chemical Bank. The boats still rested on moorings, which presented another problem.

Doris said, "A local guy named Trader John had a messy marine antiques store on the main drag of City Island, and on the side, he sold and winterized moorings. Every spring they seemed to be 'lost' and he sold them back to us."

Trader John wasn't the only guy who found the Colgates ripe for ripping off. "In those early years of our young business life," Doris remembered, "we were taken twice by bookkeepers—one who wrote checks for herself and another who had two sets of deposit slips, one for herself ($50,000 was discovered) and one for Offshore. We were so naïve, to let others write checks and take money to the bank. We were too busy having fun."

Some of the other employees, while at least honest, were also more colorful. Doris said, "Although we have been blessed with fantastic instructors over the years, occasionally we would hire someone who didn't quite fit the mold, like an odd guy who wore a bosun's whistle around his neck, and made his students—all adults—respond to him with 'Aye, Aye.' When describing stability on a Soling, he used the word 'stabability.' He did not last long."

Despite the kids, kooks and bandits, Doris enjoyed her fledgling new career, especially when it came to introducing fresh innovations, which was the fun part. She said, "I made lots of changes early on because we needed to keep up with the times. Our customers no longer seemed to have the luxury of setting aside four weekend days and four Wednesday evenings throughout a month to learn to sail. So I figured how to turn that course into a three-full-day weekend course, with some options to take the same course during the week. That made a big difference in our bottom line!"

And those three-day courses were, even then in 1971, a bargain: $99 per person for Fourth of July weekend, and $125 for Memorial Day weekend.

Soon there were other programs: navigation courses, first on the schooner *Bill of Rights*, and later on her sister ship, *Harvey Gamage*; a "Sail Away Club" for sailing-school grads that was basically a "time-share" deal where, for $75, you could share a Soling every other weekend with other Club members for three months in the summertime, an idea way ahead of its time; and in 1970, a new "branch" of Offshore based in Edgartown, Massachusetts, at the Harborside Inn (and later the Kelly House). This Martha's Vineyard location was their first Stateside venture outside of New York. That operation lasted for a decade but eventually came to an end for an unforeseen reason: Once the comedian John Belushi became a major movie star—he called the Vineyard his second home—the island became so popular that the resorts no longer needed a sailing school to fill their rooms or coffers.

Then there were the boat shows, especially the annual New York Boat Show each January, easily the nation's largest and most important at the time.

Trader John was a City Island fixture who showcased his eclectic collection
of marine bits and parts in his yard on City Island Avenue.

Steve teaches navigation aboard the schooner *Harvey Gamage* in 1978.

A rather fawning *New York Times* story titled "School of the Sailor: Landlubber to Old Salt" in the paper's boat-show section on January 28, 1973, briefly summarized Steve's America's Cup and Olympic campaigns by concluding that his was "a seafaring portfolio worthy of Davey Jones."

It continued: "While Colgate would like to slip away to sea at the mere suggestion,

he's somewhat landlocked these days while operating the tiller of two busy, well-established and respected sailing schools. He is the owner and president of Offshore Sailing School, Ltd., and part-owner and vice-president of Sailing Symposiums, Inc., both with headquarters in New York and race-week schools in the Bahamas."

Both Steve and Doris have vivid memories of those boat-show days in New York in the early 1970s. Doris had first attended while still on the staff of *Yachting*; one year she invited her dad, who had an inner-ear problem and got "seasick" on a huge powerboat set up in the auditorium while he was below deck (dubbed the "Queen of the Show," it was not an insubstantial vessel). Later, she remembered her old boss, Bob Bavier, warning his staff against complacency when a new magazine called *SAIL* was launched in 1970; *SAIL* (and later in the '70s, another new sailing publication called *Cruising World*) eventually cleaned stodgy *Yachting*'s clock, and Doris learned a hard business lesson she always held dear: Never grow complacent.

Coincidentally, *SAIL*'s founder, Bernie Goldhirsh, approached Steve around that time and asked him if he would display a *SAIL* promotional piece in his booth, to which he readily agreed. It led to Steve writing a monthly learn-to-sail column for the magazine, so at least inadvertently, he helped play a role in *Yachting*'s decline.

And the *SAIL* connection, and the recognition that came from it, led to another unusual gig, when Kool cigarettes approached Steve about writing up an instructional manual for a little one-person dinghy called a Sea Snark, a promotional advertising campaign they ran in the early 1970s. It was a straightforward deal: buy a carton of Kools, send in the attached coupon off the package with the whopping sum of $99.75, and get yourself a sailboat. Steve's handbook, complete with assembly instructions, presumably provided enough information that the recipients, between puffs,

Steve was never shy about having a side hustle, like the time he wrote the instruction manual for a dinghy called a Sea Snark in exchange for ten of the little boats.

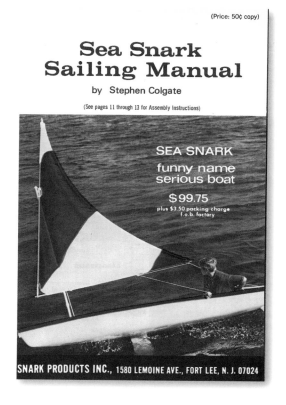

(Price: 50¢ copy)

Sea Snark Sailing Manual

by Stephen Colgate

(See pages 11 through 13 for Assembly Instructions)

SEA SNARK
funny name
serious boat

$99.75
plus $3.50 packing charge
f.o.b. factory

SNARK PRODUCTS INC., 1580 LEMOINE AVE., FORT LEE, N. J. 07024

would be able to launch the boat off a beach and return from their outing without drowning themselves. For this project, he received a small fleet of Sea Snarks…10 of them! Whatever happened to them, eventually, is anyone's guess.

But what, exactly, were those Sailing Symposiums of Steve's that were mentioned in the *Times*? They were, to say the least, a whole other story.

SPORTS ILLUSTRATED magazine's annual Swimsuit Issue was, for decades, arguably the single-most anticipated and popular publication in all of America, if not the planet. The 1973 edition, entitled "A Little Learning…" was staged in the Bahamas, and the opening spread—before you got to the hot babes in their wet, see-through tops—featured a picture of Steve, in sideburns, shorts and a tropical shirt, muscling up the mainsail on a Pearson 33. The opening text, headlined "School for Salts, Old and New," set the scene:

> "Steve Colgate's classroom is Elizabeth Harbor, off Great Exuma Island, 130 miles southeast of Nassau in the Bahamas. Instead of chalk dust it offers brisk breezes, clear water and white, sand-girt islands to circumnavigate and explore. Boats and sailors are based at the Out Island Inn, near George Town. Colgate (right, raising a sail) is a transatlantic racer and Olympic crewman who runs the Offshore Sailing School, Ltd, for beginners and directs Sailing Symposiums Bahamas Race Weeks, a course for experts. His Offshore course, reputed to be the best such program there is, consists of a solid week of basic seamanship aboard one of nine Solings. Three instructors manage to cram everything you ever wanted to know about sailing into 20 hours of instruction followed by two days of solo practice."

Pretty good plug, right? (Though they neglected to include Offshore's contact info.) There was plenty more to come:

"The Symposiums schedule involves six half-day sessions of racing aboard the Solings, which are equipped with the latest in racing gear. Sailors advanced enough to have any technique to sharpen are coached by experts on an Olympic-style course; points that can't be made at sea from the instructor's boat to the student's (through a bullhorn) are thrashed out at chalk talks in evening sessions. Tactics and techniques are taught by Colgate and such guest experts as well-known racers Bruce Goldsmith, Peter Barrett, Dick Stearns and John Marshall. New this year is an advanced cruising course for those who may not want to race but do wish to master a larger boat."

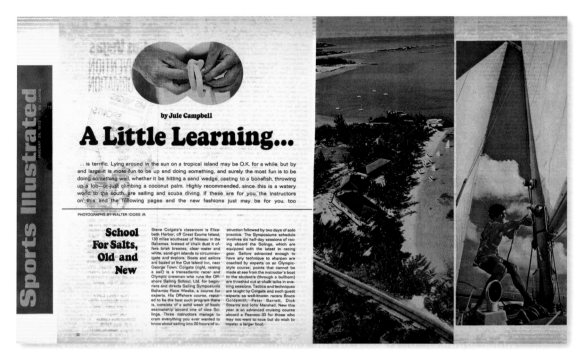

You can't buy this kind of publicity: Steve and Offshore are featured in the 1973 Swimsuit Edition of *Sports Illustrated* magazine in a 6-page spread entitled "A Little Learning…"

In the subsequent layout, interspersed among the terrific Walter Iooss Jr. photos of the lovely ladies, were action shots of Steve, the Solings and his instructors putting the students through their paces, and a long postscript at the end described all the various options in more detail, complete with info on pricing ($165 a week for Offshore's learn-to-sail course, $255 per week for the Symposiums), the excellent lodging accommodations ($56 a night for a single, including breakfast and dinner) and travel. One could not possibly have asked for a better, more complete testimonial. You literally couldn't buy this kind of favorable coverage. It bordered on a long, glowing advertisement.

The entire photo shoot and article, and the absolutely priceless exposure it provided, were largely Doris's doing.

She recalled the morning Steve answered the phone and replied, "No, we can't do that in September, we aren't open then."

She wrote, "I rushed into his office and asked, 'What can't we do?' (There are no 'No's' in my vocabulary, usually.) Jule Campbell, who produced the Swimsuit edition of *Sports Illustrated* wanted to do the next shoot at Out Island Inn on our boats! Was

After an afternoon sail Jane Gill warms up—in White Stag's pastel warmups

Steve Colgate coaches an advanced Symposiums racing crew with a bullhorn (not shown) from a chase boat on Elizabeth Sound off Great Exuma. Below, Libby Oris wears White Stag's terry-lined parka to practice between classes.

Below, Offshore Instructor Herb Stonebrook hangs on and hopes his students learn quickly as they work to put up the spinnaker for the first time on an Olympic class 27-foot Soling. Bottom, he shows them how to trim the boom vang.

Libby is decked out in a one-piece stretch swimsuit by Brigance for Waterclothes

he kidding? No? I made him call her back and say, of course, we can, and we did! We had the Pearson 33 there at the time and they shot all the sailing shots on that boat. (One of the models got a bit banged up, but these were the days before people regularly sued the bejesus out of one another.) Jule enjoyed working with us so much when we moved to South Seas Plantation on Captiva Island, Florida, they came down and did another swimsuit edition shoot there."

Doris also confessed, "I wanted them to include me. I thought I was gorgeous in a bikini. They told me to stay below."

Their loss.

Steve almost always had a little side hustle going—in addition to the books and magazine articles he was now writing rather prolifically, during that 1970 New York Boat Show when he displayed the *SAIL* promotion, he was also peddling yachts for Islander, a California builder, and later he had a scheme to import cruising boats from Greece—but nothing quite to the scale of the very ambitious Sailing Symposiums.

It all began in 1967, when a consortium of Chicago lawyers who were on the board of the country's leading sailboat-racing magazine, *One-Design & Offshore Yachtsman* (which later became *Yacht Racing/Cruising* and then *Sailing World*), and its editor, Bruce Kirby, approached Steve about organizing and running week-long training clinics in the Bahamas. They entered into a partnership, with the magazine providing the eager students, who were recruited from regular ads in its pages, and with Steve in charge of the curriculum and expertise. The hook, along with Steve himself, were the other guest experts he recruited to run the sessions, who were happy to do so for the fee of a pleasant, all-expense-paid winter escape to the islands. In addition to the roster of all-stars listed in the *Sports Illustrated* piece, Buddy Melges, Hans Fogh, Ian Bruce, Dick Rose, Charlie Ulmer and many others signed on for stints at the Symposiums.

The first couple of years the program was staged in West End on Grand Bahama Island, then a year in Nassau, before moving on to the Exumas, where the *S.I.* shoot took place. The major logistical challenge in this stretch was moving, launching and storing the fleet of 10 Solings on a regular basis. As it turned out, the actual running of the race weeks was comparatively simple. But dealing with the gaggle of 27' 6" keelboats was always an adventure that teetered on a fiasco.

Doris's very first trip with Steve on this mission, shortly after they were married, was the most notorious and bizarre. After the first few years of the Symposiums, they took delivery of 10 new Solings, which meant the old ones needed to be moved to their new home in Florida, a trip of around 60-nautical miles of very open water. For the tow to West Palm Beach, they hired a local Bahamian fishing boat with a local captain and two crew, and recruited several volunteers to join them to steer each of the Solings, which Steve hooked up with staggered lines affixed to a long, central tow line. Doris remembers the trip well: "I was still green in many ways, and while others tied off the tiller so their boat stayed in the V-line without moving towards the other line, I steered all the way. The sportfish crew said they were coming right back to West End, so we didn't take any luggage, or even a toothbrush. Of course, when they were met at the dock by three rather sexy women, we knew we were in for at least one night or maybe two in West Palm."

Not even a toothbrush or a change of clothes? What to do? Luckily (or not, as it turned out), the America's Cup sailor and yacht designer Halsey Herreshoff—from the famous family of Rhode Island naval architects—was there on his own powerboat, and invited the Colgates to a party. Drinking ensued. Then one of the guests, the captain of another adjacent power yacht, invited them to dinner and to crash that evening in the owner's cabin. They happily accepted. More drinks flowed.

All was well until Steve woke, groggily, to find the dude tugging at his underwear. He stammered something about fixing the air conditioning, split, and Steve fell back asleep. But soon he was back, sliding into the bunk between the couple, whom he started drunkenly groping with both hands. They screamed and he left, and they spent a few sleepless hours behind a locked door until they realized he'd passed out and they made their escape. Sure, Doris and Steve were a pretty attractive pair, but c'mon man.

And then there was the exodus from Nassau to Elizabeth Harbor and the Out Island Inn in the Exumas, a longer delivery of about 125-nautical-miles a couple years later, which was harrowing in a different way. The Colgates' cohort in this at-sea affair was a gruff "Conchie Joe"—a white Bahamian—named Woody, who whipped up meals of souse and chicken feet ("surprisingly good" vouched Doris) and lent them the berth usually reserved for his German shepherd, who unfortunately also used it as a urinal, so they had to crash in a makeshift bed fashioned of spinnakers in the 25-foot race committee boat, which had been stored on deck with a forklift.

Woody's boat was a rough inter-island freighter, and they strung out the Solings behind it on a long hawser with the Boston Whaler they also used for instruction tied alongside. All was well until, about 40 miles into the trip, the hawser snapped and the Solings scattered like frightened geese. Steve had a helper with him, an expat English sailor named Ian, and they both hopped into the Whaler.

Steve wrote, "The boat had a 40-hp. outboard motor, but the steering was broken, so I draped myself over the outboard, arms around the sides, and I turned the motor and operated the throttle and gear shift while Ian worked on reconnecting the line of boats. Luckily, the first break was in daylight, so we could develop a system. Woody's boat had a high-powered spotlight on the cabin top. I sat up there and played the beam on the line of boats, so we could stop immediately if it happened again."

Which, of course, it did. And again. And again. Six times.

By the time they got to the Exumas, after several days of this madness, they were all wiped out. And Woody, who'd been a solid and reliable teetotaler during the trip, really tied one on, so much so that he didn't recognize any of them the next day. Less than a year later, after a different misadventure, he was found floating face down in Nassau harbor. It was all part of doing business in the Bahamas.

HERMAN WOUK'S hilarious 1965 novel, *Don't Stop the Carnival*, tells the tale of one Norman Paperman of New York City, who escapes the rat race and his dull existence to run a hotel in the islands, and is a classic send-up of the stereotypical tropical dream that becomes a nightmare. It could've taken place in the Out Island Inn. Both Steve and Doris have loads of memories from the place. Vivid ones.

"The sewer system went on the blink and all our students and guest experts had to take buckets of water out of the swimming pool to flush their toilets," Steve wrote. "We had so many students each week that the dining room had to do two sittings, like a cruise ship. Waiters would go in the kitchen, wipe off the plates with a dirty rag and fill them for the next course. Needless to say, we had almost fifty percent of the participants laid low with diarrhea. Our worst outbreak was from an outdoor buffet with a mayonnaise shrimp salad that had been sitting in the sun. That got almost everybody.

"Once a month they closed the restaurant during the day to fumigate it for very large roaches or 'mahogany bugs,' as some islanders called them. One evening we were in the middle of a meal when we heard screams from a female sailing student. A large cockroach had fallen down from the rafters and landed on her plate upside-down, legs wiggling in the last throes of life. It was something out of Kafka's *The Metamorphosis*.

"One day the maître 'd quit, just walked out never to return. Why? The kitchen floor was covered with grease and he slipped, landing flat on his back. Whenever I went in the kitchen I thanked God I had been an ice hockey player and could handle the conditions."

The tennis pro, a guy named Prince, took bets on the regular crab races he conducted and fleeced all the guests; he kept his horse hobbled outside by the road so it could munch on the grass, secretly hoping some car would run it down and he could collect compensation. The tiny airport in Georgetown was serviced by a small Bahamian airline. One time, Doris sat next to a dead-heading pilot who was returning from vacation and pounding drinks the whole way. After he gasped upon the particularly rough landing, she asked him what was wrong and he said, "We just hit a tree." On another flight, the contents of the large paper bag one woman had carried aboard toppled over in turbulence, and the legless land crabs it contained rolled up and down the aisles.

Then there was the time Steve came ashore after teaching a class and was accosted by a uniformed immigration official, who demanded to see his work permit, which he wasn't carrying. "You're under arrest," he said. But Steve's well-connected 300-pound Bahamian lawyer, Nigel, who'd supposedly secured the paperwork, straightened things out…and later served 15 years in the slammer for smuggling blow from Colombia.

It just never ended.

There was but one saving grace, and it was a winner. The sailing was glorious, if sometimes a bit boisterous.

"We had three-person crews and most were quite experienced," Steve wrote. "Many were checking out the Soling…it was the new Olympic class and they wanted to see if they could compete in them. One crew consisted of a father, his brother and a 12-year-old son. We followed the races in a chase boat and coached. We saw the boat jibe and then there were two heads in the water: the adults. The kid rounded the boat up into the wind and waited. We collected the adults and put them back aboard. About 30 years later I met the boy, who recounted he was the one soloing a Soling in Elizabeth Harbor."

And Doris was, well, an attraction. Or was that a distraction?

With Doris adorned in a swimsuit, the standing joke at the Sailing Symposiums in the early '70s, the "favored end" of the starting line was always the Committee Boat with Doris aboard, even if Steve laid out a line with the port end so favored it could barely be crossed on starboard tack.

"Steve coached from a chase boat and moved guest experts from boat to boat," she said. "In the evenings, a recap and seminar were held. When starts were discussed at one of these sessions, and questions were asked of the group why they didn't consider (starting at) the favored end of the line, someone piped up, 'The favored end of the line is where Doris is in a bikini.' That became our motto, for a while."

Alas, all good things must come to an end, and in 1972, not one but two things did, simultaneously. Steve resigned from his formal association with the Symposiums, and he and Doris moved the revamped winter programs, now completely under their auspices, to new locations in Tortola (where their new consolidated venture, Offshore Sailing Vacations, Inc., would offer "Basic Race Weeks" for those just getting into racing) and the southeastern coast of Puerto Rico (where "guest experts" would continue teaching advanced sailors, in the same format as the previous Symposiums).

By this time, in the six years of operations, over a thousand students had taken the Symposiums' courses, and were enthusiastic in offering their praise; the comments were duly reported in a newsletter.

"The exposure I received went far enough to take first overall in Class C in the Lake Champlain racing series plus a number of pieces of silver (eight in all for the season)," wrote Peter H. Covert.

"After a week of your gentle teaching techniques, a good boat and some practice, two weeks ago I won the '72 San Francisco Bay Ericson 29 championship! And I owe it all to you…because of that, got an invite to crew in the Transpac next July. It all boggles the mind," exclaimed Lloyd Cunningham.

"After all your high-powered instruction I took third in the 470 Nationals—beat Peter Barrett in one race and lost by 10 inches in another—wonder of wonders," said Bruce Maguire, Jr.

It was all music to the ears, not to mention deposits in the bank accounts.

The Puerto Rico arrangement that proved to be the impetus for Offshore to break free from the Symposiums and instigate its own program had a rough start. The Colgates were already in business with a fellow Yale graduate of Steve's named Charles Fraser, who owned the Sea Pines Plantation resort in Hilton Head, South Carolina, where Offshore had already established a school. Fraser had purchased land on the eastern, windward coast of P.R. near the town of Humacao and was planning to build another resort called Palmas del Mar.

All was going well until Steve and Doris arrived in San Juan for a meeting with Fraser's

The wind and sea conditions off Palmas del Mar, Puerto Rico,
were sporty indeed, as the crew of this launched Soling could attest.

Mark roundings during Race Weeks in the roiling waters
of Palmas del Mar were always exciting.

partners in the enterprise (Steve recalls them as the "high-powered staff" while Doris remembers them as a bunch of "MBA suits"). Whoever they were, they had an issue; namely, they refused to negotiate with Doris, a woman, who was left to stew outside the conference room. It was the first—and last—time that ever happened.

In any event, Steve hammered out the deal, and before long the operation was up and running, albeit in a "resort" that was very much "under construction," with the aroma of wet paint and drying cement wafting everywhere. But that was only half of it. In the relatively docile Bahamas, the sailing breezes had been moderate and reliable. Here on the east coast of Puerto Rico, smack dab in the face of the staunch, powerful northeast trade-winds, it blew like hell. And then blew some more.

"Palmas del Mar was a work in progress for the whole time we were there," wrote Steve. "The marina was unfinished and we surfed into the bay that would become the harbor on the heavy seas and the strong trades. The "Learn to Sail" students went out with our instructors, blissfully unaware that these conditions were unusual, while the racing crews were saying, 'You're sending us out in this wind and in these seas? I don't believe it.' I met one of the hotel staff one day who said he saw so many women with bruises, he thought it must be a convention for battered wives until he put two and two together: 'Ah, the sailing school.'"

Even so, Offshore's penchant for garnering great press continued unabated, including a splashy, full-color, five-page feature in the June, 1974 issue of *Fortune* called "Racing School: Six Days Behind the Mast" in the magazine's regular "On Your Own Time" segment. The target audience was clear from the outset.

"Too much like boot camp for most executives, perhaps, but for the competitive sailor the Offshore Sailing School can be heaven… When we visited the school earlier this spring, the class was filled to capacity with 24 sailors, including 13 businessmen, three doctors, a dentist, two lawyers, four youths—two of them sons of other participants—and one wife.

"One student confided that he paid $100,000 for his boat less than a year earlier, and had already spent $20,000 more augmenting the equipment… 'All this for a $20 trophy!" he says wryly. Viewed in these terms, Race Weeks do not seem so expensive: $245 for tuition, plus an average of around $350 for accommodations.

"The racer has a special kind of mentality, remote from that of the ordinary day sailor. He tends to strive for perfection—particularly if he is an executive achiever… Above all, racing attracts the person who thrives on competition. 'While it's a complete escape from the trials and tribulations of business,' says Larry Brown, president of an American Hospital Supply Corp. subsidiary, 'I love the same thing in racing that I do in business. Winning is what it's all about.'"

Well, gung ho, gentlemen.

One of the more memorable encounters during this period happened one afternoon when Steve and Doris were having lunch by the pool, when a fellow came up and introduced himself as the sound man for an America's Cup documentary on *Heritage* in 1970, when Steve was the tactician (stuck down below with his recording equipment, the poor fellow was wracked with seasickness most of the time). He said he was no longer in filmmaking but driving a cab in New York City and fooling around with his guitar, writing songs. In fact, he'd written one called *Taxi* that had become a big hit, and casually mentioned he was performing in New York that weekend for $25 grand. Steve remembers him fondly, as "humble and modest," and though he died tragically in a car crash the following year, it was not before he'd set up a food bank that proved to be a lasting legacy. Doris and Steve had both enjoyed catching up with Harry Chapin.

Classes from masters: Butch Ulmer (above, on dock) and Buddy Melges (opposite page) were just two of the many top-notch racers who served as Guest Experts at South Seas Island Resort after the move to Florida.

Otherwise, the writing was on the wall for Puerto Rico. Steve said, "By the end of our three-year contract there, we knew the conditions at Palmas del Mar were too rough to continue. The boats and courses were empty in the summertime and no students returned the next winter. We needed a year-round branch in the U.S."

Did someone say "Sunshine State?"

FLORIDA MADE too much sense, on several fronts, not to be in business there. No work permits required. Easy and cheap flights (not a small consideration in those recessionary times). Perfect weather much of the year. Simpler to move the boats to

other seasonal branches if necessary. Steve and Doris embarked on a state-wide road trip to find the right location. Homer's *Odyssey* might've been less epic.

They'd consulted a thick book listing all the hotels in the U.S.A., with their managers, phone numbers, and numbers of rooms and amenities, before they set out. They decided to start on the East Coast on the Atlantic Ocean side and head south, then back up the West Coast and the Gulf of Mexico side if necessary.

They started in Port St. Lucie at the Sandpiper Bay Club, which later became a Club Med. From the moment they arrived, they realized it wouldn't do; it just didn't have the ambiance of the Bahamas, which, Steve said, apart from the insistent drama, "We loved and wanted to duplicate." Every other waterfront Atlantic hotel was similarly disappointing.

Three days were spent in Key West, which was basically a disaster. It seemed like a

A fleet of Offshore's Solings in a 1976 Race Week session
in the quiet waters of Pine Island Sound off of South Seas Plantation.

town full of hippies and losers who'd headed south to escape something until they ran out of highway. Their lasting image of the place was in Mallory Square at sunset, when a young, barefoot, very pregnant young lady stumbled past swilling directly from a bottle of red wine. Nope.

Up the Gulf Coast they went. The Marriot on Marco Island, just north of the Everglades but south of Naples, looked promising, but the facilities weren't ideal and there was a bridge under which sailboats could not pass. Bummer. But the guy running the beach concessions suggested they have a look at another little island further north, a scenic, natural place with plenty of birds and wildlife, and long, white-sand beaches.

Captiva.

In his hotel guide, Steve had already checked out the island's one resort, South Seas Plantation, but realized with 50 rooms that it was way too small for their needs. Offshore would need that many each week just for their students alone. But they decided to have a look anyway.

Steve and Doris both recall their initial impressions.

"In 1974, the island was rustic and almost deserted," Steve said. "Casuarina trees bowed over the road giving the feeling of gliding along the Canal du Midi in France."

"As we drove down the shaded road called Periwinkle Way," said Doris, "through Sanibel and over a small bridge onto Captiva, we knew we were 'home.'"

They were able to track down the general manager and decided to give it a shot, and entered their meeting armed with brochures, scrapbooks and spread sheets. Before they could barely begin, he said, "I was the manager of the Out Island Inn before you came to Exuma. I know who you are and what you can do."

"But the hotel book says you only have 50 rooms…"

"That's a misprint. We have 150. We can easily block as many as you need. Come here. We want you."

On November 7, 1976, the Colgates and Offshore Sailing School threw the Grand Opening Party for their Captiva Island base with three offerings: Learn to Sail, Learn to Cruise and Race Weeks.

Mission accomplished.

A perfect setting for a sailing school.

The future.

Boss Ladies gather at an AWED presentation in the mid-90's - front row
Cindy Annchild, Doris Colgate, Dianne Morris Sullivan,
Jo-Ann Friedman Rapaport; back row Jane Wilson, Joan Robinson,
Margo Berk-Levine, Pamela Scurry, Tess Sholom.

8

Designing Woman
The Boss Ladies...and the Boss

THE TELEVISION program *Designing Women*, a sitcom starring Dixie Carter and Delta Burke, aired from 1986 through 1993, a total of seven seasons and 163 episodes. The show tells the tale of the Sugarbaker sisters and their eponymous interior-design firm, Sugarbaker & Associates, a basically all-women enterprise comprised of smart, sassy gals making a name for themselves, with the expected comedic pratfalls along the way. Carter's character, Julia Sugarbaker, the president of the company, runs the operation and is, according to an overview of the series, "known for her no-nonsense speeches from a feminist and liberal perspective."

None of this seems particularly edgy or controversial today, but at the time a show about women successfully and aggressively taking charge of their own destiny, in the cutthroat world of mostly male, wing-tipped commerce, was unusual and refreshing. Not coincidentally, for several years *Designing Women* ran back-to-back with *Murphy Brown*, another show about a ballsy, opinionated woman who abides zero guff from clueless dudes.

The thing is, the entire production was likely based on an actual group of Manhattan women who were doing precisely what Julia Sugarbaker was doing, but in a wide variety of different businesses, above and beyond interior design. They even had their own collective name, one that was bandied about in respected publications like *The Wall Street Journal* and business magazines like *Venture*.

They were known as the "Boss Ladies."

And Doris Colgate was a very proud member of their sisterhood.

In 1978, after eight years as the vice-president of Offshore Sailing School, she assumed the role of the company's president—Julia Sugarbaker had nothing on her, thanks—a position she addressed with the utmost levels of respect, gravity and responsibility. Steve's own sailing prowess, and his natural talent for teaching, had laid the foundation of the business. Now, Doris was poised to use that solid base and grow and expand upon it, to take that ground-floor establishment and erect a high-rise atop of it.

To do so, she realized she would need to raise her game as well, to learn new skills and adapt to an ever-changing world full of fresh opportunities. Basically, she wanted to embody the characteristics of a world that was becoming ever more popular in business circles, that was even the title of a new magazine launched in 1977 that was all the rage. Like the publication, Doris wished to become an *Entrepreneur.*

She was self-aware enough to know that that would require some help. It came from, at the time, a happenstance introduction.

It was Karon Cullen, who ran a public-relations company called Cullen and Taylor, whom Doris had hired to do some publicity for Offshore, who opened the door to a program that would have a profound influence on her life, not only then but for decades after.

Karon Cullen, a publicist who did some work for Offshore, played a key role in getting Doris involved with the American Women's Economic Development Corporation.

Doris said, "Karon was involved in a program for entrepreneurial women and in 1978 introduced me to Bea Fitzpatrick and the American Women's Economic Development Corporation (AWED), a federally funded program Bea started on her own. Although I was in partnership with a man, they accepted me, and oh boy, I was exposed to the equivalent of getting my MBA."

A *New Yorker* article on AWED described it as "a highly successful management-training and technical-assistance program for women entrepreneurs," but it was so much more than that. Its members were an eclectic group of women who did indeed offer plenty of technical advice and real-world solutions which they'd gained through their own hard-earned workaday experiences, but who also served as friends and colleagues who provided emotional support, endless encouragement, and a receptive ear to ideas or complaints when difficult decisions needed to be made.

The group included Jo-Ann Friedman (later Rapaport), who ran a marketing company providing market supported health information; Deann Murphy, who owned a crafts business called Distelfink Designs; Cindy Annchild, who had an innovative holistic soap shop called The Bath House in Greenwich Village; Margo Berk-Levine, who founded and led a booming personnel service; Dianne Sullivan (later Morris), whose first company created and supplied the little bottles of shampoo and lotion for hotel chains and whose later company designed and supplied decorative bedding for retailer chains; Pam Scurry, who specialized in wicker, with an antique shop called The Wicker Garden, and a kid's store, too; Jane Wilson, a caterer who created "green" menus and wrote a cookbook called *Eating Well!*; Joan Robinson whose company specialized in HR; and many others. Most regular AWED meetings were organized for the entire group, but later, there were extra, regular break-out sessions for a smaller gathering of about a dozen women, who continued to meet well after their time in AWED had passed. Though three have passed away, and one left the group years ago, seven have continued their relationship to this very day.

The Boss Ladies at their annual get-together in 2018: Margo Berk-Levine, Deann Murphy, Jo-Ann Rappaport, Cindy Annchild, Tess Sholom, Doris and Dianne Morris.

It was this smaller group, plus Tess Sholom, a jewelry-designer and manufacturer friend of Jo-Ann Friedman who joined later, that ultimately banded together, and bonded with one another to become the Boss Ladies. The name came from one of its members, an artist and writer named Laura Torbet who wrote a pilot screenplay for a fictional TV series by the same title, which got shopped around to several production companies and agents, though never picked up. Yet everyone involved with the Boss Ladies believes at some stage the script was pilfered by somebody influential along the line and eventually morphed into *Designing Women.*

In a story for *Venture* called "A Sense of Self," author Barbara Presley Noble took a deep look at the clan. "The Boss Ladies (are) an 11-woman group of entrepreneurs who run, or have run, businesses ranging in size from about $250,000 to $7 million in revenues or receipts annually," she wrote. "In one sense the Boss Ladies do what groups of women have done for centuries when they gathered to quilt, drink coffee or raise consciousness. The difference here is content: The Boss Ladies reserve at least one evening a month, stealing from calendars stuffed fuller than a pastrami on rye, to talk business. They may meet to analyze a problem, report on recent events, or celebrate achievements.

"The Boss Ladies," she continued, "are not, as individuals, much alike. Beyond the shared demographic of being educated, white, and middle- to upper-middle class, they diverge: Their ages range from 39 to 60… They are also variable in personal style: vivacious, intense, commanding, shy, smooth, laid-back, confident, funny."

Hmmm. The summation sounds eerily like the description of a certain female executive at a New York-based sailing academy.

In the *New Yorker* article on AWED, which ran in the magazine's May 11, 1981 issue, Doris said, "I am a classic example of a woman who was not conducting her business in a very businesslike manner. I had never written a business plan, my prices were too low, I wasn't looking at my financial statements. All I would do was ask my accountant, 'How am I doing?' In the two years that I've been with AWED, my gross has risen 44 percent; I'm now taking in over a million dollars a year; and I'm employing close to 50 people. The AWED program is worth a year and a half of MBA training at a top university; I got it in one-quarter of that time and it was absolutely free.

But it's very fitting that Doris would be part of a sisterly tribe that likely was the inspiration for a TV show called *Designing Women.* For Doris was, in fact, a woman with her own designs on many matters: an emerging sense of entrepreneurship; an ambitious desire to take Offshore, the company, to another level; a growing interest in alluring side projects, in books, fashion, food and travel; and more and better opportunities for empowering all women in the workplace (and on the water, for that matter), above and beyond her talented and motivated Boss Ladies.

After all, as the business of Offshore prospered, matured and grew, Boss Lady Doris was, quite simply…its boss.

PERHAPS EMBOLDENED by her successful and supportive Boss Ladies, and her entire enlightening experience with AWED, after purchasing the Ratsey & Lapthorn sail loft on City Island in 1982 as the primary base for Offshore, Doris made perhaps the biggest miscue of her entire career when she hung a sign reading "Doris and Steve Colgate's Offshore Sailing Center" emblazoned across the front of it.

"Yes," Doris conceded, sheepishly, many years later, "I put my name first…for the first and last time ever."

Alas, Doris may have been the one now figuratively baking the business's bread, but she also eventually came to truly recognize that it was Steve Colgate—both the consummate sailor and, in contemporary parlance, the company's very own *brand*—who buttered it.

But the entire Ratsey & Lapthorn tale is one worth telling.

For the Colgates, 1976 was a big year, above and beyond all the associated hoopla with the many Bicentennial celebrations. Not only did they launch their large new southern operation on Captiva Island, after seven years in their $350/month one-room apartment on Manhattan's 51st Street, they moved into more spacious digs on the 20th floor of an apartment building at 400 East 54th Street, one with a small view of the East River, which delighted Doris. (The rent did not: "$800 a month," she recalled. "Scary.") The place was a convenient walk to Offshore's offices and classrooms at 820 Second Street, near the U.N. building, where they'd relocated a couple years earlier.

"We loved living (on 54th Street)," Doris said. "We joined a club in the Sherry Netherlands building on 5th Avenue and enjoyed many formal evenings dancing and dining. I exercised three times a week during lunch at a spa one block away from our office. We lived in Manhattan in the best of times. But our lives were changing…a lot."

A big reason for that was the move that year of their on-the-water operations in City Island from the United Boat Yard, which had been sold to developers, to the old

Before and after: the Ratsey and Lapthorn sail loft immediately after
it was purchased in 1982, and in the spring of 1983
after Doris had it repainted and added the deck for a café.

sail loft on Schofield Street, established in 1902, and where Offshore rented space
from Colin Ratsey, a descendant of the English family of renowned sailmakers, Ratsey
& Lapthorn, who'd been stitching sails for nearly two centuries. (Ratsey & Lapthorn
still has a loft in Cowes, where the company originated in the late 1700s). The three-
story building was massive, tens of thousands of square feet, with 150 feet of open
floor space where sailmakers crafted the billowing America's Cup sails for the gargantuan J-Class yachts in the 1920s and 1930s.

It was business as usual for the first few years of the arrangement, with Offshore
renting a small office as well as the use of the connecting pier and docks; along with
their fleet of Solings, they'd added a 32-foot Columbia 9.6 and a Pearson 36 for
cruising courses. Later, when windsurfing burst onto the sailing scene, they added a
bunch of boards for lessons and rentals. Then came a small fleet of Sunfish dinghies.
In the summer, the place was hopping.

But it was about to get a whole lot crazier. On multiple levels.

It all started on a late-summer day when Colin Ratsey, the owner, approached Steve

with some unsettling news. "He said he had to sell the property to pay off unpaid taxes to the government," Steve said. "He had a Chicago investor who said Offshore could stay as a tenant for (maybe) six months. I asked if we could buy the property instead. He said, 'Whoever comes up with the cash by the deadline owns it.'"

Here's where the story takes an unexpected turn. Doris's parents, Bernie and Frances, were also living in New York City, and Offshore had hired her mom as their bookkeeper, a job she excelled at, even though Doris cringed a little whenever Frances reminded one of their employees, which she did regularly, "I write your paycheck, you know…"

But Frances had come of age in the Depression, and knew a thing or two about frugality. And with the sail-loft property very much in play, it turned out, Doris said, that her mother "had squirrelled away enough money in a Dreyfus account unbeknownst to us to make the down payment and get a loan for the $250 grand (the amount Ratsey was in arrears). The net result was, with an 18-percent mortgage—thanks Jimmy Carter—we now owned the place."

On the day they closed the Manhattan offices on Second Street for good and moved everything—"lock, stock and barrel," Doris said, with "everything" including their entire office staff, including the sales team and their own dedicated travel

"Long Island weather": a group of Solings are prepared
for a day of light-air lessons in the early 1980s.

agency—out to City Island, Doris cried all the way. They were most certainly not tears of joy.

The "hostile" reception they got from some of their new neighbors upon their arrival didn't help things. In local City Island parlance, the carpet-bagging, out-of-town Colgates were "mussel suckers," unlike the entrenched, long-time townie residents, who saw themselves as "clam diggers."

The loft turned out to be a lot of things…including a money pit. For instance, there was "Big Bertha": the nickname for the coal-fired heating plant on the ground floor.

Doris said, "The loft was heated by a huge, white-painted furnace on the ground floor, that looked like it had been patched with oatmeal. The heating costs alone were

An OSS launch delivers a boatload of sailors to their moored boats.
The burned-out dock in the background was courtesy
of the "fire-preventer" named "Jimmy the Baker."

Offshore instructor Lou Carretero and VP/operations Rob Eberle on the docks
prior to a press event in 1983.

$25,000 a year. One day a strange guy showed up and told us he could make the furnace work better. He brought a small glass pyramid not much larger than a paperweight, made us all stand far away outside the building, and commenced to put some sort of a hex on the furnace. It did not work."

The Boiler Wizard wasn't the only unwanted visitor. The Colgates had dealt with mobbed-up, Tony Soprano-wannabes on City Island before, so they weren't entirely surprised when a plump, threatening little character named "Jimmy the Baker" wandered in to "talk business."

Doris remembers "the short, paunchy man with sparse grey hair" very well. It was an encounter she wouldn't soon forget.

"I met personally with him on a summer weekday morning, around 10 a.m. on our deck," she recalled. "He asked for a rye on the rocks; we had a liquor license. Then he handed me a card, which read 'Fire Prevention Services,' and in his gravelly voice pointed to the burned-out dock next to ours, and said, 'See that dock? I took care of it.'" Doris knew precisely what he was getting at. Jimmy didn't mean he'd extinguished it. She pocketed his little card, hoping against hope Steve wouldn't come down to get involved.

"A week later," Doris continued, "a guy in suit arrived and said, 'I hear you met Jimmy the Baker.' I was sitting at my desk, pulled out the card and handed it to him, gingerly. He was from the FBI and said, 'Don't do that again,' and left."

Doris was more than happy to take his advice.

Still, Doris realized the huge space offered plenty of potential, above and beyond Offshore Sailing School. And she was more than ready to go for it.

"I was determined to make something out of that sail loft," she said, recounting the time when she slapped the sign out front suggesting Steve was playing second fiddle in the place. "We thought about turning the top floor into apartments and hired an architect to draw up plans. Another of my ideas was a roller-skating rink, but I didn't share that with many people. I built an exercise room on the vast second floor, with a privacy wall, so I could continue with my new self-fitness program. We decided to create a restaurant and bar on a deck overlooking the water. It was a happy place for our students and members of our sailing club, and was open to the public as well, as there were few outdoor dining establishments on City Island."

The Colgates had erected the restaurant, and made other changes, without bothering to deal with pesky construction permits and such, which attracted local

Café Offshore, the in-house restaurant and bar,
was a busy spot on a pleasant summer day.

Never one for complacency, Doris got into the retail side of the business
with a series of stores and boutiques, including this one on City Island.

building inspectors with threats of hefty fines for the indiscretion, but nothing much came of it.

"Somehow, we got by," Doris said.

And somehow, she was just getting warmed up.

THE FOREDECK CAFÉ (later known as Café Offshore), the sail loft's in-house bar and restaurant, may have been a popular hangout for Offshore's clients and the more welcoming neighborhood denizens of City Island, but it was also a lot of work, and sometimes had to seem like more bloody trouble than it was worth. At the outset, they rented it out to a young man to run; he was the friend of a lawyer they'd hired to investigate other development opportunities at the loft. (The counselor, in his ubiquitous plaid pants, was also pals with the crooked Bronx Congressman Mario Biaggi, and tried to persuade the Colgates to throw a fundraiser in his honor at the Foredeck, shortly before he wound up in the pokey for corruption. They happily passed on that offer.)

The arrangement with their budding restaurateur did not end well.

"After the first year of the restaurant," Doris said, of an incident that landed in a *Wall Street Journal* story about the Boss Ladies, "I decided during the winter to close off the door into the store because of the greasy path that persisted throughout the season. We did not consult the lessee, we just did it. When the young man came back to reopen the restaurant, he sued us with his finger on the zeros: one million dollars! We settled for $8,000. (The *WSJ*, though it did not identify Doris or Offshore, reported that the course of action was endorsed by her fellow Boss Ladies, who told Doris "not to let her anger stop her from doing what was best for the business [but] pay the settlement and get the problem behind her"). It was a ton of money for us at that time, and I took over running the restaurant. We hired a chef who turned out to be a drunk, and after finding him sleeping way back on the ground floor of the loft with his knives by his hand, I took over the cooking, and sometimes even the waitressing.

"I had never been a waitress," Doris added, with a very rare negative postscript to her usual endeavors: "I failed at that." One time a customer called her out when she failed to jot down his order. "You're not going to remember that," he scolded. "He was right," admitted Doris.

But her other new addition to the place, a retail clothing store, played more to her talents and interests.

The Offshore staff at South Sea Plantation in 1981: Barry Bunnell, Mick Gurley, Bill Gladstone, Chris Angell, Sue Paul, Lou Carretero, Sarah Pederson, Dave Flynn, Philip Wieland, Jim Ellis and an instructor who shall remain nameless.

Doris's love of fashion—and looking and feeling good—started early: as a teenager in Paris, when she'd peruse the aisles of the best shops and department stores on sprees with her mother during their year living in France. Prior to opening the City Island store, she'd started selling boat shoes, gloves and basic sailing apparel out of an office at the Florida operation at South Seas Plantation on Captiva Island. "I always loved to shop," she said. "I liked buying. It was fun." Before long, she'd added shorts, t-shirts and other accessories to the mix, and opened a proper store at the resort called "On and Offshore." During the high season, they were raking in a grand a day. Next came the City Island location. Followed by a bigger space at the Florida marina, then a whole string of shops, including one for kids called "Kiderrific" and another, "Simply Swim," for bathing suits and swimwear, at a Captiva Island strip mall called "Chadwick's Square." Later, there was yet another location at a high-end collection of restaurants and boutiques called "The Village on Venetian Bay" in Naples, Florida.

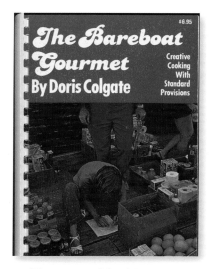

The cover of Doris's book, *The Bareboat Gourmet*, shows the author sorting out provisions for the first Maine flotilla charter in the early 1980s.

"Whenever I traveled with Steve, I sought out lines of clothes or gift items I could carry in our retail stores," she said. "In Australia, it was a fun line of clothes, umbrellas and other items with beachy motifs. In Hawaii, it was a collection of colorful pareos and Hawaiian shirts for men." Before long, she was hitting at least four buying markets a year: in New York, Atlanta, Dallas and Miami, the latter for the "amazing swim show" each fall. ("That was the only one Steve accompanied me to," she said in an aside, no doubt recalling the bevy of lovely young women who modeled the latest styles. "I wonder why?" she asked, knowingly.)

Eventually, despite early dreams of vast expansion, Doris sold or shuttered all the retail businesses. The big outlet stores had started to appear, muscling out more modest specialty shops, and on top of everything else happening, it was a pressure-packed environment. "I drove people hard," Doris confessed. "Too hard, sometimes."

Besides, as if she wasn't busy enough already, she became an author, too.

Perhaps Doris didn't know much about waitressing, but good food was another thing altogether. By 1982, Steve had already knocked off half a dozen technical sailing and racing manuals, but *The Bareboat Gourmet*, published that year, was Doris's first book. Joe Williams, a food writer for *The News-Herald* newspaper in Panama City, Florida, wrote a profile of the tome and its writer.

"Doris Colgate learned to cook from her mother and has always enjoyed preparing tasty dishes," he wrote. "She was well-versed in onshore cooking, and quickly became 'cook of choice' on sailing trips as crews began to recognize her talents and abilities… Doris has (now) published a provisioning manual and a cookbook titled *The Bareboat Gourmet*. Both are crammed with information useful for the weekend sailor or for a crew which intends to make a substantial voyage in either their own or a chartered vessel."

At that point, Williams probably should've left well enough alone. But he couldn't quite help himself.

"I found the cookbook to be most interesting," he added. "In it Doris Colgate reflects the imagination and enthusiasm which she projected to me in our brief conversation. She comes across as a pert lass with an easy smile and an engaging personality. The foods she describes appear to have that same flavor and zest."

Pert? Lass?

Crazily, there was an actual gal—not Doris—fitting this very suspect "compliment" who around this time did wonders for Offshore's bottom line. Topless and perky, with a wide, fetching smile— on the deck of a sailboat, no less—she provided the sort of publicity, it's been said famously, one couldn't buy at any price.

A brief mention of Offshore in the May, 1976, edition of *Cosmopolitan* magazine—featuring this topless "perky lass"—caught plenty of attention and garnered fantastic publicity.

COSMOPOLITAN MAGAZINE, founder and editor Helen Gurley Brown's paean to a specific brand of feminist liberation—and sex; a sampling of typical *Cosmo* cover blurbs included "Have Sexier Sex!", "Best. Sex. Ever.", "Sex It Up!", "Next Level Sex!" and "Sex That Rocks", among countless others—was a supermarket phenomenon in the 1970s. It's difficult to grasp today what a cultural touchstone it was back in its heyday, but remarkably, Offshore Sailing School was a grateful benefactor to its scope and reach.

It happened in the May 1976 edition in the up-front "Cosmo Tells All" section (right next to a quickie profile of singer/actor "Bachelor of the Month," Mac Davis). A mere 76-words long and titled "Sail Away!", the text could not have been more basic (the lead sentence: "Doers who can't just sit in deck chairs on vacation might contemplate taking to the high *seas*!"), with a very simple description of Offshore's learn-to-sail program and the advanced racing and cruising courses, plus the company's address and phone number. What caught everyone's attention was the—it must be said—*pert lass* who was clad in nothing more than extremely cut-off jeans hoisting a mainsail, with a wide, toothy grin to beat the band. It was a stock agency photo of an anonymous model; unlike the dedicated *Sports Illustrated* swimsuit shoot, Offshore had nothing whatsoever to do with it. But it sure struck a chord with *Cosmo*'s readers.

"We got more response from that one photo than from any of our fantastic publicity over the years," said Steve.

Apparently, even the sex-obsessed could use a brief break from sex now and then.

But Steve was right about one thing: Above and beyond the rather expected coverage and articles in the sailing magazines, in these early years Offshore enjoyed great press in a wide variety of mainstream titles, from *Cosmo* to *Playboy* to *Glamour* and many others. Doris's investment in P.R., above and beyond the happy, positive reinforcement it offered, provided real, bottom-line dividends.

It was well-deserved, too. By the early 1980s, growing by leaps and bounds, Offshore had one hell of a story to tell. And the company did do a good job of promoting itself, too. Doris took it upon herself to produce the firm's first full-color brochure, with the best tools of the time.

Doris said, "Our first computer was a huge IBM (machine) I bought for some astronomical sum, for Steve. I placed it on his desk and he thought I was nuts. What was he going to do with that? Our first color brochure—all 8 x 11 of it—was written by me on a Selectric typewriter with an assortment of interchangeable font balls. Then I laid it out on my drafting table, cut rounded corners around all the images—those were in vogue in those days—pasted everything down and sent it off to a printer in Jacksonville, Florida. I even went down there to watch over the first run on their presses."

A few years later, the leap was made to video—with celebrities! (well, sort of)—when a Hollywood production company approached the Colgates about partnering up for a learn-to-sail movie starring Sam J. Jones (perhaps best known for playing Bo Derrick's husband in the blockbuster movie *10*) and Audrey Landers (of *Dallas* fame), ostensibly because the latter was up for a role in a feature film that required a fair degree of athleticism, and somebody thought a few days on a boat would do the trick. Naturally, Steve played the sailing instructor, a role he was born to. For $39.95, the 106-minute video, in VHS or Beta, was all yours.

These side projects, though, were a mere footnote to what was now happening in the day-to-day running of Offshore, which was exploding. Doris eventually compiled

Ready for their close-up: Steve gives actors Sam Jones and Audrey
Landers a few pointers before filming the Learn to Sail video in 1978.

a detailed, year-to-year company history, a Word document that is a book unto itself: nearly 80 pages and almost 45,000 words. The 1965 entry is exactly one sentence and three lines long, with a single, lonely bullet point. The 1985 entry, on the other hand, takes up 3 pages and consists of 38 separate bullet points. Among the highlights, which include the Landers' video:

A new alliance with Hunter Yachts to lease cruising boats and introduce an offshore passage-making course on a Hunter 40. The First Annual Offshore Sailing Club Rendezvous, a 10-day escapade on Long Island Sound. New locations in Panama City, Florida; Newport, Rhode Island; and Bar Harbor, Maine. The availability of Doris's new booklet, *Easy Cruising*. New deals for introductory courses in Tortola, British Virgin Islands, including a scuba-certification class. The 17th season of the Race Weeks (Advanced Racing), now conducted on a fleet of spanking-new Laser 28s, with sailmaker Bill Shore and future America's Cup Hall of Fame skipper Ed Baird joining the ever-expanding list of guest experts. A "Live Aboard Cruising Course" for

Bareboat Certification on a Moorings 50. And on and on and on.

Offshore had been launched, precisely two decades earlier, on the simplest of premises: A guy on a boat, imparting the knowledge required to operate said boat.

Thanks largely to Doris's never-ending initiatives (she never forgot, from her days at *Yachting*, that those who fail at constant innovation eventually get their clock cleaned, and deservedly so), it was now something altogether different: an international, social, instructional juggernaut that was growing each year by leaps and bounds. There was nothing else in the world of sailing even remotely like it.

Nothing.

TWO YEARS into the program at AWED, and firmly ensconced as a proud member of the Boss Ladies, in the spring of 1980 Doris stepped to a podium in Washington, D.C., to testify before congress and a house subcommittee on State, Justice, Commerce and the Judiciary, in a hearing regarding the possible expansion of a woman's business enterprise program into a national initiative, beyond the boundaries of New York City.

Boss Ladies Deann Murphy, in a hat, and Dianne Morris served on Offshore Sailing School's advisory board.

"I came to AWED with a 14-year-old company that was growing, but only enough to keep up with inflation," she explained. "Offshore Sailing School was founded by my husband in 1964 to teach people how to sail or better their sailing skills—usually in conjunction with a vacation at a fine resort. In the beginning, Steve Colgate was the only instructor, the school used one boat and had one location. When I joined it 10 years ago, it had a few more branches, a few more employees, but was still operating at a marginal level. Steve Colgate was, and still is, the foremost sailing educator in the country, and he was totally engrossed in the education aspects of the company, tending to let the business end slide. Working side by side, with me assuming the managerial and marketing tasks, we began to grow, by trial and error, and with no training whatsoever.

"We survived the 1974-1975 recession and continual lack of capital because we are entrepreneurs and particularly because I, as a woman entrepreneur, have a burning desire to prove that women are very capable business men."

And after detailing her own challenges, successes and growth, she added, "AWED helped me become a better employer, taught me how to manage, helped me solve a host of personnel problems. AWED has made me think business, do business in a businesslike way, confronting all the angles, and taking the good with the bad like a man. I have seen in myself and the other women in my group a rising sophistication. We are becoming savvy, analytical, discerning, confident and assertive."

She was talking about AWED, but might've been speaking of her fellow Boss Ladies, when she added, "It's not over."

No. Not by a long shot.

As the decades passed, Doris kept in close contact with those bright, worldly sisters. By 2021, through the attrition of age, their original group of 12 had dwindled to about half that number, and Doris said, "Of all of us, I am the only one still working 24/7 and running a business."

She also said, "Our times together now are warm, caring and fruitful. We have always been available to each other, to explain what we are doing, what we need help on, what our plans are, personal issues we may be having with children, parents and spouses, with wonderful support and advice from everyone, sometimes hard to take, but right on. We will always have each other to rely on, as long as we're alive."

Back in the 1980s, of course, the history of Offshore was still being written, with plenty of twists and turns yet to unfold. And, in spite of all the ongoing changes in the firm's business evolution, there was still plenty of sailing going on.

As we shall see.

Plenty.

The Royal Yacht Squadron cannons that sound the start of the Fastnet Race, with the British royal yacht, the *HMY Brittania*, in the background.

9

The Sleuth *Saga*
The Wicked '79 Fastnet...and More Sea Tales

LOOKING BACK at what came to be called by author and Fastnet sailor, John Rousmaniere, "the deadliest storm in the history of modern sailing," perhaps the most remarkable fact of all is that it could not have begun more tranquilly.

The 28th and most infamous edition of the Fastnet, organized and run by the proper Royal Ocean Racing Club, had set forth from the quintessential English seaport of Cowes, on the Isle of Wight—the very first America's Cup race had been a 53 nautical-mile contest around the picturesque island in 1851—on the pleasant Saturday afternoon of August 11, 1979. With a BBC Radio shipping forecast of moderate to fresh southwesterly breezes ranging from roughly 10- to 20-knots, with occasional higher gusts—simply perfect for sailboat racing—a huge spectator fleet gathered in ideal summer weather off the starting line in The Solent, the narrow body of water separating the island from mainland England, to bid farewell to the impressive Fastnet roster of over 300 yachts and 2,500 competitive sailors. One couldn't have conjured a prettier scene, the very epitome of classic British yacht racing.

In retrospect, it could've been a mirage.

By the time the last boat completed the race, on August 17th, 15 people had died, 24 crews had abandoned ship, five yachts had sunk, 136 sailors had been rescued, and only 85 yachts had successfully finished. Overall, the '79 Fastnet had been nothing less than pure, unbridled carnage. Those who sailed the race witnessed something that, thankfully, had never been seen before nor hasn't since.

Including skipper Steve Colgate, and his crew aboard the 54-foot ocean racer, *Sleuth.*

The dozen sailors aboard *Sleuth* were a truly international crew with several Americans including navigator Peter Nalle; vastly experienced English sailor,

Steve puts *Sleuth* through her paces in a day race
prior to the infamous 1979 Fastnet.

Peter Wilson; Bruno Caire, an opinionated Frenchman who'd competed in the tough, prestigious Whitbread Round-the-World Race; and a young, hungry South African named Onne van der Val, at the very cusp of a legendary career in yachting and journalism that would include a winning Whitbread effort, before becoming one of the world's most renowned marine photographers.

They were all about to have their hands full.

Much has been written, discussed and analyzed about what went wrong in the 1979 Fastnet. It's been said—and it's true—that with the tools modern navigators possess,

Before he became a renowned international yachting photographer, South African sailor Onne van der Wal was a trusted member of the *Sleuth* crew.

including advanced forecasting models, satellite imagery, routing software, broadband communications and related technologies, that such a catastrophe couldn't possibly happen today. But it was a very different nautical world into which the Fastnet crews set sail over four decades ago. At that time, Fastnet sailors received a single daily shipping forecast via high-seas radio that was basically valid for 24 hours…and even then, was sometimes lacking in detail or just plain inaccurate. Which is woefully inadequate for the rapidly forming storm that the atmosphere dished up off the United Kingdom in mid-August of 1979

What happened, in a nutshell, was that with exquisite, horrible timing, a deep low-pressure system and its corresponding cold front rendezvoused with the racers as most were well into the Irish Sea on the way to Fastnet Rock, the midway turning mark of the race. When that occurred, the southwesterly gale that had not been expected or forecast, but which most boats were in the midst of successfully negotiating, almost instantly became a similarly undetected northwesterly gale following a slamming 90-degree wind shift. The big breeze was an issue, but the larger, more dangerous problem was the sea state, and the colossal, confused waves created by the confluence of the rapidly colliding systems from different directions. And of course, there was the further complication that nobody had any clue that it was coming. Yikes.

For the Fastnet fleet, their collective fate at that stage basically came down to that familiar, all-purpose summation of woe: wrong place, wrong time.

Later, Steve would write a straightforward account of *Sleuth*'s Fastnet experiences for an article that ran in the November 1979 issue of *Yachting* magazine. "Our first sign that a low-pressure area was approaching came as the wind increased late Monday afternoon, August 13th," he wrote. "We were running on port tack (before the breeze) when the wind started coming forward," he continued, pinpointing the moment when the wind direction began to switch from south to north. Which is when the heavy spinnaker they'd set "blew in half" and the crew quickly cleared up the mess and hoisted a medium-sized headsail.

"The barometer was dropping fast as we spotted the light of Fastnet Rock about 18-miles ahead," he continued. "By 2300 (11 p.m.), the wind velocity across the deck measured about 45 knots on our anemometer. We had taken two reefs in the mainsail and changed from the (medium headsail to a smaller one) in preparation for rounding."

As the wind strengthened to 50 knots, *Sleuth*'s crew successfully tucked a third reef into the main, but it wasn't easy. And now, everything was moving fast. Very fast.

Steve described what happened next: "By the time the reefing job was completed, we were in the process of coming up close-hauled to tack around Fastnet Rock. It was hard to judge how far we were from the rock, but we gave it a wide berth. I then had to judge when to tack onto starboard. When the rock was well abaft (our beam) we tacked, but we seemed to be going sideways almost as fast as we were passing the light. We appeared to be getting very close to the rock, which we couldn't see at all. We could only see the light, rotating far above us, drawing us in like a magnet. I ordered the engine started *in case* we went into irons trying to tack at the last moment. Fortunately, neither a tack nor the engine was necessary. We rounded about midnight."

Soon enough, as the boat started pounding to windward in the messy conditions, a third of *Sleuth*'s crew went down hard, incapacitated by seasickness. And a new challenge arose: as *Sleuth* sailed southward back toward England, she was more or less on a reciprocal heading to the dozens and dozens of smaller boats bound north, towards the rock. At the wheel, it was Steve's job to identify the lights of the oncoming fleet, determine what tack they were on, and dodge them the best he could. It was draining, exhausting work, with no room for error, which could be catastrophic.

Even so, while Steve knew the situation was precarious, he also realized he had a good boat and crew, and things were as under control as they possibly could be. Back ashore, however, as the first news reports began filtering in that something was seriously amiss in the Fastnet race, the suddenly worried loved ones fretting over their sailors at sea had no such comfort or reassurance. Including Doris, and Steve's mother, who just happened to be on a road trip down the south coast of England to welcome *Sleuth* back at the finish in Plymouth. It was a journey neither would ever forget.

But Doris had been all in on *Sleuth* when they'd purchased her. Most of Steve's other adventures and accomplishments in yacht racing had been, paradoxically, as the critical crew, the ringer who came aboard to ensure victory. She wanted him to be in command of his own boat, to make his own decisions, and savor his own results. Yet now, incredibly, he was smack-dab in the middle of one of the worst storms of the century.

And it was his show to run. All his.

What's the saying? Careful what you wish for?

The 54-foot, Germán Frers-designed ocean racer, *Sleuth.*

Steve (third from right) posed with fellow members of the 1968 Olympic sailing team next to fellow crewman Stuart Walker. Skipper Gardner Cox is on the far left.

THE SAILING road that had led Steve to his precarious situation off the coast of Ireland—though he still had no real clue about the dangerous days yet to unfold—was long, winding and eventful. Among the "other" sailing of Steve's that Doris had referenced just happened to be the two most prestigious inshore regattas on the planet: the Olympics and the America's Cup. For most sailors, to race in either one or the other would be the very pinnacle of their careers. To compete in both, as Steve did, is rare and prodigious.

All that said, they were interesting but mixed experiences.

The 1968 Olympic Games in Mexico is one such example. Steve had initially been approached to rejoin Ernie Fay's crew for a repeat attempt to make the U.S. team in the 5.5 Metre class; they'd finished a heartbreaking second four years earlier in the Olympic Trials for the '64 Tokyo games. But Steve wasn't interested, having come to the conclusion, he said, that Fay "was always going to be a bridesmaid, never a bride." A second invitation, to join the team of Philadelphia skipper Gardner Cox, and his acclaimed tactician/trimmer Dr. Stuart Walker, was much more alluring. Steve committed to the campaign.

The 5.5 Metre *Cadenza*, US 68, approaches the finish line
off Acapulco in the '68 Olympics.

At the outset, at least, it couldn't have gone much better. Cox was a fine helmsman but Walker was an even better all-around sailor; he would become one of the sport's icons not only for his success on the racecourse but as an authoritative author who'd eventually write nearly a dozen technical racing books and serve as a monthly columnist at *Sailing World* magazine for four decades. (The good doctor also acted as an instructor at Offshore's Race Weeks, and was still racing competitively in the Soling class at the not-so-tender age of 95, a few months before passing away in 2018.)

On paper, when the 5.5 Metre Trials commenced off Newport Beach, California, Cox's team was a longshot to make the U.S. squad; the favorite was a sailmaker named Lowell North, who launched his eponymous company, North Sails, in nearby San Diego, and supposedly had a decided advantage when it came to "local knowledge." But Cox's boat promptly went out and won the first two races, and clinched their spot on the Olympic team with relative ease. (Ironically, for North, losing the 5.5 trials was one of the best things that ever happened to him; he quickly pivoted to the Star class and won a gold medal in Mexico with crew, Peter Barrett.)

But marching into the Olympic stadium with the rest of the U.S. athletes in

Right in the middle of things: Steve racing aboard *American Eagle*
in the 1967 America's Cup trials.

Mexico City proved to be the highlight of the games for Cox, Walker and Steve. In the regatta that followed, off Acapulco, Cox and crew never had a better race result than fourth, and ended up finishing seventh in the 14-boat field; the gold medal went to the three Sundelin brothers of Sweden, who ripped off five bullets in seven races to win it going away.

Steve's first America's Cup experience, as the bowman on George Hinman's 12 Metre *American Eagle* in 1967, was another effort that did not conclude with a victory toast. But Steve, who was by then accumulating positions on high-profile sailing campaigns the way some folks collect stamps, viewed it as another step up the rungs of his own crewing ladder. (The fact that he was basically commuting from New York, where Offshore was taking ever greater commitments of his time, to Newport, for the Cup racing, just added to the degree of difficulty…which in some ways made it better and more challenging.)

And new challenges were always fun, which comes across in a story profiling Steve by Knowles Pittman in the 1967 edition of the racing magazine *One-Design & Offshore Yachtsman*.

"In addition to temperament, a delicate sense of timing and teamwork, Steve thinks the 12-Metre crewman has to be uncommonly agile," wrote Pittman. From there, Pittman quoted Steve describing his duties:

The crew of the America's Cup contender *Heritage* in 1970: (front row) Jim Brass, Steve, Andy MacDonald, Fred Bickley; (back row) Jim Guard, Tom Dudinsky, Conn Findlay, Rory Burke, Paul Curry, Charley Morgan.

"On an ocean racer like *Dyna*, I'd feel safe even in a hurricane. We can always shorten sail and do other things to keep her under control and there are lots of things to hold onto when you're working on deck. On a (roughly 67-foot) 12 Metre, everything's loose and wide open. It would be an easy thing to get swept overboard. I've come close a couple of times already this year… The point is that on a 12 Metre, the crewman has to rely on his own sense of balance, rhythm and speed to work effectively. He has neither the sense of security, nor the lifelines and footholds he's used to on an offshore boat."

All the fancy footwork on the high seas wouldn't have helped *American Eagle* in '67, though. The boat was unceremoniously eliminated from the competition to determine the America's Cup defender in late August, and Bus Mosbacher's *Intrepid* went on to successfully defend the "Auld Mug" for the New York Yacht Club later that year. But Steve was back for the 1970 America's Cup defender trials, and while the end result was not much different than in 1967, the event as a whole was much more rewarding. For one, Doris was by his side for the entire Newport summer of fun and sun. And secondly, his role aboard Charley Morgan Jr.'s *Heritage*—the last wooden American 12 Metre which Morgan, a Florida boatbuilder, designed, built and skippered—was far more substantial than it had been on *Eagle*.

But it was also somewhat bittersweet from a "might-have-been" perspective. Steve had originally been asked to join California skipper Bill Ficker's crew on *Intrepid*. Ficker, as bald as a cue ball, became an almost cult-like figure on the Newport waterfront that summer—his many fans wore "Ficker is Quicker" buttons—and he went on to successfully defend the Cup in '70. But Steve had made a commitment two years earlier to Mark Ewing, the owner of a yacht called *Harpoon*, to sail the Newport Bermuda Race that June (a race in which they went on to win Class D). When he asked Ficker for a week off to do so, the request was denied, which Steve understood and accepted. But there was also no way he would bail on Ewing.

"I'm like an insurance agent," he quipped. "My word is my bond."

But then Morgan called, and he had no such qualms about Steve taking the time to race to Bermuda. He signed on with *Heritage*.

The campaign, however, did not break onto the scene like gangbusters, as explained in a rather cheeky article by reporter Steve Cady that appeared in the June 12, 1970, edition of the *New York Times* under the headline "*Heritage* Beaten Twice in America's Cup Trials."

"*Heritage* made her debut in the America's Cup trials today and *Intrepid* and *Valiant* promptly tore into her like a couple of piranhas attacking a goldfish," it began, before a rapid summation of the gory details: *Intrepid* won by over a half mile despite a jammed spinnaker halyard, and *Valiant* "trounced" *Heritage* by over 5 minutes.

The good news? "*Heritage*...won first prize in the beauty contest," wrote Cady. "Her mahogany hull glistened in the hot sunlight and her light-air spinnaker was the prettiest seen so far, a top-to-bottom dazzler of blue, orange and white."

That was the dark cloud's silver lining. Otherwise, concluded Cady, "At day's end, Morgan was shaking his head like a baseball pitcher who has started a game by serving home run balls on the first two pitches... These are only preliminary trials (but) on the basis of today's developments, it would appear *Heritage* has a long way to go."

A big part of how Morgan hoped to rectify the situation came down to two words: Steve. Colgate. Steve was aboard for those first disappointing races covered in the

Times, which took place on Long Island Sound, but then broke away to fulfill his Bermuda Race commitment.

"Steve came aboard as the tactician to help relieve me of that load," Morgan said, many years later. "We were still trying to tune the boat. I was stretched thin managing technical matters, and we were behind on a lot of things. It was an ambitious campaign. But Steve was inspirational. He was an all-around great addition to the effort. He had this raw experience, he'd done a lot of ocean racing, he was young and energetic and very prescient about what was going on. He fit into the crew perfectly. It would have been great to have had him on the boat earlier that summer (when he sailed to Bermuda)."

By the time he'd returned, the entire America's Cup circus had moved north to Newport, which Doris recalled vividly.

"I worked all week long at Offshore in Manhattan and then drove up on the weekends," she recalled. "I wrote to *Redbook* magazine and offered to do a story on living with an America's Cup team in Newport. They declined, thank God. Because it would have been quite a story, had I had the nerve to go through with it. We all lived in a large girl's school, Salve Regina College, near the mansions and Cliff Walk. The guys had a strict regimen: running along the cliff early in the morning, then to the yard to work on the boat, out sailing, back for boat and sail changes, then dinner, when we women could join them. Then everyone was supposed to go to sleep, but Charley always had a twinkle in his eye as did a couple of the others, and we'd sneak out for a drink or two at a local bar."

The social life was great, no doubt. The Colgates and Morgan forged a lifelong bond of friendship and mutual admiration. "Doris was a favorite among the ladies and the logistics side of the game," said Morgan, "and they were always charming and entertaining at the crew dinners every night. Very congenial and cultured. I love them."

On the water, however, for the *Heritage* crew, things weren't as copacetic.

Morgan conceded that he had perhaps too much on his plate managing the entire program—"I'm not sure my helmsmanship ever got up to the level it needed to be," he admitted—though in stretches, it was clear *Heritage* was every bit as speedy (if not more) than *Intrepid* (particularly in the rare instances when Steve got a trick at the wheel).

In the end, however, it was clear they faced one roadblock that the *Heritage* crew deemed insurmountable. There was no way the staid, blue-blazered Yankees running

Doris, on *Heritage*'s tender, and Steve, on *Heritage*, in Newport, RI, 1970.

the New York Yacht Club defender's selection committee were going to choose a tanned Floridian rebel to represent their interests. They instead chose *Intrepid*, and Ficker, and the rest is Cup history.

But Steve and Doris still had more than a little sailing history of their own to record. On their own yacht. On *Sleuth*.

IT'S ALWAYS a bit of a puzzle to name a new boat. The immaculate 54-foot, Germán Frers-designed aluminum sloop that Steve and Doris purchased in 1978 was named *Scaramouche* when she won the 1974 Newport Bermuda Race, and was called *Demon* a few years after when the couple signed the papers to make it their own. (As a joke, they considered calling it *Five Kids in College*; they reckoned the six-figure annual costs to pay back the boat loan, operate it and keep it in decent sails would've been similar to sending a quintet of imaginary kids to school.)

Steve liked *Legerdemain*—he defined it as "sleight of hand"—but it was simply too long for the yacht's pinched transom.

However, a hit Broadway show at the time—*Sleuth*—captured the same essence he was after. "To me," he said, "the name represented the quiet time at night when you can win a lot of races on Long Island Sound." It was in those still evening moments, he reasoned, if you had good drivers who really concentrated, or even threw the anchor over the side in foul current, remaining stationary when the competition literally went

Sleuth, racing in the Caribbean.

backwards, that you could pull off race-winning moves when nobody was looking, and surprise the hell out of everyone when dawn broke and you were ahead.

Stealth could've also worked. But *Sleuth* was just right.

"Steve had been doing a lot of racing on *Carina* and I felt it would be wonderful if he could start skippering his own yacht and calling his own shots," said Doris. "We'd heard about a boat called *Demon* that was berthed in Newport. We drove up and fell in love. She was in beautiful condition, with a warm wood interior in the galley and navigation area, and gimballed berths, even in the large aft cabin. We got a mortgage and bought the boat. It cost about $300,000 a year to campaign her, which somehow we found a way to cover."

Doris dove right into the *Sleuth* battles as a very active crewmember, timing the starts, manning the running backstays and feeding the team. After that year's Newport Bermuda Race and some tune-up contests on Long Island Sound, *Sleuth*'s first "road" regatta was the windy '78 Chesapeake Fall Series, during which Doris cracked her

Stuart Walker joined the *Sleuth* crew during the windy Chesapeake Fall series in 1978, an experience he found beyond the pale.

sternum when she was tossed into the "coffee grinder" winches that were de rigueur on big racing yachts back in the day. Stuart Walker, Steve's Olympic teammate a decade earlier, came aboard for a day race and was more or less appalled.

"He was used to being on a (3-person) Soling and totally in control," said Steve, who pushed *Sleuth* and her dozen crew hard in that initial regatta to see what she was capable of, which led to more than a broach or two under spinnaker. "It was beyond the pale for him. He didn't like it at all."

But Steve and Doris were thrilled with their new ride, and continued south for more adventures. Doris found the tight little galley "perfect" and would literally wedge herself in to whip up tasty meals, and make sure everyone was well fed. Steve recalled one race in the bumpy Gulf Stream where nobody dared swallow a bite, which did not deter Doris a bit. "People on deck were too sick to come down and eat," he said. "She'd be down there singing away. She has an iron constitution."

Doris kept the crew in good grub but in another matter, she did not ingratiate herself; aboard *Sleuth*, the rule was, other than herself, no women or girlfriends allowed. Much later, she'd see the irony in one of the marine industry's greatest all-time advocates of women sailors banning girls, but at the time she was following the lead

Steve at the helm of *Sleuth* during the 1978 edition of the SORC.

of Janet Ewing, the wife of Clayton Ewing, who never allowed females aboard their *Dyna*, where Steve was a regular. This lasted until one day in the Caribbean when she was taken aside by navigator Peter Bowker, a reasoned voice of influence, who told her, "You can't keep doing this or you'll never have anyone crew for us. Word's getting around."

"So," Doris said, "I relinquished that rule."

Aside from matters of eating and etiquette, however, there was plenty of pure, wonderful sailing. After the Chesapeake contests, *Sleuth* made her way to Florida for the annual Southern Ocean Racing Conference, or SORC, at the time far and away the premier event in Grand Prix racing in the United States. *Sleuth* competed in Class A with the largest, most powerful yachts—at 54-feet, she was a "tweener": bigger than the midsized boats, but no maxi —but she did well on corrected time and more than held her own. But the most memorable incidents came as the boat raced on into the islands.

Take the Miami to Montego Bay Race, from Florida to Jamaica. To get there, the fleet had to sail past the eastern flank of Cuba, and at the skipper's meeting the night before the start, Steve asked the race committee if the Cubans had been made aware of the pack of yachts headed their way. After all, the U.S. relationship with Cuba in the late seventies was fraught, at best. Steve was assured the authorities had been briefed and all was well. But then something unusual happened, and with a past and future nemesis involved:

"We were doing well and were about an hour behind Ted Turner's *Tenacious,* which had rounded the tip of Cuba in the dark," Steve recalled. "It was getting to be daylight as we passed about a mile off the beach on a port-tack spinnaker run in 10 to 15 knots of wind. Out comes an open cockpit biplane with a pilot wearing goggles—straight out of World War I!

"He only lacked a white silk scarf," continued Steve. "He started buzzing us and at first we waved, smiled and thought he would go home. He came from dead ahead, five feet over the water, and at the last minute would pull up over our mast so close that the spinnaker collapsed. Then he would come from abeam pointing at our mast and peel off past our stern. He came so close to clipping our backstay that one of our crew wondered out loud if he knew there even was a backstay! We wanted to jibe towards Jamaica, but had to stay on port until we could get into international waters some 12 miles off the beach. Only then did our Cuban friend, having won his point, go home. It cost us the race."

From there, it was on to Antigua for the famous Antigua Sailing Week, where the fleet raced daily on courses laid out from port to port around the island. In their first foray to Antigua, the Class A title came down to a final race between *Sleuth* and a 72-foot "mini-maxi" called *Mistress Quickly.* It was a race *Sleuth* simply had to have, and Steve had in mind a specific plan, with a specific jib, to start the race. But when he gave the sail call for his favored choice, he was basically told, "Forget it. Not that sail."

"There was an insurrection with the foredeck crew, who decided they knew better than me," Steve remembered. "I rarely have any anger-management problems, but I got really pissed off and it showed. Finally, they acquiesced and we won the race."

The tense beginning had a bizarre, perhaps fitting conclusion. *Sleuth* tied up that evening off the famous Admiral's Inn, and the victory party was on. The next morning, a *Sleuth* crewman was found asleep on deck, buck naked, for all the world—but especially the hotel guests, and the other racing crews—to see. "Very embarrassing," Steve admitted. Sailor boys, alas, will be sailor boys.

Sleuth's ambitious 1979 racing schedule, however, was just getting underway. Next up? A transatlantic race from Massachusetts to Ireland: Marblehead to Cork.

Steve, sporting a "farmer's tan" in the Miami-Montego Bay Race, with Jim Marshall just aft. Aussie Skip Lissiman, part of the winning crew in the 1983 America's Cup, who also did a stint as *Sleuth*'s pro captain, is at the helm.

Sleuth, to weather of the legendary *Kialoa*, during Antigua Sailing Week

Doris opted out of that passage—someone had to keep the business of Offshore on track—but her presence was sensed three times daily, at each meal. She'd taken charge of provisioning and meal planning—she put together a 45-page booklet with detailed instructions, menus and recipes, and later wrote a detailed story about the entire undertaking for *Yachting* magazine—and she'd done it well. In fact, she'd prepared almost everything in the compact kitchen of their apartment on East 54th well before the race. The Colgates then recruited a volunteer "cook" who handily happened to be an emergency-room doctor, a fine combination of necessary skills for an offshore race. Dick Nivala, the willing and able helper, was nicknamed "Doctor Cook."

Steve remembered it well: "For months we would come home from work and Doris would cook up some entrees which we would put into 'Seal-a-Meal' pouches and freeze in our freezer. When the freezer was full, we would empty it into Igloo containers with dry ice until we had enough meals for a crew of 12 for about 20 days, just in case. When we provisioned the boat in Marblehead, Doris had a daily menu to be followed and all the frozen pouches were placed in the freezer from the 20th day on the bottom to the first day on top. All 'Doctor Cook' had to do was take the top pouches, put them in boiling water, and serve it to the two watches. Doris's organization was superb."

The race was almost just as ideal. Steve and crew absolutely nailed the start and sailed an almost perfect race, and while *Sleuth* ultimately saved her time on the storied maxis, including *Kialoa* and *Ondine*, she finished second overall to a well-sailed entry from the Naval Academy. Still, it was a sweet result. And as soon as *Sleuth* was secured in her berth at the Royal Cork Yacht Club, the legendary skippers of the vanquished giants, *Kialoa*'s Jim Kilroy and *Ondine*'s Huey Long, respectively, appeared with congratulations. "It was a wonderful gesture of the camaraderie among ocean-racing sailors," said Steve, and one he appreciated immensely.

The idea beyond purchasing *Sleuth* was for Steve to have his own command. And it was, unquestionably, going very well.

From there, it was on to Cowes. The Fastnet Race was soon to start.

CHAOS ENSUED. By the fourth day of the Fastnet, aboard *Sleuth* shortly before sunrise on the hellish morning of Tuesday, August 14th, Steve ducked below, sidled into the navigation station and recorded the briefest of observations for the 0400 (4 a.m.) entry in the ship's logbook:

Sleuth handling the gnarly conditions in the 1979 Fastnet Race.

"Hairy."

Indeed.

Fastnet Rock was miles behind him. Several of his crew were scattered in berths fore and aft, sick as dogs, from which they would emerge no time soon. One of them was his navigator, which meant that in addition to long spells at the wheel, Steve also had to keep keenly abreast of *Sleuth*'s speed, course and position; GPS receivers, with precise, pushbutton navigation info, had yet to be invented. He'd already shut off the radio after one of the crew said he was hearing "mayday" calls and something about a drowning. He realized it wasn't exactly altruistic, but was of the mindset that he and his crew, at this juncture, could only take care of themselves. That was the one and only priority.

A nap might've been refreshing but sleep, now and in the immediate future, was not an option. To stay awake, and avoid puking, Steve had administered to himself his go-to pharmaceutical remedy for just these situations: a half-tablet of Ephedrine, a stimulant, and another half-tab of Promethazine, for nausea. He'd read somewhere that the astronauts ingested a similar cocktail to address motion sickness, and Steve concurred that it balanced things out well.

The one thing he wasn't was scared. After all, at the end of the day, this was a sail-boat race. A very, very challenging one, to be sure. But still a boat race. And he was still racing. *Sleuth* was most definitely not in survival mode.

Back on deck, the cockpit was perpetually full of water from continuous boarding seas. God only knew what the wind speed was. *Sleuth*'s anemometer, which measures the strength of the breeze, had pegged out at its top-range figure of 60 knots. That had been a while ago. Steve guessed it was now 80- or 85-knots, with corresponding seas of 25 feet.

"It was getting worse and worse," he said.

The next geographical mark on the racecourse that had to be honored and avoided was Bishop Rock, a low, ominous, rocky sea stack in the westernmost Scilly Isles, roughly 30 miles off the mainland coast of Cornwall. It was not only a physical waypoint, but a psychological one. Bishop signified the entrance to the relatively protected waters of the English Channel. Once *Sleuth* had safely negotiated Bishop Rock, the end of the nightmare would be near.

Getting there, of course, wasn't easy. Steve picked up the action in his *Yachting* article:

"I believe it's lucky most of the crew had no idea what was going on inside my head. I was determined to keep them calm. Any lack of attention by the helmsman could have been disastrous. The No. 4 genoa and triple-reefed main were holding up well, but if we swung too much broadside to the wind the sails started to flog. In 70- to 85-knot winds it doesn't take long to rip a flogging sail. We had a staysail ready to go up in case that happened, but the main thing was to avoid flogging in the first place. One helmsman allowed a wave to spin the boat broadside. Another wave crashed green water down on top of us, throwing the helmsman into the steering wheel, bending it. One crewman lost his grip and was washed down the deck, but his safety harness kept him aboard. From then on I ordered only the two most experi-enced helmsmen on each watch to steer and we had no further trouble. One of them exclaimed, 'How can you expect me to steer two hours out of a four-hour watch under these conditions?' I pointed out that I was 44 years old and he was in his twen-ties. If I could do it, he could. And he did."

Years later, *Sleuth* crewman Onne van der Wal had trouble recalling specific moments of the race—the memories had blurred together—but he did recall that crazy night tearing down the Irish Sea towards Bishop Rock. "I remember sitting on the rail a lot during that whole night and dozing on and off, falling asleep against Peter Wilson's shoulder, then waking up... It was cold and shitty and dark and windy. And I remember looking up at *Sleuth*'s mast, which was this solid tree trunk of a rig, and thinking, 'Thank goodness for that.' Because otherwise we would've lost it."

Up on deck, van der Wal and mates were stoically enduring the vicious weather. Down below, at the nav station, Steve suddenly was faced with a different dilemma when unexpectedly confronted by arguably the most experienced sailor on *Sleuth*'s crew, Bruno Caire, the French veteran of the Whitbread race. "Steve," he said, in both his heavily accented English and within earshot of everyone else either off watch or ill in their bunks, "we have zees problem."

"Well, Bruno," Steve replied, patiently. "What is that?"

"We are heading for zee Scilly Isles." Caire needn't have uttered another syllable. He and Steve—and everybody else eavesdropping—were well versed in nautical lore, and did not require a further reminder of the maritime disaster of the early 1700s, when a quartet of Royal Navy ships piled into the Scillies in a blow not unlike the one they were experiencing, with the loss of upwards of 2,000 men.

It was a "buck stops here" moment for Steve. He had to get ahead of it. Immediately.

Steve actually understood Caire's concern. At the moment, though still many, many miles away, *Sleuth* was more or less bound straight for the Scillies. That's because Steve had charted a course to keep the boat on a beam reach, the fastest, safest point of sail, on which it was making a quick 10- to 12-knots. Yes, he could've hardened up onto the wind, but that would've made the efficient sailing untenable, and much slower, to boot. He also understood that he didn't have to. *Sleuth*, he knew, was sailing into the low-pressure trough. Which meant the wind would shift in their favor, and *Sleuth* would be safely lifted past Bishop Rock. What was required at this juncture was patience.

"I knew nobody was asleep and everyone was listening," Steve said. So, he asked Bruno a couple of straightforward questions: Are we going fast? Are the right sails set? Bruno answered affirmatively.

"When we have a problem, we'll address the problem," Steve replied. "But we don't have a problem now."

And that was that. "He never said another word," Steve later said.

The wind shift Steve expected kicked in, hours later, just as he forecast. *Sleuth* slipped past Bishop Rock safely and uneventfully. Then the breeze "lightened" to 40-odd-knots…and Steve called for the crew to hoist a spinnaker!

"It's all relative," he said. "When it's blowing 80 and drops to 40, it's like, damn, there's no wind…"

Sleuth cruised across the finish line a little after sunrise the next day. She'd not only finished the historic '79 Fastnet, she'd won her class.

Now came the next crazy part.

FOR DORIS, her personal memories of the 1979 Fastnet Race do not involve witnessing firsthand a once-in-a-lifetime survival storm, or a recalcitrant Frenchman, or class-winning decisions or maneuvers under extreme duress. But Doris did experience a rather surreal Fastnet journey of her own: a road trip in a rental car, stacked with tuxedos and other crew gear, with the wives of a couple of other Fastnet sailors and her imperious mother-in-law, Nina Colgate.

"It worked out okay," she'd later say. "Sort of."

It was all meant to be a treat for Nina, who'd spent much of her childhood in England, and who wished to see her son in his own element, skippering his own boat. After the Transatlantic Race from Marblehead to Cork, Steve and Doris had returned to the states to get some work done, then returned to Cowes, with Nina, for Cowes Week, the racing series that serves as a prelude to the Fastnet. They'd rented a condo on Thames Street in the heart of the little city, with plenty of room for everyone… including the cook.

"Yes, the cook," Doris explained. "Because that's what you did when you had a big crew, afterguard and a lot of mouths to feed. Steve got her through a service other owners used. She had Cordon Bleu credentials and sounded great. And she was not what we expected. When she knocked on the condo door, with my mother-in-law standing by my side to take over if she could, there stood a gorgeous, tall blonde with a huge suitcase. I politely asked Nina to leave it to me, invited her in, and showed her to her room on the top floor. The kitchen was big, but the refrigerator was a tiny under-the-sink thing, with a small stove and oven—very British. We had a budget and gave the cook money to shop, letting her mostly decide what to prepare though Steve's mom had a strong part in that. Then each day after breakfast we would go out to race and she would disappear to her room or wherever until only an hour or so before dinner. Most nights, most of the crew joined us. How in the world was she ever going to get dinner ready for 20 or more people in so little time? But she did, after gliding down the stairs in a beautiful, and different, dress each evening."

An old friend of Nina's joined them in Cowes, a big redhead who alighted from her tiny plane at the local airport in high argyle socks who eventually won everybody over.

"She kept us laughing every night," Doris said. "Steve's very proper mom complained a bit, and her friend called her 'old fussy boots' in front of us all. We loved it, secretly."

Doris was aboard for a day race two days before the Fastnet start that proved to be lucky indeed, though for reasons not immediately apparent. *Sleuth* was again in a tight match with Ted Turner's *Tenacious*—which Steve wanted to win for a thousand different reasons—dueling under spinnakers, when a big wind shift hit the fleet and everything went sideways. *Sleuth*'s crew quickly recovered, doused the (possibly torn) chute, and replaced it with the No. 4 genoa, the first time they'd set it since buying the boat. As it was being hoisted, however, its (perhaps corroded) wire pennant parted and Steve decided to call it a day, head in, and get the sails repaired. Which proved to be a very good thing, as the No. 4 became the workhorse at the height of the Fastnet storm.

Once the Fastnet had begun, Doris and Nina loaded up the rental car with all the crew's regular clothes and formal wear for the parties to come, and with two other women associated with Fastnet crews, including Pat Nye, the wife of *Carina*'s Dick Nye. They all drove down the coast of the Isle of Wight to watch the racers sail past the famous Needles, and out of sight. Then it was on to the ferry to Southampton, and westward along the coastline towards Plymouth. As they crossed the plains of Dartmoor, the wind really started kicking in and their heavily loaded vehicle was rocked, but they had no radio nor any idea what was unfolding on the racecourse. Nina requested a lunch stop at Torquay—nicknamed "the English Riviera"—the birthplace of Agatha Christie and a spot where she'd spent many a pleasant summer day.

But, Doris said, "There was no Riviera feeling that day, as we sat in a small café listening to the brown waves crashing on the seawall and into the road, and my mother-in-law's stories about her joyful early life."

By the time they arrived in Plymouth, and their rooms at the Holiday Inn, the early reports of a pending disaster were everywhere. Doris commanded Nina to "go to your room," which proved to be a bad idea as she watched, in rapt horror, as the entire unholy episode unfolded on her TV set. In the meantime, Doris and some of the wives of other Fastnet crews raced to the yacht club, desperate for news. The next night, Doris and friends were in the hotel bar when Ted Turner stumbled in, spewed forth his slanderous take on the fates of *Sleuth* and *Carina*, and made everyone feel more miserable than they already were.

They ate that evening gazing out at the harbor, desperate to see navigation lights arriving. It was a long, long night.

Bishop Rock, at dawn in 1979: the worst of the storm was over.

The next day, back at the yacht club, Doris learned there was still no word on Steve or his crew until she overheard a German reporter saying something about another boat that had been accounted for and was making its way to the finish line: "*Sloosh*." She understood what he meant. Her relief was palpable. She knew Steve and the boys were safe.

As often happened on *Sleuth*, they arrived engineless, limping in. When Steve made it back to the hotel and knocked on his mother's door, as she opened it she cried "My son, my son!" and enveloped him in an embrace.

It was, to the best of his recollection, the first real hug from his mom that he'd ever received.

TWO YEARS later, in August of 1981, *Sleuth* was back off the coast of England, in the very waters that had been, in about equal measure, the extraordinary scene of total mayhem and unbridled heroism. This time Doris was aboard, and in a quiet moment, she made a note in the notebook that served as her journal:

"We're on the Fastnet now," she wrote, "recently becalmed by Bishop Rock, along with most of the Admiral's Cup boats. It's hard to believe this is the same body of water that took 15 lives. We rounded the rock last night around 10:40. We have a bottle of champagne riding on a first-to-finish boat-for-boat with *Battle Cry*, but she's ahead of us and got this new breeze the same time we did. On the whole, so far, it's been an easy trip. Starboard-tack reach most of the way, which makes working in the galley quite tiresome. I had hoped we wouldn't need dinner tomorrow night, but I'm afraid we will after all. It'll be nice to take a bath and wash my hair."

Sleuth returned to do the Fastnet in 1981,
a completely different affair than the race two years earlier.

Ah, life at sea, and the longing for the simple things. Every sailor knows the feeling well. This '81 Fastnet would be Doris's and Steve's last big race on their well-traveled 54-footer. The *Sleuth* saga was coming to a close. It had been a wild, often exhilarating, sometimes maddening ride.

On the plus side, there'd been no lack of fine sailing. And they'd been able to incorporate *Sleuth* into plenty of programs and courses at Offshore. But they'd also come to realize that while they technically *owned* the boat, it wasn't really *theirs* anymore. They'd come aboard for races, of course, but moving the boat from venue to venue, the actual cruising part of boat ownership, fell to the lucky crew, whose expenses were covered and who reaped the rewards of enjoying *Sleuth* on a more relaxed timetable, like the time Jimmy Buffett invited everyone to dinner at his place in St. Barths when Doris and Steve were back in New York slinging sailing lessons.

The other frustrating part was that *Sleuth* had basically become a stepping-stone

Happy Birthday! Birthday boy Rob Eberle enjoys a libation
in a race off Martha's Vineyard in 1980.

for ambitious crew to gain some experience under Steve's watchful eye, then move on to bigger programs. Perhaps the most notable was an Aussie from Perth named Skip Lissiman, an excellent sailor who served as *Sleuth*'s paid skipper for a spell before moving on to crew on a maxi, and who later won the America's Cup with the Australian team in 1983. It was less than rewarding to serve as a "feeder league," as Doris pointed out, "for richer owners of larger boats."

When *Sleuth* arrived in the United Kingdom in 1981, it was supposedly the first leg of a trip that would carry on to Australia, where the Colgates were anxious to race their own boat in the prestigious Sydney-Hobart Race. By that time, the hired skipper was a very able American sailor named Rob Eberle, and he had a solid crew. But the voyage to Oz wasn't to be. The onward leg from England to Italy to fit a new keel shoe was sidelined by logistics issues, and in October, the president of Egypt, Anwar Sadat, was assassinated, which meant a major delay in transiting the Suez Canal, and no chance whatsoever of making the Hobart Race. Instead, Eberle sailed back to the

Bahamas, where *Sleuth* was dismasted. And that, basically, was that. A year later *Sleuth* was sold and converted to a cruising boat, her racing days over.

Eberle does recall his days onboard with fondness: "Steve was a great skipper and helmsman both offshore and in short course racing, always a pleasure to sail with. We didn't have a remarkable track record as the boat itself was an older design, no longer competitive with late-model racers designed to benefit from updated measurement rules. Still, spirits were never dampened under his leadership and in regattas where the older CCA rating rules were still in effect, we were always right up there. I don't remember ever having a bad race with Steve and Doris aboard *Sleuth*."

The most memorable part of the last foray to England, and that final Fastnet, may have been the shore-side attractions: watching Prince Charles marry Princess Di on TV at their rented home, and the lavish dinner and dance at the plush Royal Yacht Squadron, where Doris banked a lifelong memory when Prince Phillip stepped on her foot when she was spinning around the floor with Steve. A painful, funny touch with greatness.

But a final entry from Doris in her Fastnet journal perhaps summed up the best of times on *Sleuth*: "My Sony Walkman is great. I used it one day while working in the galley and got quite a rise out of the crew. Apparently, I was singing too loud."

Good times: Steve and Doris enjoy brunch and Bloody Mary's aboard *Sleuth* in 1981.

Doris aboard a Morgan Out Island 41 on one of the first BVI cruises.
Note the lack of boat traffic on Sir Francis Drake Channel.

10

Globe Girdlers
Sailing the World, the Flotilla Way

BY THE EARLY 1970s, as a business, Offshore Sailing School was gathering steam and hitting on all cylinders. Behind the scenes, Doris was firmly ensconced in her position as the company's vice president and becoming more comfortable in the role with each passing month, always pressing the strategy of ever expanding and never looking back. Steve was still sailing like crazy—the 1970 America's Cup trials on *Heritage* was just his latest high-profile campaign—but was also as active as ever in the day-to-day operations of Offshore, and was able to leverage his success on the racecourse to promote the firm and its growing package of programs and classes to both prospective customers and the marine industry. Offshore was generating tons of strong publicity and increasing both its curriculums and reach considerably. The whole enterprise was a far cry from its very humble beginning, which was essentially Steve on a boat instructing a handful of eager beginners.

There was, however, a problem, and while it was by no means major, it was still a knotty one. Offshore was producing plenty of fledgling sailors who'd experienced a sweet first taste of the sport, and had assembled a solid toolbox of basic skills. But…now what? Without investing in the not-inconsiderable cost of a boat, how would these new sailors take those tools and build upon that established foundation? Simply put: How could they enjoy more sailing? (The credit for the idea goes to Diane Duryea, Doris's former colleague at *Yachting* magazine, who was helping with marketing at Offshore and posed the questions.)

The answer, it turned out, was not exactly simple, certainly not from a logistical standpoint, but it was elegant, fun, and even revolutionary. Doris and Steve would take them sailing, to exotic locations all over the planet, on what were basically rented boats for adventurous cruises. And there was some tasty icing on

Doris soaks up some sun and surf on the first Sail Away Club
flotilla cruise in the British Virgin Islands in 1972.

this cake. Not only would Offshore's clients and graduates see and sail the world. So would they.

Today, such "flotilla cruises" are a vacation industry unto themselves. They've actually been around so long it's hard to remember exactly how they started. But the fact is, they were "invented," if that's the word, by Offshore Sailing School.

Decades later, the numbers would be beyond formidable. The Sail Away Club—the original name for the venture, which would subsequently be called the Offshore Cruising Club, and ultimately, Colgate Sailing Adventures—would eventually conduct over 200 trips to more than two-dozen destinations (Steve and Doris would personally lead roughly 80 of them). These included a host of Caribbean islands, New England, Chesapeake Bay, the Great Lakes, the French Riviera, Croatia, the Galapagos Islands, the South Pacific, and faraway New Zealand and Australia.

But in 1972, all of that was still ahead. It had to start somewhere, and that somewhere was the beautiful, windswept British Virgin Islands.

Just four years earlier, in 1968, an outfit had opened on the isle of Tortola in the BVI called The Moorings, which was based on a novel, original idea: chartering "bareboat" yachts to adventurous sailors for self-contained cruises through the wondrous string of islands dotting the pristine Sir Francis Drake Channel. (Crewed charters, with a captain and cook, had already been established, but offering a "bare" boat that you sailed with your family and friends, under your own command, was something new.) Like Steve and Doris, the couple who founded the company, Charlie and Ginny Cary, were pioneering sailing-business entrepreneurs. And the BVIs, with their gorgeous beaches, cozy anchorages and dead-easy navigation—most of the islands were within sight of one another—were very much a sailing paradise. They would ultimately become Colgate Sailing's premier destination, by a long shot, with over three-dozen flotilla vacations there.

The very first one, however—though a full-on bargain at $375 per person, including airfare from New York—got off to a somewhat shaky start.

In response to those many requests from their customers, Steve recalled, "In 1972, we chartered four boats and took 20 grads to the BVI. We met at Idlewild Airport in Queens (now JFK International Airport) in about 100-degree heat and flew to San Juan, Puerto Rico. The heat was worse in San Juan and I thought, 'What a disaster—vacationing in the Caribbean in August.' Yet, when we sailed in the lovely trade-winds off Tortola, it was delightful."

There was some other nice, positive energy right from the outset of the excursion. They were sailing what were then state-of-the-art bareboat charter boats: Morgan Out Island 41's, built by good ol' friend Charley Morgan.

If that wasn't enough kismet, though Steve had no way of knowing it, he almost immediately had an interesting encounter with a West Indian local destined to become a Caribbean legend: the singer, songwriter and raconteur, Foxy Callwood, who'd recently opened up his own seaside watering hole and restaurant on Jost Van Dyke, called Foxy's Tamarind Bar.

Steve said, "I remember Foxy's being recommended, and heard on the VHF radio a boat making a reservation for Tuesday night. Foxy quoted them a price of something like $3 a person for six orders of lobster. I got on the radio right after and said we had 18 persons for lobster and two for steak on Thursday night. Asking the price, he said $3.50 a person. I asked why I didn't get a quantity discount, since he had just quoted six people for less. Foxy said 20 people was much more work than six.

"When we arrived and anchored," Steve continued, "I went in to confirm that all was okay. Back then, Foxy's was extremely primitive. I walked up to the bar and told the bartender who I was and asked when my party of 20 should come in for dinner. Off to the side was an islander in a hammock stroking his pet goat. The bartender said, 'Don't bother, there are no lobsters.'

"I couldn't believe it. 'What am I going to do?' I asked. 'Any steaks?' He replied, 'Just two.'

"And then from the hammock came the words I remember to this day: 'Come on, the guy is pissing in his pants. Tell him the truth.'

"It was Foxy, taking over, and all was right with the world."

Dinner on the beach was delicious and memorable. Both Foxy and his bar were hilariously entertaining. Everyone had a blast. The sailing that followed was glorious. The entire unique trip, Offshore's inaugural foray into the world of vacation sailing, was nothing less than an unqualified success.

So much so, that when the Colgates asked everyone if they'd like to go again, and if so, where, the answers were pretty much unanimous:

Yes. And Greece.

THE SIGNS on the windmills addressed to the sailors from America on the island of Paros—"Welcome Sailaway Club!"—helped set the tone for the first of many, many visits to the Greek islands when the Colgates and their party of 40 excited clients arrived there at the very end of August in 1973. The whole thing started auspiciously, when Olympic Airways booked the entire mob into the first-class section of their 747 for, Steve later said, "a song. Literally, in that we were dancing in the aisles to Greek music all the way there."

One of the great side benefits to the flotilla voyages for Doris and Steve was the never-ending cast of memorable personalities they met in their travels. In Greece, bareboat chartering had yet to arrive, so the Colgates tracked down a charter broker and arranged for a small fleet of skippered yachts for their group. Most of the captains were retired naval officers, but Steve and Doris really clicked with the quite different couple who actually owned the boat they sailed.

"Our skipper," said Steve, "was an artist named Bill Papas, who was accompanied by his wife, Tessa. Bill was born in South Africa, the son of a prominent Greek immigrant, and was a political cartoonist. He moved to Greece in 1971 after he had a falling

Greek charter Skipper Bill Papas and his Doberman perform a duet,
while wife Tessa tends to a rather damp foredeck.

out with the South African authorities over apartheid, which he mocked in cartoons.
He bought a ketch he called *Petaluma* and chartered it out. Doris and I bought many
of his paintings and followed his travels over the years. Bill had an incredible zest for
life. He took us up in the hills to his favorite restaurant and at the end of the meal,
started throwing plates on the floor, breaking them to shards, hollering 'Oompa' the
whole time. The restaurant owner was appalled as this old practice was now against
the law. Bill happily paid up."

It was on the other side of the world, however, where the Colgates experienced
one of the best, most unique journeys of the dozens they undertook: the Kingdom of
Tonga. Of all their globe girdling, it was their favorite. It was not actually one trip but
two: back-to-back flotillas on a half-dozen Moorings bareboats over a 20-day span.
Steve recalls the most surprising moment of the charters:

"One afternoon we entered a harbor called 'Hunga' that could only be navigated
through a narrow passage at high tide. We were the only boats in the harbor except
for a small cruising boat. An islander came out to our fleet and said he would make us
a 'feast' later that afternoon. We negotiated a price of $3 a person. When we arrived,
I pulled our dinghy up on the sand and a young woman from the sailboat walked up
to me and asked where we were from."

When Steve explained that they were from Offshore Sailing School, and introduced himself, "She grabbed me in a bear hug and said, 'You're my cousin!' She, her

In Tonga on a charter, Steve was stunned to rendezvous
with his long-lost cousin, Sarah, here with Steve, his brother Gil,
Sarah's twin daughters and a local friend.

three kids and her husband were sailing around the Pacific in a little Catalina 30. Her father, Stirling Colgate, was a famous nuclear physicist from the Los Alamos laboratory. It's a very small world indeed."

Before departing for Tonga, Doris had asked the Moorings if there was anything they could bring, and was told a Polaroid camera—to take photos of the islanders and present them immediately as gifts—and books and teaching supplies, which she was assured would be much appreciated. They did so, and were rewarded many times over.

The food, the people, the music, the church services (Doris remembers one time at the Mormon church where "the Hungans were singing so loudly the wasps nesting in the rafters started flying around like crazy!"); every bit of it was fantastic. And the charterers brought home more than their fair share of souvenirs.

"When we anchored," Doris remembered, "many evenings we were approached by shy women in dugout canoes with beautiful displays of baskets, placemats and shells we bought for very little. Ashore, they would gather with more baskets and wonderfully painted tapas cloths, some more than 20-feet long. These are made by pressing together strips from the bark of the mulberry trees, then painted with dyes from the roots of plants in squares that depicted their culture. The cloths were much bigger

Doris purchased plenty of baskets, placemats and tapas cloth
from Tongan women that now grace their Florida home.

than we could carry home or even display at home, but no worries. They just asked us how many of the squares we wanted, and cut them to order. On one island, we saw and took pictures of a massive cloth, with more than 10 women working on it, a gift for one of the princesses that was soon to be married."

Ah, marriage. On the second of their two Tongan adventures, Doris got a surreal look at how that union played out in Tonga:

"After another fabulous feast prepared by the islanders, the next morning we climbed up a steep hill to a plateau where we found an incredible assortment of fully-decorated beds lined up in two rows. In front of each bed was a display of dishes, and other items that might be found in a dowry. And sitting on each bed was a dour-looking young woman. The men were all nearby in a thatch-roofed meeting house, drinking Kava. Apparently, this was an annual event for the men from the various islands in the archipelago to gather and choose wives, in such a way that there would not be a great deal of inbreeding. The older women told us the beds had been ordered from Sears and they stayed in storage until this event each year."

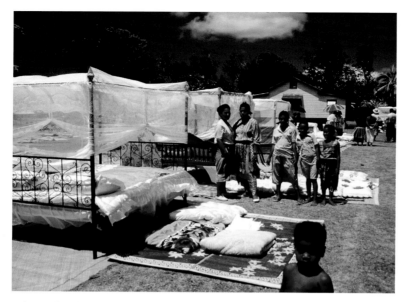

Let's make a deal! In Tonga in 1992, the Colgates witnessed an unusual ritual: the beds and dowries laid out for the island business of matrimony.

Well. Love, not so naturally.

Every little anecdote was all part of engaging with the wide, wonderful world. Steve and Doris couldn't get enough of it.

FOR DORIS, the little stories she gathered along her way, and the sheer joy in the travel itself, were only part of the fun of the flotilla charters. She was doing more and more writing, which she found very fulfilling, and began filing regular stories about her trips in sailing magazines like *Cruising World.* Weaving together the first-person tales of their own adventures with the history of the ports and islands they discovered made the entire enterprise all the more worthwhile.

In 1979, alone, she published not one but a pair of articles on destinations that could hardly have been more different; the glitzy, ritzy French Riviera, and the relatively untouched, pristine cruising grounds of the San Juan Islands in the Pacific Northwest. Each place gave her a canvas on which to paint a picture of spots just about any sailor would give their eyeteeth to cruise and uncover.

"Along the shores of the Côte d'Azur, the water seems flecked with mica. The towns glitter with old world glamour and new world opulence. The markets are overwhelming, the food magnificent. It's a wonderful place to cruise." And thus begins Doris's story of a sail from Nice to Monaco and back, entitled "Tucked in with

On a sailing trip to France, Doris took a rented bike
for a spin on the lovely island of Porquerolles.

the Millionaires at Monte Carlo." It continued: "This was our second cruise of the
French Riviera, again in late September to avoid the European vacation crowds and
to take advantage of lower air fares and less-crowded harbors. The weather was fault-
less—warm and sunny with clear skies and gentle breezes." Wow. Any takers?

Setting out from the seaside port of Golfe Juan, midway between Nice and Cannes,
the flotilla's party of four French-built Kirk 36 sloops charted a course northeast
bound for Menton, the last town in France before the border with Italy. It's a distance
of only about 75-nautical-miles, but it's hard to imagine a coastline brimming with
more antiquity or attractions.

The first stop were the islands of St. Marguerite and St. Honorat. Doris wrote,
"Both islands are wooded with sea and umbrella pines and were first inhabited in
the fourth century by St. Honorat in search of solitude, and across the way on St.
Marguerite by (his) sister (Marguerite), who headed a community of nuns. Because
his island was forbidden to women, St. Honorat agreed to visit Marguerite once a year
when the almond tree flowered, but she prayed so hard it produced a flower every

Fun sailing on lively Kirk 36s:
Steve with Al and Mary Tenbroek on the French Riviera.

month and St. Honorat had to give up his ascetic ways."

Fine. Women, right?

From there it was on to St. Tropez, and a refresher course in backing into a dock stern-to, the Eurocentric "Med moor." Then Pt. Grimaud ("a town with no history, no legends"); the island of Porquerolles ("we rented bicycles and rode on bumpy dirt roads to the lighthouse for a magnificent view"); and Antibes ("hundreds of mind-boggling yachts fill her gigantic harbor"). It was one treat after the next.

In Monaco, Doris wrote in a separate journal, "Our boat mates took a room ashore, and spent the evening gambling. We spent our first night of the entire trip alone on the boat, making mad passionate love."

That last part did not make it into *Cruising World.*

"The Pacific Northwest Abounds in Fine Scenery and Baked Salmon," which is obviously not the shortest title in the history of magazine journalism, headlined her piece in her other 1979 story for *CW.* The lead was straightforward: "In the Pacific Northwest, between Washington and the coast of Canada, are beautiful islands where one could cruise for months and never hit the same anchorage twice," she wrote, of the "northern paradise" north of Seattle. Compared to the Côte d'Azur, in fact, it was as different as night and day.

"The first European to sail this area may have been a Greek mariner, Juan de Fuca," she continued. "When quite old and destitute, he told his tale to an Englishman, Michael Lok, who believed strongly in the existence of a northwest passage (from the Pacific Ocean to the Atlantic). Lok retold the Greek's story over and over in a futile effort to get backers to support a voyage to the mysterious section of the Pacific coast north of San Francisco Bay."

It was a fine introduction to her story on the San Juans, which described the trip with their three-boat flotilla on which Steve and Doris sailed a Taiwan-built Landfall 39. It wasn't quite the eventful, momentous odyssey in France, though it did have its moments. Soon after departing from the charter base in the town of Anacortes, "We powered along the shore of Lopez Island down to Hunter Bay as a bald eagle soared above a silhouette of tall pines. It amazed us to note how calm the seas were even when it was windy. In general, we had very light air and fairly warm days. The nights were cold and usually quite still, which made for comfortable sleeping. We experienced little fog and no rain at all—a somewhat atypical cruise, we later learned."

Each and every one was different, unique and satisfying. Which was certainly the point of the entire exercise.

STEVE AND DORIS, who instituted an in-house travel agency at Offshore to streamline everything for their flotilla parties, including reduced air fares, "never thought twice" about what or who they'd encounter when they arrived at a fresh new cruising ground.

"We had become world travelers on a shoestring, and loved every minute," Doris said. "We just showed up, sometimes only a day before, sometimes the same day, even if we had never been there before. The preparation in advance involved a lot of planning, researching and then writing a handbook for ourselves and the participants, just as I do today. The books I prepare for each participant take me about a week to gather info and produce. When Steve and I went off on these trips, we left the company in the hands of our staff, hoping they would continue to sell and manage just as if we were there. And usually they did."

All that said, as Steve confessed, "We did have some characters on the trips."

Head scratcher: A bewildered Doris attempts to sort out the groceries
prior to a 1982 flotilla charter in Maine.

The standouts among them even earned their own nicknames.

"The Peanut Guy" on a Bahamian cruise insisted on emptying and segregating the peanut jar into six separate piles, one for each sailor on his boat. He regaled the crew with tales of his own adventurous travels, which became ever more exaggerated by the day. That ruse continued until Doris had a peek into his cabin and saw the copy of *National Geographic* on his bunk, which just happened to have detailed stories on all the spots he'd "visited." Busted, peanut dude.

"The Tuna Fish Gal" on a Maine charter loved the stuff so much she brought her own case of it and professed that it was all she would eat. Which was the case until the night everyone ordered lobsters and she asked for and then scarfed both of the crustaceans Steve and Doris had bought for themselves. They dined on the tuna fish.

"The Lady with the 7-Up Can" had an inordinate taste for the bubbly beverage and did not venture anywhere without carrying one. That was fine until one morning she stumbled out of the dinghy and it was ultimately revealed that the can was topped up with vodka.

Most of the time, the quirks of their travel companions could be laughed off. But one flotilla to the BVI led not by Steve and Doris, but their operations manager at the time, took a tragic turn when a client who'd taken several Offshore courses and was known to be competent and experienced—and was therefore designated the skipper of his bareboat—had a heart attack and passed away instantly while steering. About a month later, his widow arrived at their City Island offices to collect his belongings.

"I had a sleepless night imagining her suing us for putting the stress of skippering on her husband and any other bad result I could think of," said Steve. But when the woman arrived, with her two strapping 20-something sons in tow, the meeting took an unexpected turn.

"We're here to thank you," said the widow.

"Thank me?" answered Steve, incredulously.

She explained that her late husband had suffered a heart attack about a decade earlier that had "devastated" him, leaving him moping around the house and seriously contemplating ending it all.

"Then someone suggested he get into sailing to develop a passion for something," she continued. "He called Offshore and became captivated with sailing. This trip to Tortola was the highlight of his life and he was so much looking forward to it. He died happy. You gave him, and us, the best ten years of his life."

When they'd departed, Steve thought to himself: *Wow. If I ever needed justification for doing what we're doing, that was it.*

A flotilla to the former nation of Yugoslavia, hard by the Adriatic Sea, provided similar reinforcement. A woman in her 50s booked the trip with her dad, a retired doctor who was getting up there in age. A couple of days before everyone was scheduled to depart from the U.S., she called and cancelled; her father had suffered dizzy spells and was fearful of being a burden. Then, almost as soon as she'd bailed, she called back to say they were on. The reason? Her dad had done a somersault—a *somersault*—and had determined he was good to go.

"He turned out to be a delightful addition to the crew," Steve recalled. "He invented

A somersault convinced Phil Soucheray (top left, beside daughter Melanie)
that he was up for the Yugoslavian adventure,
in which Sandra Tabler and Jim McEvoy also joined Steve and Doris.

all sorts of useful gadgets out of old soft-drink cans and had no physical problems that we could detect. At the end of the cruise, the daughter hugged Doris and me, and said, 'You gave me my father back.'"

Whoa. Tearjerker.

In just about every way imaginable, then—as a business venture, as a vehicle for the Colgates' personal wanderlust, and every so often as a reminder that what they did had more than a little value to the people it touched—Colgate Sailing Adventures worked, and worked well.

And for Doris and Steve, it made them realize they had a travel itch that would forever require scratching. Luckily, Steve's next big ride on the competitive side of his sailing ledger more than took care of that.

Happy sailors, Steve and Doris, on a flotilla cruise in Turkey, 1989.

Once Marvin Green got *Nirvana* off the starting line, it was Steve's turn to drive.

11

Days of Nirvana
The Best Sailing Ever

TO SAY that Steve Colgate enjoyed a varied, distinguished and even singular sailing career is to traffic in serious understatement. The Olympic Games. Twenty-one Newport Bermuda Races. Seven Transatlantic contests. A pair of America's Cup campaigns. Multiple Admiral Cup's teams. The infamous, legendary '79 Fastnet at the helm of his own ocean racer, *Sleuth.* And that's merely scratching the surface of his racing resume. Toss in countless flotilla charters to every corner of the planet. And, as we shall see, even a rounding of Cape Horn.

But to Steve, every bit of that is overshadowed by the globe-girdling years between 1982 and 1986, starting when he was 47 years old, when he served as the principal helmsman on the record-setting IOR maxi *Nirvana.* Designed by a wunderkind naval architect named David Pedrick, *Nirvana* was built of aluminum at Wisconsin's prestigious Palmer Johnson boatyard, and owned by powerhouse businessman Marvin Green, who had a taste for the high life, as well as the high seas.

Nirvana played the high-stakes, no-holds-barred game of maxi racing, competing against a roster of yachting's major names and most famous boats: Jim Kilroy's string of maxis called *Kialoa*; Huey Long's several iterations of *Ondine*; Bob Bell's *Condor*, often helmed by, oh man, Ted Turner; George Coumantaros's *Boomerang*; *Helisara*, owned by maestro Herbert von Karajan, the longtime conductor of the Berlin Philharmonic; the classic *Windward Passage*, which arguably launched the rarified class of racers in the first place; and many, many others. It was an era of big yachts, big crews, big egos and big money. And this:

"It was the best sailing of my life," said Steve, unequivocally. "Frankly, sailing on *Nirvana* was the culmination of all the sailing I ever did."

Steve in his favorite spot to steer, to leeward,
putting *Nirvana* through her paces in Sydney in 1982.

For Steve, spinning the massive 88-inch wheel aboard *Nirvana*, in far-flung, often-glamorous venues, was a mixture of thrills, enlightenment, joy, glory, pleasure and even paradise. In other words, driving *Nirvana* was, well, nirvana.

To top it all off, as a member of *Nirvana*'s vast traveling entourage—the boat raced with upwards of 28 crewmen, most of whom were accompanied by wives or girlfriends—Doris was there nearly every step of the way for all the jet-setting, shore-side adventures and shenanigans, from New England to Europe to Australia to the Far East to Hawaii to California and back. She even wrote about it; her long, full-color feature article, *Life in the Maxi Lane*, appeared in the October 1985 issue of *Yachting*. In it, she summarized both the unusual boat and the skilled team that sailed it:

"Owner Marvin Green, a fine sailor who enjoys the company of friends aboard as much as winning, reminded us of the qualities he wanted his boat to have: 'beauty... comfort...and it would be nice if she were fast, too.' Racing yachts with teak decks, tiled galleys, clothes washers, desalinization plants, VCRs, stereo and disk players, separate cabins, upholstered berths, bookcases, paintings and saloon tables are not supposed to be fast. But *Nirvana* has all of them and is very fast indeed."

And then there were the sailors themselves:

"Of all the boats Steve has sailed, *Nirvana* stands out as very special," her 1985 article continued. "Green is an active sailor who doesn't seek out racing celebrities to make his boat win, preferring to sail with friends. *Nirvana* crewmembers are dedicated, loyal, of great strength and fortitude, well-educated, highly respected and very sure of themselves. They are men and women who have reached the top—the biggest and fastest boats around. They go about their tasks with quiet competence. Aboard *Nirvana*, a loud, boisterous or argumentative crew doesn't last."

Like Steve, Green had grown up racing in Long Island Sound; he was a lifelong resident of Stamford, Connecticut, and once served as commodore of the Stamford Yacht Club. He had a lavish 5,300 square-foot home on a peninsula in the city's ritzy Shippan Point neighborhood; "Saddle Rock House" was designed by society architects Hunt and Hunt, was once owned by William Randolph Hearst, and served as the inspiration for Jay Gatsby's mansion in F. Scott Fitzgerald's *The Great Gatsby.*

So, yes, a wealthy guy with fancy digs.

There, Green showcased his growing collection of yachting trophies in a grand room with a piano and threw plenty of lavish parties (Doris broke down and bought a mink coat for the express purpose of "keeping up with the Jones's" when attending them). Green had made his considerable dough running the business side of his television-production company, Reeves Communications, which produced *That's Incredible!* as well as *Sesame Street* and plenty of other PBS fare. As Doris wrote in her *Yachting* piece, he

Steve kept in touch with the foredeck via walkie-talkie while *Nirvana* owner Marvin Green handled the start during a 1983 SORC contest.

also liked sailing with his pals.

But the couple responsible for the broader onboard culture of the *Nirvana* program—not to mention its complicated day-to-day logistics—was sailing master Michael Keyworth and his wife, Nancy, who was officially titled the "cook" though her actual responsibilities were more akin to vice-president of operations.

The Keyworths were a formidable pair on multiple levels. Both had degrees in psychology, were poised for long careers in education, and met while working at a school for severely handicapped kids in Baltimore, Nancy as a teacher and Michael as a consultant. They were married soon after. Importantly, both were also fine sailors, having grown up in and around boats on Chesapeake Bay. Michael's consulting gig allowed him free time to sail, and on a delivery trip to the Caribbean, he was offered another job running a charter boat, an ideal opportunity for a skipper and mate. Coincidentally, back north, the school where the Keyworths met was undergoing administrative changes that would require advanced degrees if they continued. The timing was perfect. "We decided it might be fun to take the job in the Caribbean," said Nancy. "We were 25 at the time. Why not?"

It was, in every way, a life-changing decision.

The Keyworths took to life afloat like, ahem, ducks to water. But after a couple of years, it was actually Nancy who had the greater wanderlust: a wish to sail around the world. She even knew the boat she wanted: a rugged Swan 65. She instructed her husband to find one that needed a captain and stewardess. Perhaps very wisely, the obedient husband did as he was told and put the word out to a well-connected broker friend. And shortly thereafter, he got a phone call and an interview. Some guy with a fancy office on the 32nd floor of a high-rise in Manhattan. Name of Green.

They took the job, the outset of which was one misadventure after another. When Michael first laid eyes on it, Green's 65-foot Swan was a mess and needed plenty of attention, but once that was sorted, they sailed it across the Atlantic a couple of times ("It's a remarkable thing for a captain the first time he sees the Rock of Gibraltar," said Michael) and competed in several international regattas in the Med.

Then came the fateful day in Sardinia when Green approached his skipper and said, "Michael, I'm thinking about getting a maxi."

Originally, the idea was to buy an existing maxi—maybe one of Kilroy's old *Kialoa*'s—and refit it. They called designer Pedrick, a rising star in the America's Cup arena with an office in Newport, Rhode Island, to see what he thought. Eventually, he

Nirvana's 88-inch wheel dwarfed driver Steve
during Antigua Sailing Week in 1984.

took Michael aside and told him an overhauled maxi really wouldn't be competitive;
if Green really wanted to play the game seriously, he'd need a brand-new vessel.

A year passed. The following summer, once again in Sardinia, Green was at the
helm driving his Swan under spinnaker when out of the blue, he said to Michael,
"Okay, I want you to fly back to Newport and meet with Pedrick. I want the fastest,
prettiest boat in the world."

Michael was nonplussed: "Fine. What's the budget?"

"I just told you," said Green. "I want the fastest, prettiest boat in the world."
Much later, Michael recalled, "And that was that. It became this mission from God."

Pedrick proved to be the right man for the job. He'd launched his career in 1970
by cutting his teeth at the prestigious Sparkman & Stephens naval-architecture firm,
under the tutelage of the legendary Olin Stephens. When Jim Kilroy approached S&S
a few years later about a new maxi, he specifically asked for the firm's key designer on
their latest Cup boat, which is how Pedrick became the driving force behind *Kialoa
III*. He then spent several years as part of the highly successful yacht's racing crew. So,
when Green commissioned *Nirvana* from him, Pedrick was an established entity with

a lot of personal experience in the rarified maxi wars.

From the get-go, Pedrick understood that Green wanted a very unusual yacht: not a stripped-out racer, but an all-around racer/cruiser. He said, "Marvin had come from his Swan and he liked that dual-purpose style of boat. Wooden bathtub? Removable accommodations, that you could take out for racing and install for cruising? Sure, we can do that. I came up with a light enough aluminum structure where there was no compromise in the displacement and righting moment and all those kinds of things that were the sweet spot of the maxis." Indeed, *Nirvana* was equipped with the long list of accommodations and amenities that Doris had outlined in her *Yachting* article. There was literally nothing else on the water that rivaled *Nirvana* in her unique, sheer diversity and versatility.

Yeah, okay. All well and good. But was she also quick?

That question was answered, with authority, on the boat's inaugural offshore contest, the 1982 Newport Bermuda Race. *Nirvana* took line honors in the 635 nautical-mile contest as first-to-finish, in record-setting fashion, with an elapsed time of 2 days 14 hours 29 minutes 16 seconds, and in the process, knocked over five-and-a-half hours off the previous record, a mark that would stand for the next 14 years.

And that was before the fellow Pedrick described as "our rock star" even came aboard. A sailor with an excellent, unparalleled track record, not to mention a sailing school just down I-95.

AS WITH so many other defining moments in his life, that rock star—aka Steve—is hard-pressed to pinpoint exactly how or why he wound up in the cat-bird seat aboard *Nirvana*. Luck? Fate? In this case, he guesses that Green noticed his prowess when competing against *Sleuth* on Long Island Sound in light winds—an annoyingly regular feature of those waters, but the ones where *Sleuth* earned her name—which are easily the trickiest conditions in which to coax a sailboat to perform well. Steve reveled in those zephyrs, where his gift at the helm separated him from the pack, and was also noted for his consistently good, clean starts. In any event, a few months after *Nirvana* demolished the previous record in the Newport Bermuda bash, Steve got a surprise call from Green with a very specific request: his boat was in Malta, the historic archipelago in the sparkling Mediterranean Sea between Sicily and North Africa, for a series of races including the Middle Sea Race, another offshore contest. Was Steve available to come aboard to help with their starts?

"I'd never been aboard a boat that size in my entire life," Steve said. Daunting. But it just so happened that the Colgates were scheduled to be in Greece the week before, leading yet another of their flotillas, and right after that Doris's father, Bernie, was scheduled to receive a prestigious science award in Urbino, Italy. So, once their duties in Greece had concluded, Doris flew to Italy and Steve caught a flight to Malta.

He arrived the afternoon before the next day's inshore race to discover *Nirvana* was out practicing. "So, I went to the Royal Malta Yacht Club overlooking the starting line and met some of the wives of the crew," he wrote. What he saw gave him pause: the starting area for the race was extremely compact, with plenty of recreational boat traffic. "Marvin had told me that he wanted me to 'start the boat.' They pointed out the starting line, which ran from the yacht club across the harbor to the point of a little inlet. It was possible, but not likely, to get through the main harbor entrance about two miles upwind on one starboard tack from the start.

"I hardly slept a wink all night," he continued; already nervous about the yacht's sheer size, his anxiety grew from missing the practice session and witnessing the short starting line, not to mention that he was still unsure about how fast *Nirvana* sailed or her handling characteristics. But then he caught his first break. "Arriving at the boat the next morning, Marvin said he didn't mean for me to steer. He would steer and I would tell him where to go, in other words be the tactician. Whew, what a relief!

"With about four minutes to the start, I had *Nirvana* heading full tilt towards the line on starboard tack. My god the boat was fast; I could see we would be about two minutes early. I asked our navigator, Peter Bowker, if there was enough water for us in the inlet where a bunch of smaller boats were mulling around. Getting an 'affirmative,' we tacked onto port tack. I had another revelation: might makes right, as all the small boats, even those (with right of way) on starboard tack, scattered out of our way! Then, with about 30 seconds to go, we tacked onto starboard and hit the starting line right at the gun. We hardened up on starboard and sailed right out the harbor, mostly on one tack. My job as starting tactician was established."

Having nailed what was basically his audition, Steve secured his permanent spot on the *Nirvana* roster in the subsequent Middle Sea Race, a 605 nautical-mile contest once again conducted in the lightest of airs. Midway along, as *Nirvana* wobbled relative to her competition, Marvin said, "Steve, why don't you give it a try?" Relatively speaking, he immediately lit the boat up, as *Nirvana* began to eat up the miles. It was clear he was playing a different game than the other helmsmen. Sailing on all those windless races back off Long Island had paid off. Whatever it was that had inspired Green to reach out and recruit Steve, it was working.

Going forward, a pattern was soon established. Steve wrote, "Marvin would steer the start and then turn the helm over to me at the windward mark for the remainder of the race. We were usually fourth or fifth at the windward mark but ended up winning most of the races. Doris later overheard someone on the spectator's boat wonder how *Nirvana* could be in a losing position early in the races and constantly end up winning? (Doris couldn't help herself. "They turn the wheel over to Steve," she interjected.) It was the talent I never really realized I had until brighter sailors than me spotted it and made use of it."

With that, *Nirvana*'s highly successful inaugural season of racing came to an end. But the program was just getting warmed up, and 1983 would bring nothing less than one amazing experience after another.

KING OLAV V ruled Norway with an open and benevolent hand during his 33-year reign, so much so that he came to be known as the "People's King." In addition to his kindly manners and reputation as a savvy statesman, he was also a fine athlete who enjoyed cross-country skiing and was a ski-jumper in his youth. Yet the King's real passion wasn't with winter sports but summer ones, especially sailing; he earned a gold medal in the 1928 Olympics in Amsterdam at the helm of his 6-metre yacht, *Norna*, and like his son, Crown Prince Harald (later King Harald V), he was a fixture in the 5.5 Metre class for decades.

Which is why, indirectly, in July of 1983, the King ended up seated aboard *Nirvana* not on a throne, but on the beer cooler. From which Steve was quietly but firmly requested to diplomatically remove his butt, post haste, because the *Nirvana* lads were hot and parched, and ready for a few cold ones.

Nirvana's busy and eventful year commenced in Florida, with a middling, rather unsatisfying performance in the annual Southern Ocean Racing Conference, and would conclude in Australia, in a controversial finish of that year's testy edition of the Sydney-Hobart Race. But a highlight for Steve and Doris began when they arrived by seaplane to the charming island of Hankö, near Oslo, for a big regatta in honor of the King's 80th birthday. On multiple levels, it proved to be quite the bash.

The Colgates were treated like, well, royalty: they were given one of the private cabins aboard *Nirvana* (the majority of the crew, as well as the container of sailing

In Norway in 1983, Steve was tasked to diplomatically
remove King Olaf from his seat on the beer cooler.
Marvin Green was fine with his ubiquitous can of Tab.

and rigging gear, were stationed aboard Green's chartered Baltic Trader, a cargo ship that doubled as a dorm); at one point Doris was whisked away to Oslo with Green's wife for a private shopping spree; and they were invited aboard the King's graceful royal yacht for a party. That led to Green asking Olav aboard *Nirvana* for a day sail. His highness brought his own lunch, complete with a bottle of scotch that he pretty much polished off by himself over the course of the afternoon.

It was a pretty rigorous sail, with plenty of spinnaker sets and douses: thirsty work, as they say. Here Steve picks up the tale:

"The crew was working pretty hard for the King and he was obviously enjoying it. The problem, and this was pointed out to me from the crew, was that the King was sitting on the beer. Apparently, now I'm the spokesman, too, in addition to tactician and helmsman. The cockpit cooler was electric but all the beer was there and they were ready for it because they'd been doing a lot of work all day. So, they came to me to ask his royal highness to please move your ass off the beer. Which he very pleasantly did."

All that for this? In Norway, sailing master Michael Keyworth, Steve, Marvin and wife Kate were not overly impressed with the prize for winning the Maxi series.

Once the racing began in the Maxi class, matters aboard quickly returned to form. Summer evenings never get totally dark in Norway, and when Steve went off watch on the distance race, he'd steered *Nirvana* into a commanding position, to windward off the competition, which included *Ondine* and *Kialoa III*. A couple hours passed when Steve, sleeping fitfully, heard Green say, "Well, let's get Steve up here."

"So I pop on deck," he wrote. "And everything is reversed. All these guys are to windward *of us.* It was a long beat to the next turning mark. So I got on the helm and by the time we got there, about 2 or 3 hours later, we're in the lead again. And we went on to win the whole series."

For which they received a pair of drinking glasses.

Green could hardly believe it. "I think I spent $17,000 to get this boat here, this crew here, new sails, all to get in this regatta to honor King Olav," he told Steve, "and look what we get! Two glasses!" Humorously, one of the Norwegian officials running the event must've overheard the remark, because soon enough, somebody showed up with a silver plate and presented it to *Nirvana's* owner.

Crisis averted. But the high living was just getting going. Next stop? Palma, the resort city on the Spanish island of Majorca.

"Our rococo Spanish-style rooms at the Hotel Valparaiso overlooking the harbor surrounded an elegant swimming pool lined with oiled, bronzed bodies," wrote Doris in *Yachting*. "The elegant marble lobby was a meeting place for guests—mostly Arabs in long flowing robes, followed dutifully by governesses and over-fed children. The town is also famous for its discos."

Steve didn't get much, if any, dancing in, but he did cross paths with a couple of sailors from his past: Enrique Urrutia, the owner of *Mare Nostrum*, the 72-footer he'd raced across the Atlantic three decades earlier, and King Juan Carlos, with whom he'd enjoyed a double date or two at the end of the race.

From there it was on to Sardinia. "This is Aga Khan country," wrote Doris, "with pineapple-shaped mini-turrets, clay-colored tile roofs, whitewashed buildings, glamorous shops from Rome, Florence, Milan, and many luxury yachts. The guests were from all over the world, stylishly understated in dress, and always in white to set off deep suntans."

Steve with the Aga Khan on his yacht *Shergar* off Sardinia in 1983.

The Aga Khan himself invited guests Steve and Doris, and the Greens, out for a spin on his 125-foot yacht, *Shergar*, then excused himself to fly to England to watch a horse race…which naturally included one of his horses. That evening, at a lavish awards ceremony at the luxurious Yacht Club Costa Smeralda following the day's racing, who strode in but the Aga Khan. Steve was gobsmacked. Who has the wherewithal to go yachting in the morning, then zip off to another country to watch his horse compete, and be back for dinner? "Now that's jet-setting," said Steve.

Despite all the fancy landside diversions, after their initial triumph in Norway, it had not been an equally fabulous summer for *Nirvana* on the racecourse. But an opportunity for redemption was right around the corner. Or, more accurately, across the equator in another hemisphere. It was time to take the whole traveling *Nirvana* roadshow to the scorching land Down Under.

MOUNT GAY RUM has long been the elixir of choice for many a wayward sailor, but back in the day, outside of the Caribbean and other select seaman's watering holes, it wasn't always the easiest bottle to find. When *Nirvana* arrived in Sydney in December, 1983, after a grueling 50-day passage from Europe, Michael and Nancy Keyworth (who weren't on the delivery trip) had already established a base of operations. Their 40-foot gear container for the yacht's 40-sail inventory and spare parts and rigging was there. They'd procured for the Greens a beautiful home with a swimming pool overlooking Sydney Harbor, where the parties would rage. Their berth at the Cruising Yacht Club of Australia on Rushcutter's Bay was waiting. Everything was in order.

Whatever the venue, Doris was able to search out a bottle of Mt. Gay rum, to Michael Keyworth's approval. On the left is *Nirvana* crewman Dave Hutchinson before his devastating accident.

Except a stash of Mount Gay. Until Doris arrived. She'd already uncovered the coveted amber spirit in previous stops on *Nirvana*'s grand tours, and she worked her magic again in Oz. It was one of her duties as part of the team. "Doris is great to have around," said Steve, laughing.

And it was a good thing, too. In Australia, it turned out, before all was said and done, everyone in the *Nirvana* camp was going to need a good, stiff belt or two.

The first—and worst—casualty was Dave Hutchinson, a talented Scottish sailor who was a solid contributor to *Nirvana*'s core crew. On a practice session before the Boxing Day—December 26th—start of the Sydney-Hobart Race, the team was practicing spinnaker maneuvers when everything went downhill, fast.

Steve remembers it well: "*Nirvana* was a powerhouse with wire sheets and rope tails…this was before wire was replaced with super-strong synthetic ropes. We'd set a spinnaker, but Marvin, who was steering, was sailing too low to fill the chute. As tactician, I asked him to head up and fill it. It was a fresh breeze of about 15 knots and the large spinnaker filled with a 'bang.' "Unfortunately, 'Hutch' was standing in the coil of the lazy guy and when the wire guy broke with the explosive force of the chute filling, he was flung like a rag doll all the way from amidships to the headstay. I'll never forget seeing him being spread-eagled against the jib, that was still set, for

Nirvana on a practice day in Sydney, shortly before "Hutch" was launched overboard.

an instant and then pulled around behind it and into the water. A photo boat was following the practice, and rushed over to him and two others who'd jumped in the water after him."

Hutch, who'd been launched 40 feet in the air before crashing and going over the side, was unconscious, and it was a good thing, too—he couldn't feel the 16 compound fractures in his leg. He did make a full recovery, and went on to a long career skippering big boats across vast oceans. In the moment, however, nobody needed a reminder that *Nirvana* was a mammoth machine with a rig that was regularly pressed into service carrying lethal loads. But with Hutch's near miss, they got one anyway.

But every summer day on the crazy harbor resembled a high-wire act without a net, as Doris described in her *Yachting* article: "Prior to the Hobart Race, the maxis and other classes held a series of races in and around Sydney Harbor. It was mayhem. Ferries, hydrofoils and other vessels sporting red triangles have right of way. Every conceivable racing class was holding its annual championship. Eighteen-footers (a light, 3-man skiff) scooted about, capsizing left and right, and the spectator fleet was everywhere. (The Aussie maxi) *Apollo* ripped her spinnaker on the top of a spectator boat's mast. Sailboards tacked directly in front of *Nirvana* as she rounded a mark, just yards from shore. Racing at times was a free-for-all."

Finally, it was time for the famous race from Sydney to Hobart, on the rugged, weathered, exposed island state of Tasmania, nestled in the windswept waters known as the Roaring Forties. From the very get-go, as the Aussies say, it was all on for young and old.

To spice it all up, there was a familiar nemesis involved: Ted Turner was in command of *Condor*, which had quickly become *Nirvana*'s archrival. And nothing that transpired in the next few days would change any of that. Quite the opposite. When the race commenced, there was no way of knowing that, at the finish line, controversy awaited. The Australian sailing magazine *Modern Boating* summed up the contest well in the title of its 1983 Sydney-Hobart: "Race of the Red Flags." As in, protest flags, which racers hoist to call an infraction on a competitor.

There's nothing else in the world of yacht racing that begins to rival the spectacle that is the start of the Hobart Race. Boxing Day is equivalent to the Fourth of July in the United States: a national holiday celebrating the rites of summer. The harbor is awash in spectator boats. Helicopters whir overhead. The start and first few hours of the race are televised nationally. The air is charged with electricity and emotion. It's nuts.

The *Nirvana* crew, and Green in particular, had come to Australia hoping to knock off the race record, but that specific goal is weather dependent, and the '83 Hobart did not dish up the hard, northerly breezes required to do so. But it was a fascinating race nonetheless. In fact, it was a classic.

The Sydney-Hobart racecourse can basically be broken down into three separate sections. After the wild start on the harbor, the fleet exits through the iconic Sydney Heads and turns south down the coast, to the Bass Strait, the body of water that separates the mainland from Tasmania. The middle section is the strait itself. Finally, the competitors sail the final stretch down the coast of "Tassie" and up the Derwent River, some 15 miles to the finish line off Hobart. It seems like something crazy or unexpected always happens in the Derwent. This year, especially, would be no different.

A good-sized fleet of 179 yachts set sail on the '83 race, but from the very outset, it was a two-boat match race for line honors—or first to finish—between *Condor* and *Nirvana*. It was nip and tuck throughout, with *Condor* generally holding a small lead of 3 miles or so, but with the boats in visual contact almost the entire race. Finally,

Steve in control as *Nirvana* barrels out of Sydney at the wild start
of the epic 1983 running of the famous race to Hobart.

in the Derwent, as the breeze fizzled away to barely nothing, *Nirvana* made her move
and eked into the lead.

To this day, it's impossible to say exactly what happened next; everyone who was
involved, it seems, has their own interpretation. There are some irrefutable facts:
Condor was clawing back and went aground. There was brief contact between the
two yachts. With *Condor* stopped cold, *Nirvana* crossed the finish line and docked
on the honored spot at the head of the wharf reserved for the line-honors winner.
Pandemonium ensued. Champagne flowed, the press swarmed the decks, the battle
flag was raised. (The flag, stolen from a concert of a band called Marvin and the Mad
Dogs, depicted a snarling canine with blood dripping from its fangs; the crew loved
it; Green and Doris, among others, were less enthralled.) It was a wonderful moment.

Until, that is, it wasn't: In the next instant, *Nirvana* learned they were being
protested by *Condor*.

Condor and *Nirvana*, tangled alongside in Tasmania's Derwent River
in the closing controversial moments of the '83 Sydney to Hobart classic.

The protest meeting was a circus. At one point Turner excused himself to regale the waiting press corps with all manner of tall tales, mainly involving his own heroics, which ended with him offering a hundred grand for anyone who could bring him evidence of a real Tasmanian tiger, which was supposedly extinct. And completely beside the point. But everyone lapped it up. Was it possible the protest committee was dazzled by Turner's celebrity?

That question will never be answered. But the result of the hearing was straightforward: *Nirvana* was disqualified on the grounds that she did not give *Condor* enough room along the river bank when she went aground. Thus, *Condor* was the winner.

Hearing this, the *Condor* crew showed up on the wharf demanding the top spot on the pier. But it was blowing like hell, dark and—it must be said—everyone was drunk. Cooler heads prevailed, and the swap was made the next morning.

But a line had been drawn in the sand between the two crews. That said, going forward, the *Nirvana/Condor* match-up was like a rocky marriage where the protagonists have had their moments but have also come to realize they need each other. To maximize their potential, and earn and truly enjoy their victories, each team understood they needed someone to push them into true, hard competition. Which brings us, on the international circuit, to Southeast Asia.

HONG KONG, compared to Sydney, was bustling and frenetic. *Condor* and *Nirvana* were the only boats on the starting line in the inaugural match race in a series of them. Steve got the better of the start and *Nirvana* took off like a scalded cat; the race was literally over before it started. But as Doris wrote in *Yachting*, the race was almost a footnote to the far grander reason they were there in the first place.

"On the seventh of April, 1984, at the ungodly hour of 5:30 a.m., we boarded our 65-foot tender to watch *Condor* and *Nirvana* race out of Hong Kong harbor to the entrance of (China's) Pearl River. It was a historic encounter, the start of a two-day escorted adventure into Communist China that had taken a year of concentrated effort to prepare. *Nirvana* won the race. Then we spectators and two interpreters boarded *Nirvana* and *Condor*, and with two Chinese pilots for each maxi, we made our way up the muddy Pearl River on a drizzly, brown day."

Nirvana's ride up the river was nearly a disaster. The crew offered the pilot a

A distracted pilot from Hong Kong nearly ran *Nirvana* onto the bricks steaming up China's Pearl River to Guangzhou.

Heineken, which he happily accepted, then nearly drove the boat out of the channel and aground; luckily, navigator Bowker was keeping a close eye on things and corrected the course before any damage was inflicted.

After docking in Whampoa, the crews boarded busses to Canton (now Guangzhou), passing, as Doris noted, "rice paddies worked by water buffaloes, old ladies and men carrying goods in buckets balanced across a rod on their shoulders, and farmers knee-deep in water trenches between vegetable rows." But the China Hotel, their destination, "looked like a capitalist stronghold—pink marble floors and walls, crystal chandeliers, a fleet of brand-new brown Mercedes waiting outside." It was all a bit of culture shock.

After a couple of whirlwind days, it was back to Hong Kong to resume the series… which quickly devolved into disarray. Once again, after *Nirvana* had vanquished *Condor* on the racecourse, a protest was lodged and *Condor* got the favorable ruling, in this instance the highly questionable and almost unheard-of decision to re-sail the contested race. By this time, Green was totally fed up and refused, which left *Condor* to sail around the course the next day, alone, to "win" the series.

With that, *Nirvana's* participation in the upcoming 565 nautical-mile China Sea Race, from Hong Kong to Manila, in the Philippines, was very much in doubt. Green was ready to bag it and fly home. But Steve talked him down from the figurative ledge with an age-old argument. "Winning," he told Green, "was the best revenge. We convinced him to sail on."

It was a good thing.

Despite the fact that the pre-race meal at a beautiful Chinese restaurant the night before descended into a chaotic food fight—Green signed a big restitution check for that one—the crew was ready to go on the morning of the race. Steve remembers it well:

"The China Sea Race was very light and the lead changed hands about seven times in the last 100 nautical miles. I steered the last seven hours of the race and was totally 'in the groove,'" he wrote. There was a close call near the very end, some 7 or so miles from the finish line, with *Condor* trying to pass to windward while *Nirvana* was on a collision course with a Manila ferry. Steve managed to pass the ferry by the narrowest of margins—a hundred feet or so—while also using it as interference to increase the lead over *Condor*. The tricky maneuver worked perfectly. "Revenge is indeed sweet," he said. To punctuate it all, *Nirvana* went on to win all five subsequent day races in Manila against a totally demoralized *Condor* crew. The formal ball at the end of the series was rollicking.

Nirvana continued on to the Clipper Cup in Hawaii and the Big Boat Series in San Francisco, but with only so-so results. There were new boats and fresh crews on the scene. And many of *Nirvana*'s sailors were also ready to move on. It had been months and years of almost non-stop campaigning, and frankly, everyone was exhausted.

But it wasn't quite over. Not yet. Not by a long shot.

THIRTY YEARS had passed since 20-year-old Steve Colgate had been a winning crewman in record-setting fashion aboard *Mare Nostrum* in the 1955 running of the biennial Fastnet Race. In the passing years, Steve had competed in four more Fastnets, including the harrowing 1979 version in command of *Sleuth*. So, in 1985, when *Nirvana* set sail to begin the iconic race off the coasts of England and Ireland, Steve had a pretty good idea of what lay ahead, at least in terms of the potential weather and the racecourse itself. Many longtime followers of yacht racing will remember the 1985 Fastnet Race as the one where rock star Simon Le Bon, of the band Duran Duran, ended up trapped down below with several other sailors for 20 minutes on his 77-foot *Drum* when it lost its keel and capsized. And Steve remembers that Fastnet well, but for far different reasons.

Steve called a solid start, putting *Nirvana* into the early lead. But for some reason—Steve was never consulted—the crew had opted to sail with the light-air mainsail, a curious choice given the race's reputation for heavy winds. As they sailed out of the Solent, the sail ripped just above the reef that had been tucked in, forcing the crew to put in a second reef, seriously downgrading their speed and horsepower. Steve knew if they were going to have any chance of winning, they'd need a full-hoist mainsail, so he made the unusual call to replace the main. For a solid couple of hours, as they made the sail change—a big job alongside a dock, never mind in the middle of a race—*Nirvana* sailed on under jib alone.

Steve wrote, "The next morning, asleep, I woke up to hear Marvin say, 'Let's get Steve up here. He'll help us make a decision.' Mike Keyworth came down, shook me and explained the situation: 'The crew is exhausted from the mainsail change and it's a bit rough, so Marvin wants to tack to port and sail into a little harbor near Land's End, anchor and recharge.'

"I couldn't believe my ears. It was legal to anchor, but we were racing one of the most famous races in the world and the operative word here is 'racing.' I came up on

Nirvana and *Condor* lined up at the start of the 1985 Fastnet Race.

deck and it was a beautiful morning with the deep blue sea sparkling like diamonds. It was at least 20 feet from the companionway to where Marvin was sitting next to the helm, so I called out, 'Marvin, what a beautiful sailing day!' When I reached him, he suggested that we tack inshore to get in the lee of Land's End and smoother water, because the crew was so tired. There was no mention of anchoring, so I think I had killed that consideration.

"I said, 'Marvin, that's a great idea. Let's do it.' We tacked, and when we got a couple of miles inshore, along comes Peter Blake's maxi *Atlantic Privateer* on starboard tack. We tacked on top of him and the race was on."

Blake, of course, was a New Zealand yachting legend, winning nearly every important offshore race imaginable in his distinguished sailing career before he was

Nirvana hauling the mail while ripping past The Needles in the '85 Fastnet.

To the winner goes the spoils: *Nirvana*'s crew and supporters
after winning the Fastnet in record-breaking fashion.

For the second time in his ocean-racing career, some 30 years between,
Steve holds the course record for the singular Fastnet Race.

tragically murdered off the coast of Brazil in 2001. For the next 300 miles, *Nirvana* and *Privateer* sailed practically neck and neck. At the finish line, they were almost overlapped. But *Nirvana* held on, by mere feet, to not only win, but in doing so, establishing a new course record of 2 days 12 hours 34 minutes.

It took a while for Steve to soak that in: two records, three decades apart. When he'd digested it, he thought simply, "What a life."

There had certainly been some up and down moments in the middle of the *Nirvana* era, but bookending the campaign with record-setting victories in the Newport Bermuda Race and the Fastnet—two of the premier ocean races in their respective hemispheres—was damn satisfying. (The protest imbroglio at the end of the '83 Sydney-Hobart was the only thing that denied *Nirvana* of the "triple crown" of offshore racing.)

That was that for Steve, and for Michael Keyworth, as well, who stepped off the boat soon after to take a shore-side job running a Rhode Island boatyard and becoming a mighty force in the state's marine-trade sector. Sadly, soon after, the *Nirvana* years came to a rather ignominious conclusion. In an effort to diversify his portfolio—or something—Green flipped *Nirvana* for a shopping mall in Ohio. No, that's not a joke. And after a bitter divorce in which he lost most everything, he spent his final years not in Gatsby's place but in an assisted-living facility with all sorts of nefarious characters as neighbors. Keyworth joked that if he wrote Green's biography, he'd call it *Riches to Rags.* Even so, Keyworth said, Green spent his bittersweet final years more or less content, happy with his memories, and grateful for the good times that preceded the lesser ones.

The Colgates, too, would always look back on their rowdy *Nirvana* run with fondness and appreciation. Life in the maxi lane had been a wild ride, in every way. One they wouldn't want to have missed, not for the whole wide world to which it took them.

Doris in 1976 at the South Seas Plantation
on Florida's Captiva Island:
Offshore's first year-round location in the United States.

12

A Woman in Full
Doris Hits Her Stride

THE TITLE of the late Tom Wolfe's epic novel, *A Man in Full*—he copped the phrase from the lyrics of an old Southern folk song—ostensibly tells the tale of an ex-Georgia Tech football player turned millionaire Atlanta real-estate developer named Charlie Croker, a multi-dimensional character if ever there was one.

Wolfe was known for his meticulous research, and made at least a dozen trips to Atlanta to gather material for his second, critically acclaimed novel, compiling notes on the real-life local businessmen who were rapidly reshaping both Atlanta's skyline and its reputation as it briskly evolved into a world-class city (yes, old pal Ted Turner served as partial inspiration).

Atlanta-based journalist Haisten Willis, writing about the infamous Wolfe shortly after his death in 2018, concluded that, as a protagonist, Charlie Croker wasn't based on one, central figure, but on many: "The truth, of course, is that all these (Atlanta) men likely played roles in Croker's past and personality. A Man in Full was, in fact, A Man in Composite."

In the real world, Doris Colgate resembled the fictional Croker in one interesting and unmistakable regard: her growing list of responsibilities, at both Offshore and in the broader realm of the sailing world, were layered and multi-faceted. They were a blend of her own skills and talent, the company's growing business opportunities, and causes she found personally interesting: not just one person, or persona, but an amalgamation.

This was abundantly clear in the essay she penned for the 1989 Spring/Summer edition of Offshore's quarterly newsletter, entitled "My Life With Offshore: A 25 Year Retrospective." It starts simply: "Offshore Sailing School is 25 years old this year. Steve and I are approaching our 20th wedding anniversary. Two milestones intertwined inexorably."

Working girl: Doris at her desk at Offshore's headquarters
in Ft. Myers, Florida, circa 2016.

With those meshed fundamentals established, she starts ripping. If the story had been a record album, it would've been called "Offshore's Greatest Hits!"

There's the tale of her initial sailing lessons, and meeting Steve for the first time in the Bahamas. Getting married the same day as Tiny Tim. Those crazy early years, running programs in the Exumas at the zany Out Island Inn. The eventful, jack-of-all-trades days at City Island. The critical move to Florida. The memorable flotilla voyages to Greece, St. Tropez, Tahiti, and so many other wondrous destinations.

In the closing paragraphs, she writes, "I'm reminded of the many, many women who agreed to take (our) Learn to Sail (course) as a last-ditch effort to keep a marriage together, whose husbands now complain happily that they hardly ever get to steer. And the young adults who found a common bond through sailing with a parent that just couldn't measure up.

"Lastly, I'm reminded that our employees have been a great part of these 25 years. Ah yes, a few have worn our nerves of steel to metal filings. But most have made Offshore the success it is today."

And then this revealing conclusion, which practically reads like a manifesto:

"High flying business folks look at a sailing school as a hobby. We've stopped defending our roles, or trying to prove we really *do* work. It's a business all right, with budget, cash flow and growth problems like any other. But it's sailing too! I ought to know. I married it.

Doris, Steve and the French Riviera, September 1978.

"What do we do when we're not talking, planning or thinking sailing? We go on bike tours or to a dude ranch. But mostly, we go where the sailing is. It's a labor of love."

Labor. Love. The balancing, restorative qualities of each. The abridged story of Offshore Sailing School in two simple words.

Like Wolfe's Charlie Croker, and as underscored in her "Silver Jubilee" piece, at this stage in her career Doris wasn't a single entity, but a complex powerhouse comprised of many facets: wife, lover, businesswoman, boss, colleague, sailor, writer, editor, traveler, friend. And she would soon add activist (for women's sailing) and promoter (of the marine industry) to her ever-expanding array of priorities and causes.

Like Croker, she'd become, in fact, A Composite: A Woman in Full.

SAIL EXPO '94, the second running of a massive, sail-only winter boat show in Atlantic City, New Jersey, in mid-February, 1994, was one of the most elaborate initiatives ever by the sailing wing of nautical commerce. The organizing group, known as ASAP (short for the American Sail Advancement Program), was led by an impressive coalition of sailing heavyweights, including yacht designer Garry

Hoyt, who'd founded Freedom Yachts; Everett Pearson, the prolific boat builder who helmed Tillotson-Pearson, the manufacturer of J/Boat racers and Lagoon catamarans, among other brands; John Southam, the publisher of a pair of well-read sailing magazines, *Cruising World* and *Sailing World*; and Peter and Olaf Harken, the mischievous brothers and firebrands who together owned and operated their namesake company, Harken, the maker of a wide range of sailboat hardware.

Conducted at the somewhat bizarre and fusty Atlantic City Convention Center—the longtime site of the Miss America Pageant—Sail Expo was nevertheless a wildly successful, pioneering event in its early runnings. But the most ambitious, original program at the '94 Expo was easily the one entitled "Women and Sailing: A Day of Panel Discussions by Women for Women."

By women? For women? In the macho sport of sailing, where he-men like the Harken boys ruled and prospered? Who'd ever dreamed of such a thing? (Hint: a certain sailing-school co-proprietor was prominently involved.)

The 21 women panelists who appeared on the docket that weekend were a who's who of accomplished yacht-racing competitors, long-range voyagers, writers and businesswomen, and included five-time Rolex Yachtswoman of the Year Betsy Allison, Olympic sailing medalist Julia Trotman, charter-yacht broker Lynn Jachney, and charter-guide publisher Nancy Scott (whose husband, Simon, was now the influential CEO of The Moorings).

And then there were the moderators of the five distinct sessions, whose topics included careers in sailing, competitive sailing, living aboard and cruising, boat buying, and charter vacations. In retrospect, this quintet had already truly smashed through the glass ceiling of the entrenched, old-boy sailing network. Sally Helme, then the director of marketing communications for the International Marine conglomerate, would soon embark on a long career as the publisher of *Cruising World*, *Sailing World* and many other marine titles. Linda Lindquist, a renowned and proficient Great Lakes racer, was an executive at the giant marine-coatings company, Interlux. Against extremely long odds, Patience Wales and Bernadette Bernon were the respective editors-in-chief of the world's two biggest sailing magazines, *SAIL* and *Cruising World*.

Finally, Doris Colgate, the president of Offshore Sailing School who naturally moderated the charter vacation program, was also the chairperson of the National Women's Advisory Board on Sailing (NWAB) which, not coincidentally, was the organizer of this entire groundbreaking series (not to mention the Women and Sailing

The original National Women's Advisory Board on Sailing was formed by Doris in 1994 with women representing nine states. The membership: (bottom row) Diana Smith, Sandra Tabler, Sandra Chandler, Lyn Fontanella, Mary Lee Montague, Kate Kerr, Eileen Shivers, Doris Colgate; (back row) Martha Ehmann, Joan Vermaire, Marcia Andrews, MaryAnn Sinclair.

brunch the following morning at the, ahem, Trump Plaza next door).

And that was very fitting indeed, for it was Doris who'd founded the NWAB in the first place, four years earlier, in 1990 (the organization's name, in 1995, would be changed to the National Women's Sailing Foundation, or NWSA, to both underscore its national scope and put an emphasis on *sailing*). Certainly, there was a business angle involved; Offshore was not attracting significant expansion in its dedicated courses for women, and Doris wanted to do something about it. But there was also a very personal motivating element. For Doris knew, not only from the many positive first-person testimonials of Offshore's women graduates, but from her own experiences racing aboard *Sleuth* and roaming far and wide on exotic flotilla charters with Steve, what a dynamic and forceful change agent sailing could be in a person's life. She wanted other women to realize what she already joyfully had, and to follow her lead to make their own personal voyages of discovery.

The original mission statement was dead simple, if a bit of a mouthful: "To increase awareness and accessibility of sailing to women in the U.S. and dispel many of the misconceptions surrounding participation in this lifetime sport." It was later simplified, the message more direct: "To enrich the lives of women and girls through education and access to the sport of sailing."

All good. Now what?

Doris put the wheels in motion with a questionnaire to all 2,000 women on Offshore's company mailing list. She said, "I was looking for a diverse group of women from across the country, who loved to sail. The response was wonderful, and I chose 12 women to join me in an advisory group to Offshore Sailing School. Though the company did not have budget to spare, I insisted we fly those women to Ft. Myers, Florida, for weekend meetings twice a year, and put them up at what was then called the South Seas Plantation. It was a dynamic group, from as far away as San Francisco, the Midwest, New York City and other locations."

With that original "dynamic dozen" chosen and in place, they got to work.

Their inaugural program was called "You Can Sail Escapes": weeklong learn-to-sail sessions for women only that were conducted at Offshore's Captiva Island, Florida, base. "Yes, there were a couple of other women-owned sailing schools existing at the time, but none that could bring in 40 women all at once to learn to sail, bond and have fun together because of sailing," Doris recalled. "We also developed a beta video tape called 'Want to Sail? You Can Do It!' and gave accompanying presentations at boat shows. And kept running those women-only weeks with members of the NWAB board hosting and sailing with the women."

One success led to another. Next on the docket was "AdventureSail: Making Changes Come About," which targeted at-risk girls all over the country and aligned with organizations like Big Sisters and Boys and Girls Clubs to bring young women together for informal sails followed by a dockside picnic, where they learned to tie knots and spell their names in code flags, among other activities. Sheer fun. Not to mention a program that exists to this day.

The great Betsy Allison shares some sailing tips during an Adventure Sail outing aboard boats donated by Club Nautique in Oakland, California in the late 1990s.

To make the numbers work from a legal standpoint—and separate NWAB from Offshore for tax and business purposes—a couple of years after its creation the board established the Women's Sailing Foundation (WSF), hired a lawyer, and formed a non-profit 501c3 organization through which the growing list of NWAB activities could be run. Which was a good thing, because the next idea was the biggest and most far-reaching yet.

It was at Sail Expo '95, a year after their triumphant launch of the Women and Sailing seminars, that the group staged its first "Take the Helm" program, which debuted to sold-out, standing-room-only crowds. It was the first of many, in a series that lasted nearly a decade.

Take the Helm took what the original seminars had set out to do—raise awareness and opportunities for women sailors—and doubled down. Along with seminars, panels, speakers, receptions and cocktail parties, there were also hands-on, do-it-yourself courses in matters like servicing winches, diesel-engine maintenance, and deep dives into yacht systems. And there was more star power than ever, including Barbara Marrett, an author and long-distance sailor, and Tania Aebi, the charismatic New

Dawn Riley, keynote speaker; Tania Aebi, panelist; and Barbara Marrett, who played a huge role bringing in more speakers and panelists. All three women were important players in the Take the Helm programs.

Yorker who'd become the youngest woman to sail around the world alone, who made a celebrated appearance at the first Take the Helm weekend. In future years, as the program gained momentum and became even bigger, keynote speakers would include America's Cup and Whitbread Round-the-World sailor, Dawn Riley, perhaps the best-known and most successful example of a woman who could play the game of Grand Prix yachting as well as the big boys.

To make it all happen, Doris and her board recruited industry sponsors to join Offshore's and NWAB's efforts, including the retail titan West Marine, the Maine builder Sabre Yachts and *Cruising World* magazine, whose editor, Bernadette Bernon, remembers it all very well:

"We wanted women to come, to learn more, to ramp up their skills, to be able to take on mechanical DIY tasks," she said. "We wanted all that. We wanted it to be taught by the people in the industry. It was a Herculean organizing effort. Of course, these days, lots of shows do it. But nobody did it then. And Doris, who was at the forefront of it all, along with her board and her partners,

Doris hosts a Take the Helm luncheon at an Atlantic City Boat Show.

had a whole business to run. And she just dug in and got to it. And we all just did it. The boating industry had never had such good parties mixed together with all these instructional programs. Everything was huge. The whole industry pulled together on it in a way that nobody had ever really experienced before."

It brings to mind that old saying: A rising tide lifts all ships. Which was certainly the case here. More *women* sailors meant more *sailors*, period. Who in business doesn't appreciate an expanding market? Sure, the ladies attracted to the sport and lifestyle were definitely the primary benefactors, as was the intention, but the entire panoply of nautical enterprises that were focused on sailing also surged on that welcome, unexpected, incoming wave.

It was a classic case of a win/win situation.

WHEN DORIS was approached by editor Molly Mulhern of Ragged Mountain Press/International Marine (a division of the mammoth McGraw Hill) in the late 1990s to write a book on sailing for women as part of a series of how-to manuals the publisher was commissioning on various sports, her answer was quick and short: "Of course." It was a rather obvious choice: who better to pen such a tome?

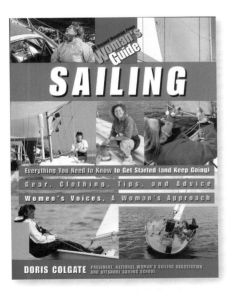

The cover of Doris's book, *Sailing—A Woman's Guide*, published by McGraw Hill/International Marine in the late 1990s.

Doris had already written several provisioning books published under the Offshore imprint—the most elaborate being *The Bareboat Gourmet*, back in 1982—but the 1999 release of *Sailing: A Women's Guide* was the first from a major publishing house. Patience Wales of *SAIL* magazine had this to say about it:

"Doris Colgate takes a premise that most women approach learning to sail differently from men, and I think she's right. In *Sailing: A Women's Guide*, Doris uses her considerable expertise to encourage, excite and educate women in sailing and to show them how their inherent female qualities are those sailors need. Written in clear, but accessible language, Doris's book will help women to start sailing or hone the skills they already have."

In other words, throughout the 90s, her mission continued...above and beyond

Instructor Jim Ellis, who later became the president of BoatU.S.,
teaching aboard a Soling at South Seas Plantation in the early '80s.

her author's byline.

There was the invitation in 1997 to join the BoatU.S. National Advisory Council, a committee aligned to the consumer-advocacy BoatU.S. organization, which Doris accepted and on which she would continue to serve for the next 17 years. Fittingly, the invite was extended by the then BoatU.S. Foundation's president, Jim Ellis, whose nautical career began as an instructor at Offshore's Florida branch at South Seas Plantation, where he eventually became the manager.

(Jim has some humorous remembrances of his early days at Offshore as a 30-year-old wayward sailor in the early 1980s, when he began there and worked with Doris's sister, Linda, who was also on the management team at the time: "Steve would come down from New York and say, 'Do it *this* way!' and then Doris would come down and say, 'Do it *that* way!' They weren't always the same. It made for some interesting times...")

And three years later, in 2000, Doris was off to Amsterdam at the bequest of Alistair Murray, a raffish Aussie who was the head of the Australian-based hardware

Some 30 years later, Jim Ellis and Sarah Pederson present a gift to the Colgates at Offshore's 50th anniversary instructor reunion.

firm Ronstan, to speak before the third International Sailing Summit prior to the gargantuan METS international marine-trade show. Her presentation on marketing to women—for which she was by now the sector's unquestioned authority—was warmly received.

For Doris and Steve, there was plenty happening back home as well; actually, in both their homes. Their primary residence, naturally, was near their business head-quarters in South Florida. But Doris retreated alone to the couple's "second home"—in the so-called "City Different" of Santa Fe, New Mexico—to put the finishing touches on *Sailing: A Woman's Guide*. "It's in the high desert at 7,000 feet and takes some getting used to," she said, "but its striking colors of adobe against bright blue skies is very alluring." And, for a writer on a deadline, it was also peaceful and inspirational.

After decamping from New York in 1988, they'd moved into a lovely home on Sanibel with a pool and great neighbors that became the centerpiece for New Year's

Homes sweet homes: Santa Fe and Ft. Myers.

blowouts, dinner and birthday parties, and all sorts of other celebrations for the next 12 years. The getaway place in Santa Fe was actually instigated by sister Linda, who'd moved to a neighborhood called Eldorado, where Steve and Doris discovered a cute, southwest-style place of their own. Steve especially enjoyed exploring the old local ruins, checking out the countless cool museums, and attending each November's Dixon Studio Art Tour, which exhibited the work of the region's many talented painters and sculptors. The Colgates even considered setting up an Offshore branch on New Mexico's Lake Heron, a roughly 3-hour drive from Santa Fe that even had its own yacht club. When that proved impractical, and with no other place to sail, they decided to sell the home and, in 2000, made a new plan.

Their Sanibel neighborhood had changed dramatically in the intervening years, which led to the purchase of a lot on the Caloosahatchee River in Fort Myers, meaning the commute to their nearby offices was quite manageable: 5 minutes! It took two years to design and build it, time spent in a rental home, but once completed, the open, inviting space, created specifically to showcase the southwestern art and other collectibles from their global wanderings over the years, and to host parties and arts fundraisers for which they'd become well known, was just perfect.

Their last big move had been completed. Ah, home sweet home.

NOT THAT they were especially there all that often. Seriously, perhaps the one constant about Doris and Steve is that, when they weren't working around the clock, they were always on the move. As Doris said, "Travel has always been in our blood. Going to places where they don't speak English, and have very different ways of life, has never been a challenge to us. The highlights of our life, aside from those many flotilla cruises we led, are adventures that have absolutely nothing to do with sailing, because we both like change."

Audacious trips to celebrate birthdays, the unavoidable milestones on one's life journey, were always intricately planned and particularly special.

Doris's 50th surprise bash in 1991 was a double feature, starting with a boat trip out to Useppa Island, on Florida's Pine Island Sound, for an elaborate dinner party at the local inn. Then it was off to Arizona and a dude ranch in Tucson followed by a visit to Sedona; a swing through the Grand Canyon; and on to Santa Fe, where the love affair with the southwest was launched.

In return, Steve was gifted with bike trips in Vermont and France later that decade,

Doris rides with the wranglers to celebrate her 50th birthday in Arizona.
Steve pulls the oars rafting on the Middle Fork of the Salmon River.

a return to the road-warrior days of his cycling youth. That was a fairly new experience for Doris, but it was, she said, "a thrill for me to learn how to change gears, make it up most of the hills, and fly down narrow roads." And Steve's 60th, in 1995, took the couple to the Middle Fork of the Salmon River—Idaho's 425-mile long "River of No Return"—for a sensational white-water rafting excursion down through the canyons.

But they did return, in time for a cruise through the Galapagos Islands on a rather

Steve and friend on a cruise of the amazing Galapagos Islands.
Steve in Fengdu City of Ghosts, before a dam immersed it forever.

Biking in Burgundy.

ancient 57-foot sloop called *Resting Cloud*. On that one, Steve got to flash some sailing skills. "What a trip," remembered Doris. "The boat was run by an ex-Navy captain who didn't speak English but really wanted to learn from Steve how to properly sail the boat. He wore a khaki uniform and hard-soled black shoes. Later in the voyage, trimming the old sails properly eventually caused the main to rip!" Whoops.

China was on the docket in 1997, one of several escapes undertaken with Steve's alumni group from Yale's Class of '57. "An incredible eye opener," Doris said. "We

Gliding along the Canal du Midi on Steve's 70th birthday; naturally, he's aft swapping stories with the captain.

always say we have traveled and lived in the best of times. This trip was before China opened, and we were not allowed to go off on our own except for a couple of hours in Shanghai. It was also before the dam opened on the Yangtze River, though we did see it under construction, so we were able to visit incredibly historic sites that are now under water. Our guide was a beautiful woman who carefully talked about her restricted life and longed for books she could get when visiting Hong Kong. All of our meals—all of them—were arranged by the government. We climbed the Great Wall, met artists and bought paintings. I could go on and on."

She did just that, on another topic, in a grand, 8-page, full-color article in the February, 2007 edition of *Power Cruising* magazine called "France's Canal du Midi: Gliding through Languedoc in Pampered Splendor," which recounted a different, memorable jaunt marking another very special occasion.

"When my husband, Steve, and I decided to celebrate his 70th birthday with the cruise of a lifetime, we chose the Canal du Midi, which links the Atlantic Ocean with the Mediterranean, because of its architecture, its history and the beauty of the land-scape it passes through," she wrote. "Though we could have chartered a comfortable, self-drive power cruiser from any number of agencies along the canal, we chose the 100-foot *Clair de Lune* because we wanted to savor every aspect of this vacation—pampered, fed and guided by professionals."

Happy Birthday, Steve. Lucky rascal.

BACK IN real life, there were awards aplenty for both Doris and Steve, and much recognition and praise for what they'd accomplished. Take the cover story in the May 2009 edition of *BoatU.S.* magazine heralding the "Top Women in America Boating." The article recounted the deeds of an all-star group of A-list women, including Elizabeth Meyer, who restored the J-Class sloop *Endeavour* and co-founded the International Yacht Restoration School in Newport, Rhode Island; Paralympian Maureen McKinnon-Tucker, and Olympic sailing gold medalist Anna Tunnicliffe; the aforementioned inshore and offshore racing sailor Dawn Riley; and many others.

But writer Louisa Beckett kicked everything off in the lead of her piece, noting that "few women in boating are better known than Doris Colgate," who Beckett referred to, concisely, in bold type, as the "Dean of Women's Sailing."

"The Dean." Well, tough to top that.

A few years earlier, in 2004, Doris was honored with the Leadership in Women's

Sailing Award, presented by BoatU.S./National Women's Sailing Association (she'd resigned from the association four years earlier, after a decade, to devote more time to Offshore). This had followed *Boating* magazine's Betty Cook Memorial Lifetime Achievement prize—which actually gave Doris pause for a moment, as she pondered whether it meant her life was over! With Steve, she shared both *SAIL* magazine's Industry Leadership Award, which was awarded to the couple in Atlantic City in 1996, and, in 2003, the Timothea Larr Trophy from US Sailing—the national governing body of sailing—for their leadership and excellence in sailing education.

But Doris's most prized award may well have been the one she received in 2019, when she was named a PACE Grande Dame from the PACE Center for Girls, a Florida organization that was devoted to safeguarding young girls from perhaps troubled situations, who may be on the brink of incarceration. Soon after being notified about the award, Doris received a note from a young woman named Sue Rugala, who'd started working at Offshore back in City Island before moving on to several roles with the company at Offshore. It read: "It does not surprise me that you are honored, yet again! I am a prime example of investing in a young girl's life. She will

Doris, a "Grand Dame" in 2019.

Doris at home, 2021.

build confidence and achieve things she never thought she could! Because of you, I mentor people and teach the values of hard work! I don't say it enough, but I want to thank you and Steve in giving me a chance when I was 16! I'll always be humbled because of you!" Later, the married Sue Kortleven went on to the Marriott organization and then on to an executive sales position at the Marriott Marco Island Resort. She and Doris have remained close friends.

In her acceptance speech at the St. Charles Yacht Club in Ft. Myers, as she cited the feats of other women sailing leaders, she said, "We all have a passion we need to share. Most of us here in this room are or have been passionate boaters or sailors. And because we have that passion, and the confidence that comes from taking the helm, we CAN make a difference in the lives of girls and women who may never have the chance to experience life as we have, by sharing our convictions and strengths to succeed and live full and happy lives."

And speaking of passion, she also recalled her very beginnings at Offshore with Steve: "I learned a tremendous amount in those days, not only about sailing. I learned to live and work 24/7 with my business partner, best friend, spouse and lover. Life was fun."

It still was.

When all was said and done, Doris had published five books. But she also, from time to time, put together little booklets with words and pictures that weren't meant for widespread consumption, that were aimed at a sole audience of one. Like the 23-pager she prepared just before Christmas in 2004 that was called *A Love Letter to Steve from Doris: Memories Moments Magic.*

It begins like this:

"The first time you touched my hand—riding to City Island in that dusty gray Volvo—my heart leapt with joy. I was handing you a quarter for the tolls—my secret wish was to share your life. A year and a half earlier I saw you for the first time and fell in love. I was married to a man I didn't love. You were accompanied by a gorgeous tall blonde. They were both foolishly in love with themselves. We explored unspoken, unrecognized sensations in each other's presence—comfort, warmth, wonder, understanding, electricity—the seeds of a romance we would not acknowledge until later. Magic!"

And it ends like this:

"You are a saint for putting up with my strong will, my idiosyncrasies after all these years. I promise I will grow up someday soon. No matter what comes in the days and years ahead—the inevitable sale of our company, whatever travel we can enjoy together, the quiet times—I will always say each morning… How lucky we are—how thankful I am that our paths crossed so long ago. Magic! I will love you forever, thank you for marrying me… Doris."

So, like, after all these years, she was still crazy mad for Steve.

Her best, happiest accomplishment of them all.

Magic.

The 45-foot cat-ketch *Denali*,
overall winner of the 1990 Newport Bermuda Race.

13

Hall of Fame
Steve Sails into Yachting's Annals

THE *NIRVANA* YEARS. Steve Colgate would always say that the stretch from 1982 to 1985, when he served as the powerful 81-foot maxi's principal driver at the sport's absolute pinnacle of Grand Prix competition, was the shining highlight of his stellar yacht-racing career. Given that, at the time it might have been easy to walk away from the game and maybe rest on his considerable laurels. But… step away from sailboat racing, at the still-vital age of 50, when it continued to provide the thrills and adventures—and sate a deep craving—that had hooked him in the first place?

Not bloody likely.

In fact, as he embarked on the next stage of his sailing journey, in some ways he was just getting warmed up. Which is cool, because some of Steve's most interesting, far-flung racing and cruising, on a variety of vessels and designs large and small, lay ahead.

But not much could compare with winning the Lighthouse Trophy—the cherished prize presented to the overall victor of the legendary Newport Bermuda Race—in 1990, as a member of the crew of the unusual, controversial 45-footer, *Denali*.

Denali owner/skipper Larry Huntington.

Denali was owned and skippered by Steve's friend Larry Huntington, a successful New York banker and a renaissance man in his own right, who was comfortable in two wildernesses: the open ocean (a veteran offshore racer, he also served as commodore of the New York Yacht Club) and soaring mountain peaks.

The *Washington Post*'s esteemed sailing journalist, Angus Phillips, alluded to the latter in his Sunday column in late June, 1990, in a wrap-up story about the recently concluded Bermuda Race, entitled, "Oh So Odd, *Denali* Takes a Bermuda Shortcut." He opens with a quote from Huntington dismissing "the grumbling" from the dockside peanut gallery about his triumphant sail, which Phillips immediately addresses.

"The source of the discontent is simple: While some wealthy entrants in this venerable race spent millions on new boats and the latest electronic gadgetry and space-age sails, Huntington took 1990's grand prize with a goofy-looking, 13-year-old castoff he'd bought for a song six years ago from a former prime minister of England, Edward Heath," wrote Phillips.

"The 45-foot aluminum racer is *Denali*, named for the highest peak in North America because Huntington climbs mountains too," he continued, alluding to the Alaskan monolith that Huntington had summited. "It's goofy-looking because instead of one mast, as all proper racers have today, *Denali* has two, the front one being held up by a wacky array of home-designed crossbeams welded to the bow."

The rig Phillips described is known as a cat-ketch: cat, because the forward mast is right on the bow, like an old-fashioned catboat; and ketch because of the second spar, like a traditional ketch. Garry Hoyt had popularized the configuration in his line of Freedom Yachts, but those were primarily cruising boats. Nobody was racing Freedoms, or any cat-ketch, in serious, high-level competitive sailing. Well, nobody but Huntington—who'd converted Heath's original sloop to the twin masts so he could cruise the boat on Long Island Sound with his family, but could also race it hard offshore—with the able assistance of rock stars like Steve.

From a strategic, tactical standpoint, the Newport Bermuda Race is one of the world's trickiest offshore contests, for it has a feature like none other: the Gulf Stream, the pumping, northerly flowing "river in the sea" in the deep-blue North Atlantic that basically intersects and crosses the 630-nautical-mile racecourse about a third of the way between Newport and Bermuda, wreaking havoc with its thorny meanders, freight-train currents and warm water, which basically creates its own chaotic weather.

The navigator of a Bermuda racer—probably the most important sailor on its crew—basically has to nail not one but three races: from Newport to the Stream; the all-important crossing, where races can be won or lost; and then the final approach to the reef-strewn island, where the winds can be fickle and elusive.

Much of that sailing can be close-hauled, or hard on the breeze, very bad news for

Denali, with a rig optimized for off-wind, reaching conditions. When Huntington and Steve pored over charts and forecasts on the eve of the race, they devised a highly unique plan for negotiating the Gulf Stream, with its pulsing current of three knots or more. As much as possible, they'd skirt the damn thing. If they'd been football coaches, you might say they'd called an end run. Steve remembers it all well:

"Sailing races with Larry Huntington was always a pleasure. He was extremely competent and an incredible navigator. We knew from experience that we could not save our time on our rating if we were beating upwind; we realized the standard strategy of following the Gulf Stream meander…would put us southeast of Bermuda (after crossing the Stream) and beating against the forecast southwesterly breezes. We had to figure out a different way.

"Larry and I discussed it," Steve continued. "His wife, Carolyn, had told him not to take any chances. That was the same advice she gave him when he attempted to climb Mouth Everest at the age of 50; he and I are almost exactly the same age. He was near the summit and reportedly found himself in an unsteady shale field and they were no longer tied together for the final push, so he abandoned the effort. We did not think the same advice applied here, so we sailed right through the Gulf Stream rather than following it for the extra three- to four-knot current. We sailed well west of the rhumb-line course and reached into Bermuda."

In other words, the *Denali* crew took a chance, threw conventional wisdom out the window, sailed far to the west of the 144 other yachts, and rode their flier to the very front of the fleet.

To that point, Steve had done well over a dozen Newport Bermuda Races and was on class-winning efforts three times, in 1958 aboard *Touche* (Class B); in 1960 aboard *Dyna* (Class A); and in 1970 aboard *Harpoon* (Class D). But it was on *Denali*, two decades later, that he nailed his first overall win. And because it came not aboard a rocket like *Nirvana*, but on a relatively crazy boat they sailed the absolute hell out of, it was especially rewarding.

FUNKY BOATS—and big races, and for that matter, close calls—were still on the horizon. And nothing Steve sailed, not even the eccentric *Denali*, was funkier than the Russian entry in the 1989-90 Whitbread Round the World Race, a light, skinny, 82-footer with a sloping bow and stern called *Fazisi*.

Under the command of American Skip Novak and with a largely inexperienced

Russian crew, *Fazisi*'s Whitbread voyage was a long, strange trip; at the conclusion of the first leg from England to Uruguay, the Russian co-skipper hanged himself. After the shock of that tragedy, the crew of *Fazisi* pulled themselves together and ultimately sailed a respectable race, finishing 11ᵗʰ in the 23-boat fleet, and becoming the first boat from the Soviet Union to do so in the process.

By the time *Fazisi* sailed into the Gulf of Mexico on a U.S. tour following the race, however, the crew was basically broke and forlorn. Once they'd tied up in Fort Myers, Steve and Doris extended a dinner invite, and Doris whipped up a steak barbecue that basically floored everyone. Not long after, a local brain surgeon, Dr. Tony Chiruco—who'd been a student at Offshore and self-deprecatingly referred to himself "a plumber for brains"—chartered the boat for the Miami-Montego Bay race to Jamaica, and asked Steve to come aboard.

Having sailed through the Bahamas on multiple occasions on *Sleuth* and other yachts, Steve knew these waters well. By cutting inside Cat Cay in the middle of the night, when the other boats were forced to tack to get around it, and making a key jibe off Jamaica at the perfect moment, *Fazisi* sailed a fast, fine race, much better than expected. In fact, at the finish, they were just four short miles behind a quick, well-known 82-foot maxi called *Congere*, the crew of which thought they were going to hammer *Fazisi* by a hundred miles.

Steve at the helm of the Russian round-the-world racer, *Fazisi.*

Steve at the controls of the maxi *Congere*
on a day race in Australia.

Once in Montego Bay, Steve introduced himself to Bevin Koeppel, *Congere*'s owner, who had to be impressed by *Fazisi*'s unexpectedly solid performance. Steve casually mentioned to Koeppel that if he ever needed an extra hand aboard, he was available. And so, in the time-honored sailing tradition of making connections and paying it forward, Steve landed his next nifty ride.

Steve knocked off a bunch of races on *Congere*, including the 1991 Fastnet Race and the 1992 and 1994 Newport Bermuda Races. And he was also aboard for the granddaddy of them all, the 1994 Sydney-Hobart Race, the 50th Anniversary of that offshore classic, which drew a mammoth, record-setting fleet of 370 yachts.

Once owned by Australian businessman Alan Bond, who'd won the America's Cup in 1983, *Congere* had several *Sleuth* links; in addition to Steve, the navigator was Peter Bowker, who'd served in the same capacity aboard *Sleuth*, and its foredeck was run by Skip Lissiman, *Sleuth*'s former skipper. Steve's fondest memory of that adventure to Oz was probably sorting out a massive spinnaker wrap with an old trick he'd learned on a modest Soling. But it was also a fantastic sail, which he wrote about in the spring '95 edition of Offshore's newsletter, in a piece he called "Sydney-Hobart Demolition Derby."

The outset, especially for a Hobart race, was particularly benign. By the time *Congere* sailed into the usually notorious and dreadful Bass Strait, the sailing was downright delightful. "Shirts are off and the crew are getting suntans," Steve wrote. "A pleasant sail even for a 31-footer. It reminds me of many Bermuda Races. 'A piece of cake' suggests one American crew member to the Channel 10 TV cameraman who is along for the ride. I remember thinking, 'Now that's a kiss of death.'"

Unfortunately, Steve was correct.

"Soon we're running down the Tasmanian coast with freshening northerlies," he continued. "The 1.5-ounce chute is set. We hit 17.7 knots on our watch—what a ride! The bow submarines into the wave ahead and white water surges 40 feet up the deck, filling sail-trimming cockpits. The boat slows, pops up and gathers speed on the next wave. The other watch takes over and hits 18.8 knots before the spinnaker says 'I'm tired of this' and sails off to spinnaker heaven in a multitude of parts."

And things were just starting to get, ahem, stimulating. In frigid, dropping temperatures, *Congere* sails into the infamous Roaring Forties. Which is when the boom breaks. "The race is starting to live up to expectations," Steve reports. "For the next two hours the excellent crew works on cleaning up the mess, lashing the boom to the lifeline stanchions and setting a storm trysail while I steer. We're still making three knots close to course, under bare poles. The cold wind hits 45 knots. It seems like 60. The sea spray stings your face unless you look away to avoid it. The storm trysail gets our speed up to eight knots and a storm jib adds three more. And so on through a very cold night…"

Congere soldiers on, up the Derwent River to the finish line, changing sails right up to the end, about which Steve wrote, "Enough is enough. We're about eighth across the line. By evening, 48 yachts have retired. We hear of boats hitting whales and giant sunfish, dismastings, injuries, crew overboard and retrieved, etc.

"As they say," he concludes, "the only difference between fairy tales and sea stories is a fairy tale starts with 'Once upon a time...' and a sailing story starts with 'Now this is the God's truth...' Unless I'm the one narrating the sailing story... This report IS the God's truth."

While all that, in Steve's words, was certifiably undeniable, so too was the memory from that excursion to Oz for slipping off to the Whitsunday Islands for a bare-boat-charter cruise with Doris to celebrate their 25th wedding anniversary, which was particularly special as they had the trip to themselves, not as the leaders of an Offshore flotilla.

But back to the sailing stories. Doris was not far from Steve the day he almost got killed in a sailboat race, once again memorialized by the *Post*'s Phillips in his May 26, 1996 piece entitled, "The End of *Donnybrook* Comes Right Before the Finish." At the outset, Phillips cut to the chase: "*Donnybrook*, the sleek, black, 70-foot ocean-racing sailboat of Washington businessman Jim Muldoon, is dead, cleaved amidships by a vessel more than six times its weight just a few hundred yards from the finish line of a wild race in the Caribbean."

It was far from Steve's first race on *Donnybrook* (though it was obviously the last), a Santa Cruz 70 Muldoon had owned since 1990. The two men knew each other through US Sailing, where Muldoon, who served a stint as the organization's president, was quite supportive of Steve's efforts when he led the Training Committee. Steve rarely drove, which was Muldoon's job onboard, though he once took the wheel, knocking the owner aside, moments before *Donnybrook* was about to get impaled in a tight crossing in a Caribbean regatta where Muldoon's vision was impaired by the jib.

"No one had ever done that to Jim before and instead of me getting thoroughly reamed out as one might expect based on Jim's personality, he praised me for saving his boat," Steve said.

Sadly, nobody was going to save Jim's boat when it got T-boned by the 80-foot, 47-ton *Creighton's Naturally* (coincidentally, a rival of *Fazisi* in the 1989-90 Whitbread) on that fateful afternoon during the 1996 running of Antigua Race Week.

Naturally, Steve remembers it second by second. He said, "We had rounded the last mark, the wind had increased to 35 knots, and we'd torn the mainsail, so we were sailing close-hauled on starboard tack under jib alone. Along came the large, yellow,

Fun on the well-named *Donnybrook*. Steve grabs the wheel to avoid a crash. The infamous crossing that didn't cross: the t-boning by *Creighton's Naturally* during Antigua Sailing Week, and the aftermath. That'll buff out? No, it won't.

aluminum *Creightons Naturally*, which was sailed by a small group of pro sailors with a group of paying charterers along for the ride. They were on port tack and decided to change course to leeward, go under us and pass astern. Only they didn't make it. Nobody eased the mainsail when they bore off, so the helmsman couldn't turn far enough in the big breeze.

"I was sitting to windward just aft of the traveler. Jim was steering further back. The rest of the crew, including Doris, was sitting on the starboard rail with legs over the side much further forward. The behemoth hit our boat right at the traveler on the leeward side, which crushed it and tossed me on my back on top of the traveler. I was looking up at the starboard lifelines and hearing the bow of the maxi crunching through *Donnybrook's* hull. The one thing I remember thinking was, 'The next crunch is me.' And then it stopped.

"It turns out that she struck the strongest part of *Donnybrook* where the running backstays, the traveler and mainsheet are located. I was saved. We tacked immediately and got the major hole out of the water and were towed into port. This incident is the closest I have ever come to 'buying the farm.'"

God's truth.

In more pleasant circumstances, Doris also joined Steve for the America's Cup Jubilee in Cowes, England, in 2001, which also represented a sense of matters coming full circle. The sesquicentennial regatta, to celebrate the 150th anniversary of the first America's Cup race, in 1851, drew some 200 yachts, and Steve sailed as tactician aboard the 12-Metre *American Eagle*—aboard which he'd crewed in the 1967 Cup defender trials—which had been chartered by Marvin Green, who'd of course owned *Nirvana*, the platform for some of Steve's best sailing days. The *Nirvana* reunion did not go spectacularly from a competitive standpoint, as the old Twelve was a far cry from the big maxi, and the crew less familiar with it, but the racing was fun and Doris took much of it in from the deck of a cruise ship, an ideal platform for shooting photos.

"It was all a highlight," said Steve. "All the famous sailors and all the famous sailboats from the past and present attended. We were always excited being back in Cowes and what an extravaganza it was."

Once upon a time…

THE PROFILE of a local celebrity—Steve—by reporter Chad Gillis that ran in the October 26, 2006 edition of the Florida newspaper, the *Naples Daily News*, provided a fine recap of his sailing career, his marriage to Doris, and their many shared accomplishments at Offshore, "the most successful sailing school in the country." But along with the history, the article also broke some news about Steve's next, surprising sailing highpoint.

"It would seem his sailing resume is more than full, but there's one more notch Colgate wants on his sailing belt, one last ocean crossing. He plans to sail to Patagonia in February and round Cape Horn, possibly the most treacherous stretch of water on

Aboard the 56-foot aluminum expedition boat, *Seal*,
Steve fulfills a lifelong ambition of rounding Cape Horn,
which he celebrated with a champagne toast (right).

the planet.

"Cape Horn is at the tip of South America and is where the Pacific and Atlantic Oceans collide," the story continued. "Lots of ships have sunk there, lots of lives have been lost. He'll crew on a boat loaded with world-class sailors, and they'll only attempt the rounding if weather permits. Still, Colgate's eyes light up at the mention of such a trip. 'We'll go if it's safe,' he said, smiling like a nervous 6-year-old about to sled down an icy hill for the first time."

As happened more often than not in Steve's peripatetic existence, the tale of the Horn trip is another case of being in the right place at the right time.

At a private dinner Steve and Doris attended with the sales and editorial staff of *SAIL* magazine at the U.S. Sailboat Show in Annapolis, Maryland, in the fall of 2006, the publication's editor, Peter Nielsen, casually mentioned that he was bound for South America in a few months' time to write a story about sailing around Cape Horn. And, oh yes, would Steve like to join the trip?

"I pounced on it," Steve said.

The vessel aboard which Nielsen's party would attempt a Horn rounding—part of a two-week cruise of Patagonia—was called *Seal*, a 56-foot expedition-style cutter owned and run by an extremely experienced married couple, Hamish and Kate Laird. Nielsen's story about it all, "The End of the World," appeared in the 2007 edition of *SAIL*. From the first sentence, he wasted no time getting to the point.

He wrote, "The change in the weather is as emphatic as it is fast. One moment we're meandering along, running wing-and-wing before a light northerly breeze that's just enough to get our heavy 56-footer trundling at five knots. The next, the sky to the west takes on a gunmetal hue and the jib shakes itself as the wind starts to back. Our skipper, Hamish Laird, and fellow charter guest Steve Colgate furl the jib and muscle the big mainsail down to the second of four reef points as the clew pennants dance madly. Why the second reef? The sea is flat, and the wind isn't that strong—yet. You need only look under the eased-out boom to figure out why Hamish favors discretion over valor. Not five miles away lies the brooding silhouette of Cape Horn, ship killer and seaman's graveyard, and the souls of a thousand sailors whose bones lie in these waters would tell you that you take this place lightly at your own peril."

To prepare for the trip, Steve had read Charles Darwin's *The Voyage of the Beagle*, the famed naturalist's account of his own journey on the HMS *Beagle* through these very waters he was about to traverse. Once he'd arrived, he appreciated it all the more, which is clear from his thoughts about sailing in Tierra del Fuego and rounding Cape Horn.

"It was fascinating to be sailing into the same harbors in the Beagle Channel as the *Beagle* had many years before," he said. "It was not windy at all at first, then the wind came up unexpectedly and with great power. The cold made the wind force much denser and more powerful for the same amount of wind speed in warmer climates.

"In fact, on the day we planned to go around the Horn, we had to power to get to the exit (of the channel) and we did all the superstitious things that were supposed to get wind, like whistling for it. It worked and as we were passing the Horn it increased to over 60 knots. I was happy that Hamish had the same seamanship ideas I had from storms I had been in. I thought a storm trysail was a waste of time and a dangerous effort to set in the midst of a storm, and preferred a triple-reefed mainsail. Hamish did not have a storm trysail and used *Seal*'s reefing system instead. The only disappointment was it was too windy to go ashore to the coast guard station at the Horn and get our passports stamped with the special Horn stamp."

Still, he'd seen something few sailors ever get the opportunity to witness: Cape Horn to port.

And what, exactly, did he think of sailing in the high latitudes, including slipping past the great cape at 56-degrees south?

"I wouldn't want to make a habit of it."

A FEW MONTHS after putting Cape Horn behind him, Steve and Doris received a truly out-of-the-blue letter from a former Offshore employee. It was but a paragraph long, but a startling and powerful paragraph it was:

"I'm writing as part of a 12-step recovery program for addiction. I'm not sure you even remember me, as it was 20 years ago that I used to work for you on City Island. While I have great memories of doing so for several summers, I also remember that I stole equipment and clothing, damaged the van, and would sometimes 'hide' while I should have been performing maintenance work. For these things and anything I may have overlooked, I am truly sorry. Enclosed is a check for an approximate reimbursement."

Steve's reply:

"It takes a lot of guts to do what you're doing. I'm so lucky I never had any addictive problems, unless one calls a daily rum and coke more than a habit. I don't know if I could have the perseverance to recover from addiction. My hat's off to you and it shows you have a deep moral compass to make things right. Frankly, I may have been wrong about hiring you in the short run, but it's clear that deep down I was right, because you are renewing my faith in human nature.

"I wish you all the success possible and a wonderful life in the future. As for Doris and me, we are still running the Offshore Sailing School and are ready to retire. We just haven't found the company with deep pockets that wants to buy and run a sailing school. I had a heart attack and five bypasses about three years ago and a total knee replacement this March, but really am fine. I just sailed around Cape Horn in January with the editor of *SAIL* magazine. I've always wanted to do that and now, at 72 years of age, I can say I have. Good luck to you and thanks for your honesty and compensation."

Two men, two letters. Different paths, not always easy ones. But both striving, and largely succeeding, at arriving to the same destination. Self-awareness. Honesty. Peace.

In and of itself, Steve's response to his former employee was a fine representation of a man who, like Tom Wolfe's Charlie Croker, was also in full. The punctuation mark for his long life's journey happened several years later, at the Bay Head Yacht Club in Bay Head, New Jersey, when Steve was inducted with five other yachting luminaries as members of the National Sailing Hall of Fame's Class of 2015.

Steve's acceptance speech was predictably unpredictable. Never a man of too many words, it had not occurred to him to prepare anything elaborate in advance, and he was somewhat startled when he was the first inductee called to the dais. In an address that lasted two minutes, tops, he spoke a bit about his mother and Aunt Lou, who'd chided him about getting a real job way back when. He hoped they were proud of him. And, well, that was that. Only later did he realize it would've been good to recognize Doris, and others who'd guided him along the way. Flustered, he remembers feeling embarrassed that he hadn't risen well enough to the occasion. Which was pure Steve: never one to toot his own horn or hog the limelight.

As the evening unfolded, the master of ceremonies, Gary Jobson, actually had to "give the hook" to a couple of inductees who rambled on indefinitely with their thanks and appreciations, a transgression for which Steve was most definitely not guilty.

Writer Roger Vaughan, in a short profile he crafted of Steve as part of his NSHOF induction, was more loquacious in his remarks:

Stephen Colgate, member of the National Sailing Hall of Fame Class of 2015.

"Steve had lucrative career choices. Instead, he applied his calming approach to the Offshore Sailing School he founded in 1964, in New York. From two boats and two instructors, the school now has eight locations and more than 40 Colgate 26s, a highly-regarded boat Steve collaborated on with designer Jim Taylor. He authored a much-needed textbook on sailing (one of nine books he's written) that is required reading for students. 'I instinctively set up the school for all types of learning,' Steve says. 'Visual: the book. Audio: instruction. Kinesthetic: on the water. First there's classroom theory, then we go on the boat and do it, all in three days.' It worked, and it's still working. Steve Colgate has taught 130,000 people how to sail." That figure would top 150,000 in years ahead.

Books and a boat, sportsmanship and fair play, lessons learned and taught: These are Steve's true legacy.

The books, of course, started with the mimeographed sailing instructions he cobbled together for Offshore's very first students. It perhaps culminated in 1996 with the publication, from the major publisher W.W. Norton, of the revised and updated edition of his fully illustrated, hard-cover, 384-page book, *Fundamentals of Sailing, Cruising & Racing*, a testament to all he'd learned and taught. Something tangible in a man's career.

But something even more quantifiable and, in the long run, more important also happened that year, with the launch of the Colgate 26, the eponymous training sailboat to which Vaughan referred.

The Colgate 26 evolved from Steve's concept of the ideal training sailboat, one that would be extremely fast and very stable. Offshore had been using 27-foot Soling class sailboats since 1966 for basic and intermediate learn-to-sail courses, and race training. Steve wanted something better, a safe, highly responsive open-cockpit keelboat that he believed would become very popular with competitive sailors, as well as be the perfect boat for training.

The Colgates hired Precision Boat Works in Bradenton, Florida, who recommended noted naval architect Jim Taylor from Marblehead, Massachusetts. The Colgates gave Taylor their list of parameters, and the first 10 boats were built in September 1996; the 150-boat milestone was reached in 2006; and by 2021 the production run was nearly 400 vessels.

Reviewed favorably by top sailing magazines, and shown at the major American boat shows, the Colgate 26 (now built by Waterline Systems in North Carolina) won "Best Pocket Cruiser" in *Cruising World's* 1997 Boat of the Year Awards. In 1999, the U.S. Naval Academy chose the Colgate 26 for its training fleet, and purchased 42 boats over the ensuing years.

Gary Jobson was on the committee that recommended the boat to the Academy; they'd been looking to introduce a new trainer and were considering the J/22, the Rhodes 19 and the Sonar, which Jobson believed was the frontrunner.

He said, "So I put my hand up and said, 'Have you looked at the Colgate 26? No? Well, I strongly recommend you get one (to inspect). The Colgates have spent their entire lives teaching people to sail and I'm sure this boat is perfect for the midshipmen. You can put an instructor on the back of the boat and load it up with 3-5 mids. I bet it would be perfect.' To their credit they tried it out and agreed with me. The only stipulation was that for the Academy, they'd be called the Navy 26, which Steve said

The crowning achievement of a life teaching sailing:
The Colgate 26, in a fleet race (above) and slashing upwind (on right).

was fine. They're still there and have been terrific. An excellent boat and Steve gets credit for that."

The United Kingdom Sailing Academy agreed, and also ordered several. Steve and Doris were actually in England, at the America's Cup Jubilee, when the first boats were introduced at a special launching ceremony. In his opening remarks, the UKSA director, David Green, said, "Without a doubt, the Colgate 26 is the best training boat in the world."

That boat, then, more than any ceremonial remarks, was the real, true capper to a Hall of Fame career. So fitting. Sailing's ultimate teaching tool. From—it's hard to argue otherwise—the sport's ultimate teacher of sailing.

Doris and Steve with former Offshore student Capt. William "Bill" Pinkney, the first African American sailor to complete a solo circumnavigation around the five great southern capes.

14

Offshore High
A Half-Century Teaching Sailing...and Counting

ON JUNE 10, 1992, William "Bill" Pinkney sailed his 47-foot cutter into Boston Harbor—and into the record books—after a 22-month solo voyage around the globe, becoming the first African American sailor to ever circumnavigate alone via the five great southern capes. As he glided alongside the Charleston Navy Pier, he was greeted with waves and cheers from a thousand local public-school kids who knew his story well. Pinkney's boat was named *Commitment*, but it could've easily been called *Unlikely*, which would have been equally fitting. In the story about the voyage in that day's *New York Times*, it was noted that the 56-year-old Chicago native "was reared in a single-parent household on welfare, (and) has become a hero for thousands of schoolchildren who have followed his voyage in their classrooms."

Bill Pinkney had never had the opportunity to sail a lick as a kid. None. But nearly 30 years before triumphantly sailing into Beantown, he'd begun accruing the skills necessary to complete his record-setting voyage...at Offshore Sailing School.

A few months after Pinkney's accomplishment, Steve was down below inspecting a racing yacht at the annual fall boat show in Annapolis, Maryland, when he was approached by a stranger who'd recognized the Offshore name tag he was wearing. "He shook my hand and said I had gotten him interested in sailing in 1965," Steve wrote in a piece for Offshore's newsletter. "His name was Bill Pinkney and it didn't register immediately, so I asked, 'Have you kept on sailing since then?'" When Pinkney described his historic trip, Steve was deeply moved.

"It wasn't (the circumnavigation) that made me tingle, however," Steve continued. "It's what he imparted to kids, many of whom are at risk of ruining their lives in a cycle of poor education, poverty and drugs. During the voyage, he radioed back to inner-city school districts in Boston and Chicago so those kids could stay in their education, and learn geography, navigation, ecology, oceanography and many other subjects related directly to his sailing and the conditions he was encountering. His greatest achievement is the example he set for kids—that no matter what your skin color, if you set goals for yourself and have commitment you can achieve them. Bill had no money, had lost his job and took six years to raise the cash needed for the project. What better name for his 47-foot Valiant cutter than *Commitment?*"

At Steve's urging, Pinkney penned a letter to share with other Offshore students and graduates. "Dear Steve," it began.

"It was great seeing you after so many years. It's ironic how life takes such strange turns. When you first started your sailing school, did you ever dream it would become what it is today? When I came up to the little office you had in midtown Manhattan I would never have dreamed it was the beginning of my great adventure. We started with the basics, but I never got to the on-the-water part of the course. That didn't seem to make much difference. I had the foundation of the rest of my sailing career and the on-the-water (experience) came later.

"Things just went on from there," he continued. "The beauty of sailing for me is that it is a lifelong process of learning, and gaining the proper basic education is key to the joyful pursuit of knowledge. I hope all of your students will reach for the pleasures that world-wide sailing brings. It's not all easy, but when you have a solid background you can go as far as your spirit of adventure takes you. I'd like to say thanks for giving me the solid basics that have led me around the world alone."

As it turned out, Pinkney's sailing story was far from over. Soon after his circumnavigation, he traveled to Mystic, Connecticut, to take command as the first captain of the replica slave-ship *Amistad*, inspired by the epic Steven Spielberg movie of the same name.

Pinkney was hardly the only notable personality in Offshore's ranks of graduates, a list that also included tennis champion Martina Navratilova; supermodel Christie Brinkley; NASCAR driver Carl Edwards; TV host Bob Vila of *This Old House* fame; newsman Ted Koppel of the influential ABC News *Nightline* program; businessman David Chu, founder of the Nautica brand; and Dr. Paul Marks, the president/CEO at Sloan Kettering, the renowned cancer hospital. High achievers all.

Coincidentally, it was another African American sailor, the thriving chairman of the investment-management firm, Alliance Capital, Frank Savage—like Pinkney, he went from rank beginner to accomplished international yachtsman—who became one of Offshore's most successful sailing alumni in the Grand Prix racing ranks.

Savage was coming home from vacation on a flight with his wife, Lolita, thumbing through a magazine, when he happened upon a photo of a sailboat heeling into the low light of a sunset.

"Doesn't that look great?" he asked her.

"Why don't you take a lesson?" she replied.

A week later he was on one of Offshore's Solings off City Island, a short hop from his home in Stamford, Connecticut. "We hit that first puff of breeze," he recalled, "the boat heeled over, and I fell in love. That's the only way I can describe it. I thought, 'This is incredible. I love this feeling.'"

Savage worked his way up the boat-owning ranks, purchasing a Cal 33 and then a Swan 46, aboard which he was cajoled into entering his first race in a Swan regatta, which he didn't finish. Nor the second race. Or the third. But he was hooked, and determined to get better. Incidentally, all of his yachts were named *Lolita*, after the woman who'd nudged him into the sport in the first place. "I've made a lot of stupid mistakes, but I'm not that stupid," he joked.

In 2000, he commissioned his third *Lolita*, a Swan 56, and recruited some fine

sailors to compete with him. And started winning. A lot, with multiple class victories in the prestigious Swan Cup series. It all came together in 2003, when *Lolita* earned top honors as the overall winner of Antigua Sailing Week. A long way from a pretty picture in a magazine.

Looking back at his start in sailing, he said, "It was an intense time in my life and I found something that I really loved and could be absolutely

When businessman Frank Savage, who went on to own and skipper a series of race boats called *Lolita* took his first Offshore lesson, he said, "This is incredible. I love this feeling."

committed to."

For Savage, taking lessons to learn to sail at Offshore Sailing School was nothing less, right from the outset, than pure pleasure, a total rush. Which led to countless more experiences, one feeding upon another, and another still: the exhilarating path of a confirmed sailor knocking off personal milestones. The fun, as he proved, is all about the steps, the progression.

In Savage's case, you could call it all his "Offshore high."

ABOVE AND BEYOND the basic courses that introduced Bill Pinkney, Frank Savage and so many others to the sport, as the years rolled on, Offshore's curriculum was also in a continuous process of evolution and expansion. Doris's basic business philosophy, originally planted way back in the 1960s at *Yachting* magazine—never get too comfortable being comfortable, lest the comfortable days will cease—continued to be the company's overarching goal. New opportunities and ideas ruled the days.

Steve and Doris quite literally never stopped.

From the company's earliest incarnation, thanks largely to Steve's love of yacht racing and his prowess at it, competitive-sailing programs were an Offshore staple. But the vast majority of sailors don't race, they cruise, using their boats to live aboard and explore. It was a segment of the market that couldn't be ignored. "And early on," said Doris, "I realized we would never be able grow without moving our students into bigger boats so they could truly live the sailing dream. I consider sailing a 'lifestyle,' not a 'sport,' as so many in the industry refer to it. That's an argument I have had over and over with the management of US Sailing and other organizations. I'll let it lie at that."

In any event, Offshore's first foray into dedicated group cruising courses was in 1984, partnering with the Canadian company Performance Sailcraft—the builder of the Bruce Farr-designed Laser 28 cruiser/racer—for live-aboard sessions based in City Island. A year later, they aligned with the major American production boatbuilder, the Florida-based Hunter Marine, for their first Passage Making courses from Jacksonville to Newport, R.I., and Tortola, in the British Virgin Islands, respectively, aboard Hunter 40s. The alliance with Hunter turned into a 15-year partnership leasing big, dedicated cruising boats, eventually topping out at a half-dozen vessels a year.

Soon after moving Offshore's base of operations from New York to South Florida in 1988, the Colgates formed another important allegiance, this time with the Moorings, a charter company they knew well from the many flotilla charters on their boats. The plan, which worked well, was to have a year-round base in the BVI from which to offer more cruising courses on well-found cruising boats. With that, Offshore became the official sailing school for the Moorings, a collaboration that exists to this day.

In the meantime, Offshore was also becoming a greater force on the instructional side of the marine industrial complex. In the mid-1990s, Steve was asked to head the Training Committee at US Sailing, the sport's governing body in the United States. Once again, the notion of a true certification program was raised. This time the concept bore fruit, and in 1995, Offshore was named a US Sailing certified school; the organization's Certification System had seven different levels, including basic sailing and cruising, navigation, and offshore voyaging. Steve actually headed up the committee that developed the Keelboat Certification System.

While still chipping away at his US Sailing responsibilities, Steve was asked to join the board of the fledgling industry organization ASAP, or the American Sail Advancement Program (which later became Sail America). Around the same time, he chaired for US Sailing the Commercial Sailing School Committee. Doris replaced him about a year later, and also joined the board of Sail America, and served on the marketing committee (while concurrently addressing her duties on the BoatU.S. Advisory Council). Whew. Busy people.

Have Soling (and RV), will travel: the rambling Learn to Sail tour.

The recession of the early 1990s, soon after moving Offshore's headquarters to Florida, put a serious dent in business at the company's resort locations, which required more creative thinking. If students weren't coming to Offshore, well, Offshore would take the lessons to them. Which is when the Learn to Sail Tour was launched.

Doris said, "Steve put our Learn to Sail course on the road, with an instructor driving a small RV, while towing a Soling, up the East Coast, then into Texas and the Midwest. The RV doubled as his home and a classroom. Yacht clubs and marinas were happy to have us there, launching the Soling and letting the RV stay in the parking lot. This was before there were so many mom and pop sailing schools across the country. One day, the RV caught fire in the parking lot of a McDonald's while the instructor was in getting his breakfast. Steve and our operations manager at the time, Tyler Pierce, jumped in the company van and went to his rescue."

Never a dull moment. However, the next aggressive initiative was far better.

"The biggest innovation of all was when I came up with the Fast Track to Cruising course, which we registered right away because we knew we would be copied," Doris said, referring to the major course package that Offshore adopted in 2007, which remains the company's bread-and-butter, go-to program even now. "It was a combination of the three-day Learn to Sail course and five-day Cruising course, with students either staying at the resort or living aboard during the cruising portion. It's since been shortened by one day so the Learn to Sail portion is two days now. That course is our true income engine."

Of course, in the middle of all this enterprise, into existence came a tool that would transform the way the entire planet stayed connected, consumed and shared information, and practiced business: the Internet.

The Colgates credit a young employee named Lynn Halter—who joined the company in 1991 at the ripe old age of 19, with her maiden name of Devens—with playing a major role in the launching of Offshore's initial swing at a website. The young lady started in the stockroom of the retail operation, but she was a serious go-getter who quickly rose up the ranks and eventually became the firm's number one, star salesperson before moving on and into the corporate arena. But not before making her mark.

"While Lynn was with us, she also took on the task of working with a guy we hired to set up our first website," said Doris, about the site that launched in 1997. "Joe Robinson was a tall guy who retired after creating a point-of-sale system for a

The Fast Track to Cruising course, which combined the Learn to Sail course
with dedicated instruction aboard large cruising boats, was a major innovation.
Here, students Lindsey Lee and Patrick Blasdell learn the ropes
under the watchful eye of instructor Hunter Botto.

well-known video-store chain. He lived on Fort Myers Beach and invariably left
sandy flip-flop footprints when he came to our office. That was a great website, with
online booking capability, but way before 'secure' booking functions existed. We did
about $12,000 (in bookings) in the first year it went live," an impressive start into
digitizing their client interface.

Alas, when the site needed to be upgraded over a decade later, the next iterations
were migraine-producing, ending in expensive litigation as contracted companies
failed to produce a site that could keep track of inventory and handle their more
than 10 course options, and eight different locations with multiple accommodations
choices. Finally, the Colgates cut their losses, and went with the Tampa company
Bayshore Solutions, which ultimately got it sorted.

Back in the real world, as opposed to the virtual one, the quest to keep adding more substantial cruising boats to the Offshore fleet continued unabated. Production boats from Dufour, Beneteau, Jeanneau and Catalina were also added to the fleet. All of those boats were monohulls of varying dimensions. But a powerful new trend was growing in the sailboat market, one that would not be reversed anytime soon. Catamarans.

A series of cats were introduced into the Offshore ranks: a Leopard 46, a Lagoon 47, a Leopard 48. Each presented their own set of challenges vis-à-vis purchasing or leasing arrangements, as well as the logistics of moving and docking rangy, beamy twin-hulled vessels. Ultimately, a South African-built Leopard 40 fit the bill perfectly, which proved to be an ideal teaching platform for Offshore's purposes.

SEPTEMBER 11, 2001: 9/11. At Offshore's Hudson River base of operations for New York and New Jersey at the Liberty Landing Marina on the waterfront in Jersey City, it was a stunning, early fall Tuesday morning as the staff began preparing for the day's activities. But there would be no sailing that day. Instead, the crew had a clear, unobstructed view, and watched in horror, as the pair of jetliners under the control of a band of terrorists flew directly into the Twin Towers. Neither Manhattan, nor anywhere else on the planet for that matter, would ever be the same.

Everyone wanted to do something to help. But what?

"As New Yorkers," Doris said, "we wanted to find a way to support those who were involved in the clean-up of Ground Zero and announced we would give $50 of every full-course tuition received, over several months, to the World Trade Center Foundation."

In a statement announcing the plan nine days after the Towers fell, she said, "America remains strong and though saddened and scarred, our country is resolved to go forward. There's solace in sailing, a chance to reflect on the beauty and goodness nature can bestow. We are one of a group of sailing-related companies dedicating portions of revenues to this worthwhile cause."

In July of 2002, in a ceremony at the Liberty State Park walkway overlooking the Hudson, where the Towers once stood, Offshore presented a check for $10 grand to Staten Island firefighter Paul Wittek, a previous Offshore grad, who was in the thick of it all on 9/11 and accepted it on behalf of the WTC Foundation. Afterwards, fittingly, the Offshore staff treated Wittek to a sail.

A Fast Track to Cruising Course on a Hunter 50 and a Learn to Sail course on a Soling take place on the Hudson River in the shadows of the Twin Towers.

There would be more giving back. And no single organization benefited greater than the Leukemia and Lymphoma Society.

It all started in 2003 when Sally Helme, then the publisher of *Sailing World* and *Cruising World* magazines, approached the Colgates at the Annapolis boat show about providing their Colgate 26s for one of the LLS's major fundraising efforts—a Fantasy

Sail Weekend—in conjunction with their regular, national slate of Leukemia Cup regattas. Helme reckoned that, in addition to raising money for a good cause, it would also introduce the Colgate 26 to dedicated racing sailors. The Colgates agreed. "We jumped at the idea," said Doris.

With Marty Seiderer, the LLS's former longtime development director, they scheduled the event for the first week of December, 2004. Which was fine. Until Hurricane Charley barreled through South Florida in mid-August, steamrolling everything in its path…including the South Seas resort on Captiva Island, where ten Colgate 26's were berthed.

Remarkably, most of the training sloops survived, and Steve was able to sort through the rubble and tow them with Offshore's Hunter 50 cruising boat from the leveled resort to berths at the nearby St. Charles Yacht Club, where they were members. But that was only a temporary solution. As a longshot, Doris called the general manager at the Pink Shell Beach Resort on Ft. Myers Beach with an unusual question: Would he like to have a sailing school there?

"The answer was they would open again soon, and yes, they would like to have us," Doris recalled. "That started a long relationship that exists today. We moved our South Seas fleet to their rickety docks, which had been pretty badly damaged but were usable, and on the appointed date in December, we ran our first of five—to date—Fantasy Sail weekends for LLS. It was a huge success. We became national sponsors."

For Steve and Doris, the LLS was more than a worthy charitable foundation; it was personal, as they had several family members and friends afflicted by the disease, including Steve's fellow member of the National Sailing Hall of Fame, Gary Jobson, who became one of the great supporters of LLS, and a survivor, too.

"For the first four years of our relationship we set aside $25 of every regular course tuition and sent checks on a periodic basis to Marty at LLS," Doris said. "All the while we were giving them up to 20 courses to auction off at various Leukemia Cup events." At last count, the sum Offshore had contributed had risen to $141,000, with in-kind donations of sailing lessons matching that amount. Altogether, more than $70 million has been raised through the Leukemia Cup regatta program." For Offshore, and countless other sailors who competed and donated, it was a symbiotic relationship that filled the coffers, emotionally as well as financially, of all concerned.

Another organization that benefited from Steve and Doris's time, effort and largesse was the Florida Repertory Theatre, the only professional repertory company

The Colgates present a check from Offshore to Gary Jobson of $100 grand
for the Leukemia and Lymphoma Society.

in Ft. Myers. In this instance, it was truly a labor of love. The Colgates both adore live performances. For ten years Doris served on the organization's board, and eventually became its secretary, and was influential in both decision making and fundraising. For Doris, the reasoning was dead simple. "I will do whatever I can to keep theatre in southwest Florida alive," she said.

Meanwhile, the business of Offshore continued apace.

As underscored by the events of 9/11, though the Colgates had officially decamped to Florida well over a decade earlier, New York (and nearby New Jersey, right across the Hudson River) still played a prominent role in the business, and fittingly so, as it was Steve's hometown and the birthplace of Offshore, as well. It would continue to be a huge factor for the first couple of decades of the 21st century, too, though not without some ups and downs.

The base at Liberty Landing, in the figurative shadow of Manhattan, was the longest-running venue, from 1997 to 2016. On the opposite side of the mighty Hudson River, in an effort, as Doris said, "to try and capture more of the Manhattan crowd," another Offshore branch was established at the vast Chelsea Piers Sports and Entertainment Complex, which also had some staying power, running from 2000-2014. Yet another venue on the New York side of the Hudson, at Pier 25 in Lower Manhattan, had a briefer burst, from 2013-2014. The Colgates were never shy about throwing the figurative spaghetti at the wall to see what would stick; lots, obviously, did.

Perhaps one of the more ironic milestones on Offshore's journey was a brief partnership in New Jersey in the mid-1990s with The Colgate Center at Colgate-Palmolive Exchange Place in Jersey City.

Here's Steve's recollection: "In 1994 a realtor we knew got wind that the Colgate company was trying to develop the property, but it had to adhere to New Jersey codes that required public use of the Hudson River waterfront. We were looking for a branch location away from City Island now that we had sold our property there, and other boatyards were not very good options. The problem with the Colgate property was no harbor was associated with it. So, not worrying about small obstacles like no harbor to thwart our plans, we rented a couple of large barges with retractable pilings in each corner to anchor them in place, creating our own harbor.

"We leased two buildings, one for offices and classrooms and the other for winter storage of our boats. The offices and classrooms smelled of soap. We found out our building had been the soap manufacturing plant. One of the advantages for a sailing school was a mammoth clock on the property: the so-called 'Colgate Clock' was purported to be the largest clock in the world. So there was no reason for any of our instructors not to know when it was time for a sailing class to end and to sail back to the 'harbor.'"

Offshore ran something they called "The Colgate Cup," a corporate race for charity, to kick off their programs there. (They would later get into the business of staging corporate sailing gatherings and team-building sessions, first with the Wharton School of the University of Pennsylvania and later with Emory University's Goizueta School of Business.) The irony, of course, is that many decades after Colgate-Palmolive products were banned from his household when he was a youngster thanks to internal family matters, Steve at least surreptitiously was once again involved with the ancient family business.

All good things do come to an end, though, and for Offshore the formal denouement with New York—what Doris ruefully calls "the last hurrah"—took place in 2016 at the swish North Cove Marina at Brookfield Place in the heart of Battery

A special 50th Anniversary sail adorns a Colgate 26 at the entrance
to Liberty Landing Marina with the famous "Colgate clock" in the background,
a landmark Steve said gave the instructors no excuse for being late.

Park City. The marina had hosted some earlier sailing-related businesses, including an operation run by America's Cup legend Dennis Conner that involved corporate charters on retired Cup 12-Metres, and a longstanding relationship with the Manhattan Yacht Club—and its corresponding sailing school—that had ceased when the Brookfield Properties management team had taken over the property.

Once Offshore became involved in 2015, unfortunately, matters became complicated, then contentious. Naturally, Doris did not go down without swinging.

"I hired a lawyer we had worked with in the past to set up North Cove Sailing School with dreams of big profits in my mind," she said. Rather quickly, she discovered that the payback she hoped for, which was based on figures supposedly raked in by the previous sailing school, had been based on the cash they earned running a floating bar in the harbor. After running a restaurant and bar way back when on City Island, this was an endeavor Doris had no wish to recreate.

Things continued to deteriorate. The Battery Park City neighborhood insisted Offshore provide low-cost sailing education for adults and children, free rides on the weekends and many other demands. By October 2016, Offshore had had enough, and decided to close down the operation. They sold Brookfield the dozen Colgate 26s, the chase boat and most of the classroom furniture.

Across the Hudson at Liberty Landing, the writing was also on the wall, and the Colgates decided the timing was right to fold their hands there as well. "We were, at last, done with seasonal schools and sailing clubs," Doris said. And with that, Offshore's sun set on the Big Apple.

THE "FIRST COUPLE" of sailing: That's how *Bluewater Sailing* magazine described Steve and Doris in a profile piece celebrating Offshore Sailing School's 40th Anniversary in 2004. In summation, reporter Sue Davidson wrote this:

"Running a successful business for 40 years can be mentally and physically exhausting, but the Colgates claim that what keeps them going strong is, 'Our absolute belief in what sailing can do for the individual. And the (so-called) buzz words don't just come from us. Our customers tell us over and over how it gives them freedom, self-esteem... It's a happy product. 99% of our customers send us very laudatory evaluations about the course. When you read those every day you know you've done something. It's not a big money-maker business, but it's fun because we can go sailing and be a part of an industry we care about.'"

It was a fitting tribute to the past. But, other than the nod toward the enterprise being "mentally and physically exhausting," left unsaid was an open-ended question: What, on the occasion of conducting four decades in business, did the future hold?

Or, more pointedly, was there any point on the immediate horizon when the Colgates might entertain the thought of selling the whole shebang and moving on?

When the question was posed directly to her—when will you sell Offshore?— Doris replied, "Well, maybe never. But we have had some offers. Way back in the early 80's when we were still in our offices at 820 Second Avenue in Manhattan, a guy we never met came in and offered $700,000. That would be a lot of money today. But we didn't want to sell. Through the years I have gone through I think eight due diligences with potential buyers."

Perhaps the closest call in recent times came in 2008 when a vacation-industry conglomerate made an offer that the Colgates accepted...before the vacation company unceremoniously pulled the plug on all acquisitions at the time. In retrospect, Doris was relieved that it all fell through.

In 2014, ten years after the *Bluewater Sailing* story lauding their 40th, the 50th Anniversary celebration—with press events and media tours in New York and Florida, a story contest for Offshore graduates to extol their love of the sailing lifestyle, and a big reunion for all the instructors over the years—went off without a hitch.

From both a personal and professional perspective, sailing magazine publisher Sally Helme knows the Colgates as well as anyone in the marine industry. She has interesting takes on their legacy and longevity:

"I think they've been a force for good and an engine for growth for the entire industry for many, many years. In the business that they're in, sailing instruction, they have set the bar in the standards they set, the curriculum they use, their method of instruction, their level of instruction. They are the top of the top.

"Then there's their business acumen," she continued. "One of the things I've learned from them, over the 30 years I've known them, is resilience. We as an industry, as a country, as a society, have been through a lot of ups and downs: economically, recessions, 9/11, whatever. And every single time they always have been one of the first to address things and move ahead. Doris is somebody I would always turn to and say, 'Where do we go from here, how are we going to go forward?' And they both always have ideas. They don't sit around and whine, 'oh woe is me.' It's more like, 'OK, it happened. How are we going to figure it out, change what we're going to do, go onward?

"Finally," Helme said, "they're just incredible the way they're devoted to each other. They have fun together, a great time together, they love to go on their travel adventures and do all these things. It's phenomenal. And they're just great people whom I love to be around. Because they are so interesting: both well read, generous, big hearts. Doris also has such a fierce business intellect. And drive. Both have amazing drive. Their strengths are so complementary. And their devotion to one another after all these years, when you're with someone 24/7 in every aspect of their lives, all intertwined? I don't know how they do it. I couldn't."

And so, the business of fun and learning—the business of Offshore—carries on.

Now, about that compatibility to which Helme refers.

Way back in 1985, the couple gave themselves behavioral assessment tests from an outfit called the Predictive Index that evaluates such traits as aptitude, personality and skills. Over the years, many prospective Offshore employees also took the tests, and still do to this day.

Steve and Doris, on the starting line aboard *Sleuth*, 1978.

Frankly, the respective appraisals for Steve and Doris are pretty much spot on. To the point that they're actually rather comical. A few notes on their results…

Steve Colgate: "Craftsman… Guarded, serious, deeply introspective and very reserved… Immersive thinker… Most productive with fewer interruptions… Modest and unassuming… Has better-than-average aptitude for work that is analytical or technical in nature."

Doris Colgate: "Strategist… Intense, results-oriented, self-starter… Has confidence in own professional knowledge and ability to get things done quickly and correctly… Imaginative and venturesome… May be perceived by others as aloof, but will earn respect for their knowledge, word and the soundness of the decisions they make."

Well, well, what do you know? What's that old saying? Opposites attract?

Too simple. A better analogy, given their shared life's work, might be to compare them to the perfect joinery in the well-crafted furniture of a fine, classic yacht.

Dovetailed.

Steve and Doris sailing through life, forever on an OFFSHORE High!

Magic: Steve and Doris, February 2021.

Epilogue
Ft. Myers, Florida
2021

IT'S WEDNESDAY MORNING, nine sharp, in late February at the headquarter offices of Offshore Sailing School at 16731 McGregor Boulevard in Ft. Myers, Florida, a sprawling single-story space bustling with activity in what was formerly a pair of retail storefronts in an unassuming strip mall. The weekly operational meeting is about to commence.

Just across a hall around the corner, Steve's and Doris's offices face one another. Because she's wrapping up this book project for which she dug out and perused literally thousands of old photos, Doris's office is—how shall we put this—rather busy. On the walls of Steve's workplace, there are plenty of mementoes of races won, awards accepted, even a plaque commemorating the ex-Olympian's run with the Olympic torch in 1996 before the Atlanta games, an honor he relished. An exercise bike is parked in front of the desk, while a big leather recliner sits imposingly off to a corner. At some point, later today, might it afford the chance for a brief moment to get horizontal?

It's entirely possible.

As an aside, for those who wonder, Steve and Doris never seriously considered the idea of having kids, and don't regret that decision. In that respect, they're quite similar to their generational peers, Lin and Larry Pardey, who made their mark in the cruising and voyaging realms of the sailing world. Like the Colgates, they were too devoted to each other, and their never-ending shared pursuits, to entertain the notion of more plates at their table. Which was just fine. Perfect, in fact.

After all, they have a close family, one they've built and nurtured, one that relies upon and looks out for each other. In fact, seven members of that extended clan—which include the dozens and dozens and dozens of instructors, salespeople and support staff who have worked for Offshore over the past five-and-a-half decades—are spaced around this very room today.

They are socially distanced. Everyone is wearing a mask. Yes, the coronavirus scourge is still around, and on top of everything else, what havoc it has wreaked in the business of travel and leisure. The business these very folks are in. The business of Offshore.

Doris sports an extra accessory: a big, black, Darth Vader-looking walking boot on her right foot. Oh, brother. Over the years, like anybody who's lived a long and fruitful life, the Colgates have weathered and prevailed over their fair share of health indignities. Steve's include a knee replacement, a mild stroke, open-heart surgery (with five bypasses!), and a hard fall in the British Virgins that had all kinds of unwanted repercussions. Doris has dealt with Grover's disease, fibromyalgia and her own bad tumble, on the slippery rock floor of a shower in St. Vincent, which for a while robbed her of her sense of taste, an especially cruel punishment for such a fantastic and enthusiastic cook. After all that, the freak hairline fracture in her ankle that she suffered the other day while simply getting up to leave a meeting was really a bit much. Life, right? Still, they look great for their ages. Vital. Fully engaged.

This book project they're involved with has consumed an incredible amount of their time, probably more than they anticipated when it got underway, and there's nobody in this room who hasn't been at least slightly affected by their sometimes-distracted bosses. But it's something the Colgates wanted, not only for posterity, and to inspire as many people as possible to experience the positive high of the sailing lifestyle, but to thank all the students and employees who have taken or taught their courses.

Steve has mostly tolerated the "opposites attract" stuff that popped up in this manuscript from time to time. But he also wants it known that it's not entirely accurate, that Doris and he have a lot more in common than not: Their shared love of art, architecture, theatre, classical music, and fine food and wine. Their fondness for the outdoors, for exercise and healthy activity. They love the same movies and TV shows: Skip the violence, thanks. They hit the sack early and rise just the same. They are very, very prompt: why be late when you can be early? More than once, Steve has said, "We both are 'one-person fan clubs' of each other, with an incredible amount of mutual respect and love."

Correct, Steve. It's so evident to all who enter your spheres. Apologies for that "opposites" drivel.

While the pandemic has surely slowed things down—especially in the British

Virgin Islands, Offshore's go-to winter destination, where the hard COVID-related restrictions on tourists and visitors have recently been extended—there are still plenty of updates to report.

The director of marketing, Beth Oliver, leads the meeting. In a previous life, she was a hard-charging corporate executive in Detroit, first at General Motors, before moving on to several other fun and challenging positions in events and entertainment. She met Doris rather by chance after relocating to Florida just when Doris was searching for a right-hand person to help her both ease the load and build the brand. That was six years ago. She's everything Doris was looking for.

The proceedings kick off with a pretty humorous update on the dispute between two couples who chartered a boat together and each reckoned they were promised the owner's cabin. A discount has been offered and accepted by one of the couples. Truce. That trip, one guesses, should be a nonstop barrel of laughs.

On to more substantial news. Beth reports on the young, peripatetic family living in an RV and working on an ongoing YouTube documentary series, the next installment of which may be about the sailing lifestyle. They're about to take some lessons. She spent some time with them for a story and video piece that went out in an e-newsletter yesterday, and which attracted 700 visits to the Offshore website overnight. This, Beth explains later, reflects the changing nature of the business, and how the brand is presented. The marketing budget hasn't changed much over the years, but its allocations have. Print advertising is less important, though media partnerships remain essential. But more chips are now pushed to the online side of the marketing ledger. What was it Doris said about never getting complacent?

Midway through the proceedings, operations manager Bryce Jackson strolls in. He's been dealing with 1) the fried engine on one of the power catamarans, the replacement for which runs into six figures and 2) locating another boat to put into service for the courses already purchased for the out-of-commission vessel. Bryce grew up in these parts and returned several years ago after a 10-year stint in the Marine Corps, followed by more time overseas as a contractor. He hadn't sailed as a kid, but once back in Florida he got his captain's license, started sailing on his own Bristol 41, and eventually landed at Offshore some four years ago. This whole power-cat debacle has been a major pain. Somebody jokes, "If Bryce had any hair, it would be gray by now!"

Despite the current dire business scene in the BVI, Bryce has an interesting update on an Offshore initiative in Tortola. By virtue of a relationship with VISAR, the

Virgin Islands Search and Rescue squad—the marine professionals at Offshore are part of the islands' waterborne fraternity, who may be pressed into service in an emergency—the instructors on Tortola have already been vaccinated. But the cooler thing happening is that Offshore is providing, at nominal cost, sailing lessons to the local students in the Marine Professional Training curriculum at the Centre for Applied Marine Studies on Tortola's Paraquita Bay. Nearly three-dozen students have learned the ropes on a Colgate 26, practical knowledge that may help them land a job as crew on a super yacht down the line. Giving back. You got to give back.

Thinking about it, it's very clear that Beth and Bryce have assumed many of the roles and duties that Doris and Steve once addressed exclusively. Authority and responsibility have been delegated. It's also very clear that the Offshore ship is on a straight, true course, and in very capable hands.

The meeting breaks up shortly after. A couple of times over the course of the afternoon, Beth returns to the open space of the main office to ring the ship's bell hanging on the wall, signifying another big course package sold and sealed. "That's a good sound," says Doris, and indeed it is: the resonant toll of success. Hopefully this COVID mess won't last forever. Everyone wants more chimes.

The day winds down. Soon after five the place has emptied out, Steve and Doris the last today to leave. Pretty soon it'll be time for the evening news programs—BBC America, Lester Holt, Judy Woodruff—then a nice supper, and maybe some quiet moments to chat about what lies ahead: the reopening of their beloved Florida Repertory Theatre, what to dial up on Netflix, perhaps a future trip to plan. Then: lights out. No time to dawdle, you know. Like almost every other weekday for the last 56 years, there's work in the morning.

Acknowledgments

THERE IS NOT MUCH to recommend a pandemic, with the possible exception of having abundant time to hide away and write a book. I am so very grateful to have had the chance over this last crazy year-plus to author this one. Of course, it wouldn't have happened without the support and assistance of many, many folks.

Two of my longtime friends and colleagues need to be at the top of this list. Among other things, they read the manuscript closely and made a million good suggestions, and I took damn near every one. But that was only the beginning. Elaine Lembo came in at the outset and transcribed all of the interviews, conducted a couple herself, and was just a source of constant good energy and inspiration. As always, thanks 'Lainey.

It is not an understatement to this say book would not be in your hands, in this form, without the guidance and wisdom of Bernadette Bernon. When things wobbled, Bernadette calmly and patiently got everything on track. The fact that she's one of the best, most intuitive editors I've ever worked with was, um, also helpful. When you need a favor, my friend, you know where to find me.

To my current colleagues at *Cruising World* magazine, Mark Pillsbury and Jen Brett, thanks for always having my back. Thank you to publisher Spencer Smith and copy editor Queene Foster, the spinning wheels turning Seapoint Books, and the terrific book designer Claire MacMaster of Barefoot Art Graphic Design for pulling this all together. And to the McSparrens of Portsmouth—sis Nina, Bob, godson and nephew Tommy—who were and are always there for me, so grateful.

Many people took time to grant what were always solid interviews, and all were invaluable. Thanks to Bernadette Bernon, Cornelia "Nita" Chubb, Diane Duryea, Jim Ellis, Sally Helme, Bryce Jackson, Gary Jobson, Elaine Lembo,

Michael and Nancy Keyworth, Bruce Kirby, Linda Lally, Deann Murphy, Charley Morgan, Beth Oliver, David Pedrick, Captain William Pinkney, Frank Savage and Onne van der Wal. What a pleasure it was to reflect on such great times and accomplishments with all of you.

Thank you to Alexsandra Jean, the proprietor of Camp Kennebunk, a private writer's retreat in Maine, where fires roared, the kitchen hopped, wine was uncorked, and perhaps most pertinently, in a lovely upstairs (socially distanced) space ideal for writing, much of this book was completed. Thanks, Sasha.

To daughter Maggie McCormick, of the world's infamous Class of 2020. Mags was also prominently involved, from the very moment I picked her up for spring break from her New England college a few hours after the world stopped and she got the word to pack up and not come back, she would be finishing her degree remotely. And thus my kid, heartbroken about missing the fun and activities of senior year, was stuck in her room completing her studies while in the adjacent kitchen, dear ol' dad was hammering away with this. It was pretty horrible, right Mags? Except that, in retrospect, it was also pretty great. Love you, Bud, forever proud. Never stop roaming.

And, last but very hardly least, to Steve and Doris, for many, many reasons, not the least of which was hanging in with this pandemic project when it would've been easy—perhaps actually wise—to put the brakes on it temporarily, if not permanently. After all, there weren't exactly a stampede of folks booking sailing-school vacations in 2020. But, even more importantly, I want to thank you for trusting me to tell your tale, way back in Annapolis, a few months before the coronavirus became prominently involved with us all. It's been wonderful sharing time with you in your lovely Florida home but especially collaborating with you both so closely on this… My goodness, what a journey, what a story, that the two of you have shared. Having the opportunity to tell at least this version of it has been nothing short of an honor. Truly, thanks.

Herb McCormick
Newport, Rhode Island
April 2021

Appendix A
Steve Colgate—A Life in Sailing

In 1944, on Long Island Sound, nine-year-old Steve Colgate learned to sail, began competing on Atlantic Class sailboats and Lightnings. He would go on to achieve one of the most consequential racing careers in American competitive sailing:

1955 – Won first Transatlantic Race, Cuba to San Sebastian, Spain, on 72-foot *Mare Nostrum*; won class in the 1955 Fastnet, breaking record

1960 – Little America's Cup Trials (catamaran), Long Island Sound

1963 – Pan America Games, Sao Paolo, Brazil, alternate for Finn, Flying Dutchman, Lightning

American's Cup Trials (12-Metres)
- 1967, foredeck chief, *American Eagle*
- 1970, tactician and co-helmsman, *Heritage*

Olympic Trials
- 1964, 5.5 Metre *Pride*
- 1968, 5.5 Metre *Credenza*
- 1976, Solings

1968 – U.S. Olympic Team, 5.5 Metre *Credenza;* Acapulco, Mexico; with Gardner Cox (skipper) and Stu Walker

1978-1984– Owned/raced the 54-foot Frers *Sleuth*
- Competed in the Southern Ocean Racing Circuit (1978, 1979)
- St. Pete to Ft. Lauderdale Race (won class, 1978)
- Antigua Race Week, competed twice (won class, 1979)
- Transatlantic Marblehead to Cork (2nd in class, 2nd overall, 1979)
- Miami-Montego Bay Race (2nd in class 1979)
- 1979 Fastnet Race (won class A, Hong Kong Trophy)

1955-1979 – Seven Transatlantic Races
- 1955 on *Mare Nostrum*; Havana, Cuba, to San Sebastian, Spain
- 1960 on *Dyna*; Bermuda to Marstrand, Sweden
- 1963 on *Dyna;* Newport, RI, to Eddystone Light, England (watch captain when rudder was lost 1,000 miles from finish; finished 4th of 14 boats)
- 1969 on *Dyna*; Newport, RI, to Cork, Ireland
- 1972 on *Dyna*; Bermuda to Bayona, Spain
- 1974 on *Dyna;* Bermuda to Plymouth, England
- 1979 on *Sleuth*; Marblehead, MA, to Cork, Ireland (2nd in class and overall)

1955-1991– Eight Fastnet Races including skipper of *Sleuth* in infamous 1979 event
- 1955 on *Mare Nostrum* (broke record)
- 1969 on *Carina*
- 1971 on *Carina* (U.S. Admiral's Cup Team)
- 1979 on *Sleuth (*won class)
- 1981 on *Sleuth*
- 1985 on *Nirvana (*broke record)
- 1987 on *Nirvana*
- 1991 on *Congere*

Sydney Hobart Races
- 1983 on 81-foot maxi *Nirvana*
- 1994 on 81-foot maxi *Congere*

Antigua Race Weeks
- 1979, 1980 on *Sleuth*
- 1984 on *Nirvana*
- 1996, 1998 on *Donnybrook*

1958-2008 – 19 Newport-Bermuda Races, 1 Annapolis-Bermuda Race
- 1958 on *Touche* (won class B)
- 1960 on *Dyna* (won Class A)
- 1962 on *Dyna (*won 3rd class A)
- 1964, 1966, 1968, 1972, 1974 on *Dyna*
- 1970 on *Harpoon* (won class D)
- 1978, 1980 on *Sleuth*
- 1986, 1988, 1990 (overall winner) on *Denali*
- 1992, 1994 on *Congere*
- 1998 on *Snow Leopard*
- 2000 on *Donnybrook (*Annapolis to Bermuda)

- 2006 on *Snow Leopard*
- 2008 on *Donnybrook*

1982-1986 – Principal helmsman and watch captain on 81-foot maxi *Nirvana*
- 1982, won class Malta Middle Sea Race
- 1982, Southern Ocean Racing Conference, Florida
- 1983, won Maxi Series in Norway celebrating King Olaf's 80th birthday
- 1983, won Maxi Series in Palma Majorca, Spain
- 1983, watch captain in Maxi Series, Sardinia
- 1984, watch captain in Sydney-Hobart; won overall, protest with *Condor* pushed to 2nd
- 1984, won race from Hong Kong to the Pearl River
- 1984, won China Sea Race; Hong Kong to Manila
- 1984, Clipper Series, Hawaii
- 1984, Big Boat Series, San Francisco
- 1985, won class, broke record, Fastnet

Marblehead-Halifax Races
- 1991 on *Congere*
- 1999 on *Donnybrook*

Miami-Montego Bay Race
- 1979 on *Sleuth* (2nd in class)
- 1991 on *Fazisi* (Soviet entry)
- 1992, 1997 on *Congere*

Miscellaneous competitions and sailing events
- 1971, North American Men's Championships
- 1987, won International IOD Invitational with skipper Stuart Walker; Bermuda
- 1988, tactician on 59-footer *Colt International* in Swan Worlds, Sardinia
- 1988, crew in Soling North Americans
- 2001, tactician on *American Eagle* for America's Cup (150th) Sesquicentennial Jubilee; Cowes, England; 34 years after crewing on her in America's Cup Trials
- 2007, sailed up Beagle Channel and around Cape Horn on 56-foot cutter *Seal* with Kate and Hamish Laird
- 2008, Rolex Cup St. Thomas USVI on *Donnybrook*

Appendix B
Offshore Sailing School Courses and Guest Experts

Steve started teaching classroom courses in New York City in 1965, and on-water courses on a 34' yawl in 1966. For many years he continued a variety of winter seminar courses (Bill Pinkney took one of those). The following is a list of key courses by the year they were started, with notes for those that continued on for several years, and to this day.

1965 -1967 Classroom Courses
- Racing Tactics, Strategy & Tuning
- Racing Rules and Appeals
- Winning at Frostbiting
- CCA & MORC Measurement Rules
- Sailing Theory for Beginners
- Coastal Navigation
- Basic Racing Tactics
- Coastal Navigation
- Celestial Navigation
- Practical Engine Maintenance
- USCG Operator's License Course
- Weather for the Yachtsman
- Meteorology
- Engine Maintenance

1966 -1973 On-Water Training and Special Seminars
- First ever on-water course, on 34' yawl (1966-1967)
- Standard Complete Sailing Course, renamed Learn to Sail in 1970 (Solings until 1998, then Colgate 26s)
- Spinnaker Course
- Private Instruction
- Sailing Symposiums Bahamas Race Weeks (1967-1973)
- Sailing Symposiums Racing Seminars (became Steve Colgate's Racing Seminars 1974-1981)

1970-1984 New Courses Added
- Sailing Symposiums Advanced Junior Racing Clinic
- Learn to Sail Week-long Resort Course
- Advanced Sailing (became Performance Sailing in 1993-present)
- Charterboat Qualification Course
- Sailing Symposiums Coed Junior Program (1971 only)
- Junior Sailing on O'Day 15 centerboarders (1972-1978)
- Live Aboard Cruising Course (also called Advanced Cruising Course and Learn to Cruise
- Navigation Workshop on schooner Bill of Rights (1972-1975)
- Steve Colgate's Racing Workshop on Lasers and Force 5s (1973-1974)
- Guest Expert Race Weeks (formerly Sailing Symposiums Race Weeks, became Offshore/North U Performance Race Weeks in 2000)
- Basic Racing (1974-1990, became Introductory Racing in 1977)
- Singlehanded Racing Clinic on Force Fives (1975)
- Ocean Experience (day long sails on 54' Frers *Sleuth*, 1979)
- Special courses on ocean-racer *Sleuth*: Fundamentals of Ocean Racer Handling and Navigation (3-day non-stop 1979 and 1982); Celestial Navigation Passage Making (5-night course 1982 only); Live Aboard Course (5-days 1984 only)
- Windsurfer Courses (1982-1988)

1985-2017 New and Changed Courses
- Sailing and Cruising – on Laser 28s – 1985-1988
- Coastal Cruising (1985-1986, revived in 1996 with addition of night sailing)
- Sailing and Diving Course, nicknamed "Iron Man Course" (1986-1988 and 2007)
- Accelerated Sailing 1985-1993)
- Sailmaking Course (1986-1987)
- Intensive Racing Course (1986-1987)
- Advanced Racing (1989)
- Moorings/Offshore Cruising Courses (Learn to Sail/Live Aboard Courses combined 1988-1998)
- Blue Water Passage Making (1989)
- Accelerated Sailing Course (1990-1991)
- National Learn to Sail Tour (1991-1996)
- SAIL/Offshore Race Weeks (1991-1992)
- Sailmakers Caribbean Challenge (1991-2000)
- Virgin Islands Voyaging Course (1991)
- Catamaran Cruising Course (1994-1999)
- Caribbean Coastal Passage Making Course (1997-1998)

- Learn to Sail in a Day (boat show course, 2003-2007)
- Power Cruise Courses (2003-2007)
- Catamaran Live Aboard Cruising Navigation (2006-2017)
- Learn to Cruise (2007)
- RYA Competent Crew, Day Skipper and Coastal Skipper (2008-2012)

Current Courses and Programs with Start Dates Noted
- Fast Track® Cruising on Monohulls – OSS 101/103/104 (1997)
- Fast Track® Cruising on Catamarans – OSS 101/103/104/114 (1959)
- Learn to Sail – OSS 101 (1970)
- Fast Track® Sailing – OSS 101/101 Pro/OSS 105 (2020)
- Two-Day Introductory Learn to Sail – OSS 101 for Fast Track courses (2009)
- Performance Sailing – OSS 102 (1993)
- Bareboat Cruising Preparation on Monohulls or Catamarans – OSS 103/104 or OSS 103/104/114 (1985)
- Live Aboard Cruising on Monohulls – OSS 103/104 (1970)
- Catamaran Live Aboard Cruising – OSS 103/104/114 (1999)
- Catamaran Cruising Endorsement – OSS 114 (2020)
- Coastal Navigation – OSS 105 (1985)
- Coastal Passage Making – OSS 106 (1985)
- Fast Track® Coastal Passage Making – OSS 105/106 (2006)
- Celestial Navigation – OSS 107 (1990)
- Offshore Passage Making – OSS 108 (2009)
- Fast Track® Offshore Passage Making (2009)
- Performance Race Week – OSS 109 (1990)
- Go for The Gold Racing Clinics (2017)
- Fast Track® Performance Racing – OSS 102/109 (2000)
- Fast Track® Power Cruising – OSS 112 (2007)
- Team Building Programs (1987)

Guest Expert Instructors Who Coached Original Racing Programs
Until 2020, famous racing sailors, called Guest Experts, coached racing programs. All the Guest Experts listed below participated in Racing Programs run by Steve from the Sailing Symposiums days 1968-1973 through Offshore's Advanced Racing programs through the '90s.

- Scott Allan (Horizon Sails, Olympic competitor, FD Nat's champ, Congressional Cup winner)
- Tom Allen (Lightning national and world champ, Congressional Cup Winner, Trans-Pac Winner, One Ton North Americans)

- John Aras (President Shore Sails, Chesapeake; Albacore National Champ, 2nd in Championship of Champions, winner Prince of Wales Cup; winner MORC, Flying Scot North Americans, Richardson Cup Champion, Lake Erie Boat of the Year, IOR & PHRF; 420 Olympic Trials, Bermuda Race winner)
- Ed Baird (author Laser Racing, Soling Champ, won 1984 J-24 Worlds in England)
- Peter Barrett (Olympic Medalist, Pan Am Games, North Sail)
- John Bertrand (Finns Australian Champ, 4th Olympic Games, American's Cup Challenge crew, Admirals' Cup crew)
- Tom Blackaller (North Sails, Clipper tactician, '80 Star World Champ, Williwaw tactician, 6 Meter Champ)
- Ed Botterell (Hood Sails, Canada)
- Gordy Bowers (Finns Champ, sailmaker)
- Ian Bruce (POW Trophy, Canadian Olympics)
- Gardner Cox (Penguin National Champ, 5.5 Metre Olympic Contender)
- Dick Deaver (President North Sails, Seal Beach; Bronze Medal '64 Tokyo Olympics Dragons, 1st '73 ¾ Ton World Championships, '77 Admiral's Cup U.S. Team, helmsman on *Bay Bea*; '78 Congressional Cup and French Match Racing Championships, '79 British Match Racing Championships, '80 New Zealand Match Racing Championships '81 Stannic Trophy and 2nd in Congressional Cup)
- Greg Fisher (Shore Sails, Columbus, OH; Thistle Champ, Highlands Champ, SORC, CORC, Mackinac RW)
- Hans Fogh (Denmark and Canadian Olympic Medalist, crewed for Paul Elvstrom in Olympics)
- John Gluek (President Melges Sales, Winner Soling Bowl Annapolis, Winner E Scows Blue Chip, 2x Winner E Scows ILYA, 2x Winner Western MI Invitational, 4x Winner ILYA invitational, 2x Winner Midwest Ice Boat Regionals)
- Bruce Goldsmith (Lightning Worlds Champ 2x, NA Champ 4x, Gold Medal Pan Am Games 2x, Soling Runner-up Worlds, Winner CORK)
- Rick Grajirena (Flying Dutchman SPORT Winner, Laser District Champ, OK Dinghy National Champ, Canadian National Champ, 470 NA Champ 2x, Race of Champions Winner)
- Graham Hall (Mallory Cup Winner, Author)
- Steve Haarstick (Star District Champ 2x, Bacardi Cup 2nd)
- Jim Hunt (Mallory Cup Winner)
- Andreas Josenhans (Soling Champ, crew member America's Cup winner, Swan Class leader, Montreal 1976 Olympics, Canada's Sports Hall of Fame)
- Bruce Kirby (Canadian Olympics, Editor One Design Magazine)
- Jack Knights (British Olympics and journalist)
- John Kolius (Ulmer Sales Texas, Olympic silver medal Solings, NA Soling Champ,

2nd in J24 Natiionals, Mallory Cup, Sears Cup Champ)
- Perry Lewis (many North American championships and Mackinac Race wins)
- John Marshall (Olympic contender, North Sails)
- Buddy Melges (Olympic Silver Medalist Flying Dutchmen, Olympic Gold Medal Solings, National World Champ Star Class)
- Jim Miller (Thistle National Champ, winner Yachting's One-of-a-Kind)
- George O'Day (Olympic Medalist)
- Stan Ogilvy (Star North American's, author)
- Mark Ploch (Ulmer Sails FL, '80 NA J-24 Champ, 2x mid-winters, crew on *Black Star*)
- Dick Rose (author, Yachting's Racing Clinic, International 14s, racing rules expert)
- Wally Ross (President Hard Sails, author)
- Bill Shore (Lightning World Champ, 4x Lightning NA winner, Bronze Medal Pan Am Games, Albacore World Champ, Class winner Bermuda Race, owner Shore Sails)
- Harry Sindle (Albacore Mid Atlantic Champ, Flying Dutchman National Champ, Pam Am Games Gold Medal, Jolly World Champ, Laser District Champ 3x, Lightning Atlantic Coast Champ, midwinter Champ)
- Bob Smith (Star Worlds Champion)
- Dick Stearns (Olympic Medalist, Murphy & Nye Sails)
- Dick Tillman (Finns Medalist Pam Am Games, Laser NA Champ 3X, Snipe Nat'l Champ, Martini & Rossi Yachtsman of Year)
- Owen Torrey (Olympic Medalist, Ratsey & Lapthorn Sails)
- Charlie Ulmer (Tempest National Champ, Ulmer Sails)
- Carl Van Duyne (Finn Champ and Olympian)
- Sandy Van Zandt (505s, sailmaker)
- Gene Walet (Mallory Cup Champ)
- Stu Walker (Olympic Contender, Author racing books, International 14 Princess Elizabeth Trophy, Prince of Wales Cup, Yachting One-of-a-Kind, US Championship, 5.5 Metre US Olympic competitor; Soling Great Lakes Champ, Swiss Champ, Atlantic Coast Champ, LI Sound Champ)

Guest Experts Who Taught Classroom Courses in 1965-1967
- Bill Cox, American Eagle helmsman, Winner 1966 Mallory Cup
- Alan Gurney, naval architect
- Steve Haarstick, head designer Hard Sails
- Graham Hall, 1970 Mallory Cup Winner
- Arthur Knapp, frost-bite champion
- Wally Ross, President Hard Sails
- Bob Smith, Author "The Rules of Yacht Racing"

Appendix C
Colgate Flotillas Take Graduates Adventure Sailing

Steve and Doris Colgate realized early on that, although their graduates couldn't wait to use their new skills, they didn't yet own their own boats, nor did many have friends who sailed. In 1972, they had an idea to fill the gap, and organized a "flotilla sailing charter" in the British Virgin Islands. Since that first cruise, Offshore Sailing School has organized more than 200 flotilla cruises, with more than 4,000 graduates participating. Here are destinations where Offshore's Colgate Sailing Adventures® took their graduates through 2021, followed by the number of flotillas to those destinations through the years. The Offshore Sailing School website features four to eight flotilla cruise adventures each year.

- British Virgin Islands (37)
- Grenadines (27)
- Greece (18)
- Maine (18)
- The Bahamas (14)
- Leeward Islands (12)
- New England (8)
- Croatia (7)
- Tahiti (7)
- San Juan Islands (7)
- Belize, Central America (6)
- Apostle Island, Lake Superior (5)
- Chesapeake (4)
- Tonga (4)
- Turkey (4)
- Florida (4)
- French Riviera (4)
- Whitsundays, Australia (3)
- Sea of Cortez, Mexico (3)
- Gulf Islands, British Columbia (2)
- Italy (2)

- Seychelles (2)
- Mallorca, Spain (2)
- Galapagos (1)
- Honduras (1)
- St. Barts (1)
- St. Kitts (1)
- Bay Islands, New Zealand (1)
- Thailand (1)

Appendix D
Colgate Awards & Honors

- 2019 - Doris honored as a PACE Center for Girls Grande Dame
- 2016 - Steve and Doris profiled in "Leaders and Legends," *BoatU.S. Magazine*
- 2015 - Steve inducted into the National Sailing Hall of Fame
- 2015 - Doris and Steve receive Philanthropy Award, Leukemia & Lymphoma Society
- 2013 - Steve and Doris receive Chairman's Citation, Leukemia & Lymphoma Society
- 2013 - Steve, Doris, and Offshore receive Chrysalis Award, Lee County Visitors and Convention Bureau
- 2010 - Steve, Doris, and Offshore receive Junonia Award, Lee County Visitors and Convention Bureau
- 2010 - Colgates profiled in "Top 40 Sailors Who Made a Difference," *SAIL Magazine*
- 2009 - *BoatU.S. Magazine* selects Doris for it's feature "The Top Women in American Boating"
- 2008 - Colgates presented with Harken Gold Block Award
- 2007 - "Dreams Come True" appreciation presented to Offshore for dedication and support to children with life-threatening illnesses
- 2004 - Doris receives Leadership in Women's Sailing Award, BoatU.S. and National Women's Sailing Association
- 2003 - Steve and Doris awarded Timothea Larr Trophy, U.S. Sailing
- 1999 - Doris receives Southam Award from Sail America for her book, *SAILING: A Woman's Guide*
- 1997 - Steve and Doris win *Cruising World's* Boat of the Year, Pocket Cruiser division, for the Colgate 26
- 1996 - Steve and Doris receive Industry Award for Leadership, *SAIL Magazine*
- 1996 - The American Woman's Economic Development Corporation salutes Doris for "pioneering vision, ingenuity, tenacity, and spirit symbolizing success and growth in the women's business sector"

- 1994 - Doris receives Betty Cook Memorial Lifetime Achievement Award, Boating Magazine and International Women in Boating
- 1990 - Steve presented with the U.S. Sailing President's Industry Leadership Award
- 1988 - Steve and Doris presented with silver trophy by South Seas Plantation for Offshore's 25th anniversary
- 1988 - Steve and Doris made Lifetime Honorary Members, Florida Sheriffs Association, and given Golden Star Award from Florida Sheriffs' Youth Ranches

Appendix E
Bibliography

Stephen Colgate:

Steve has shared basic sailing techniques, pro-racing techniques, and stories about his competitive experiences in magazines such as Yachting, SAIL, and Cruising World. His books include:

- *Manual of Advanced Sailing Theory* (Offshore Sailing School, Ltd., 1973)
- *Manual of Racing Techniques* (Offshore Sailing School, Ltd., 1975, 1977, 1979, 1981, 1983, 1985, 1987)
- *Manual of Cruising Sailboat Techniques* (Offshore Sailing School, Ltd.)
- *Fundamentals of Sailing, Cruising & Racing* (W. W. Norton, 1978)
- *Colgate's Basic Sailing Theory* (Van Nostrand Reinhold Co., 1973)
- *The Yachtsman's Guide to Racing Tactics* (Ziff-Davis Books, 1981)
- *Advanced Sailing* (Offshore Sailing School, Ltd., 1982)
- *The International Sailing Logbook* (Offshore Sailing School Ltd., 1984)
- *Steve Colgate on the Racing Rules* (Offshore Sailing School, Ltd., 1990)
- *Steve Colgate on Cruising: The Hows and Whys of Bareboat Chartering On Your Own* (Offshore Sailing School, Ltd., 1990, 1995)
- *Steve Colgate on Sailing: The What, How, Why, and When of Sailing, Cruising, and Racing, By the Head of the Famous Colgate Offshore Sailing Schools* (W.W. Norton, 1991)
- *Colgate's Basic Sailing* (Offshore Sailing School, Ltd., 1991, 1995, 1999, 2004)
- *Fundamentals of Sailing, Cruising & Racing* (W. W. Norton, 1996)
- *Performance Sailing* (Offshore Sailing School, Ltd., 1993, 2006)
- *Performance Sailing and Racing: All You Need to Know to Sail Faster and Smarter* (International Marine/McGraw Hill, 2012)

Doris Colgate:

Through the years, Doris has written many entertaining articles for top boating magazines on sail technique, big-league racing, provisioning, and on the couple's travels by boat, including several for Yachting and Cruising World. Her books include:

- *The Transatlantic Race from Marblehead to Cork: Provisions, Menus and Recipes on $7.72 a Day* (Offshore Sailing School, Ltd , 1979)
- *The Sleuth Odyssey: Provisioning and Other Thoughts for Short and Long Passages* (Offshore Sailing School Ltd., 1981)
- *The Bareboat Gourmet: Creative Cooking with Standard Provisions* (Offshore Sailing School, Ltd., 1982)
- *Easy Cruising: Provisioning and Other Thoughts for Short and Long Passages* (Offshore Sailing School, Ltd., 1984)
- *Sailing: A Woman's Guide: Everything You Need to Know to Get Started (and Keep Going)* (Ragged Mountain Press/McGraw-Hill, 1999)

Steve and Doris:

- *Fast Track to Cruising: How to Go from Novice to Cruise-Ready in Seven Days* (International Marine/McGraw Hill, 2005)
- *Fast Track to Sailing: Learn to Sail in Three Days* (International Marine/McGraw Hill, 2009)

Appendix F
Offshore Sailing School Locations Through the Years

Offshore Sailing School over the years has had a total of 63 locations – 15 in the United States and 8 countries/territories outside the United States. In 2016 the Colgates closed down the last two seasonal branches, both in NY Harbor. Since then they have concentrated on a business model that focuses solely on resort-based locations.

Headquarters and Winter Classroom Locations
550 Fifth Avenue, New York, NY – 1964-1965
5 East 40th Street, New York, NY – 1966-1972
820 Second Avenue, New York, NY – 1973-1982
Offshore Sailing Center, City Island, NY – 1983-1987
16731 McGregor Blvd, Ft. Myers, FL – 1988-present

On-water Sailing School Locations

BAHAMAS
- Grand Bahamas Hotel and Country Club, Grand Bahamas Island – 1967-1969
- Coral Harbour Hotel, Nassau – 1970-1971
- Out Island Inn, Georgetown, Great Exumas – 1971-1973
- The Moorings and Conch Inn, Abacos – 2004-2008 (Conch Inn 2007)

BERMUDA
- Newstead, Paget Parish – 1971
- Glencoe, Paget Parish – 1981-1982

BRITISH VIRGIN ISLANDS
- Treasure Isle Hotel, Road Town, Tortola – 1974-1996
- Prospect Reef Resort, Road Town, Tortola – 1997-2004
- Mariner Inn, Wickham's Cay, Road Town, Tortola – 2006-2013
- Fort Burt, Road Town, Tortola - 2008
- The Moorings on Wickhams Cay, Road Town, Tortola – 1988-present
- Scrub Island Resort, Scrub Island – 2014-present

CARIBBEAN
- Canouan and the Grenadines – 2007 (cruising only, no Learn to Sail)

CONNECTICUT
- Greenwich Harbor Inn, Greenwich – 1994-1995
- Whaler's Inn, Mystic – 1998
- Brewer's Yacht Haven Marina, Stamford – 1996-2004

FLORIDA
- Sheraton Four Ambassadors, Miami – 1971-1972
- South Seas Plantation, Captiva Island – 1975-present (changed name to South Seas Resort 2002, then South Seas Island Resort 2005)
- Sarasota Hyatt, Sarasota – 1977-1978
- Marriott's Bay Point Resort, Panama City – 1986-1987
- Bayfront Hilton, St. Petersburg – 1996-1998
- Harborage Marina, St. Petersburg – 1994-1995
- Hawk's Cay Resort, Duck Key, Florida Keys – 1999-2009
- Mansion House B&B, St. Petersburg – 1999-2009
- Whitney Marine, Jacksonville – 2002-2004
- Pink Shell Beach Resort & Marina, Ft. Myers Beach – 2005-present
- Downtown Hampton Inn & Suites, St. Petersburg – 2011-present
- Westin Cape Coral at Marina Village, Cape Coral – 2018-present

ILLINOIS
- Chicago's Westrec Marina, Jackson Park Harbor, Chicago – 1996-2004

MAINE
- Atlantic Oakes-by-the-Sea, Bar Harbor – 1981-1986

MARYLAND
- Great Oak, Chestertown – 1978-1979
- Inn at Perry Cabin, St. Michaels – 2007-2013

MASSACHUSETTS
- Harborside Inn, Edgartown, Martha's Vineyard – 1970-1974
- Kelly House, Edgartown, Martha's Vineyard – 1975-1975
- Edgartown, Martha's Vineyard (no specific hotels) – 1976-1984
- Wequassett Inn, Cape Cod – 1988-1992

MEXICO
- The Moorings, Baha, Sea of Cortez – 1988-1989 (cruising only, no Learn to Sail)

MICHIGAN
- Grand Traverse Resort Village, Traverse City – 1987

NEW JERSEY
- Colgate Palmolive Exchange Place, Jersey City – 1994
- The Colgate Center, Jersey City – 1995-1996
- Sandy Hook Yacht Sales, Barnegat Bay – 1997-1999
- Liberty Landing Marina, Jersey City – 1997-2016

NEW YORK
- Minneford Yacht Yard, City Island – 1966-1967
- Bob Taylor's Yard, City Island – 1968-1970
- G&G Marina, City Island – 1971-1972
- United Boat Yard, City Island – 1973-1975
- Ratsey & Lapthorn Sailmakers, City Island – 1976-1980
- Offshore Sailing Center (formerly Ratsey & Lapthorn Sailmakers), City Island – 1981-1988
- Wings Point, East Hampton – 1986-1988
- Manhattan Yacht Club, South Street Seaport Museum, New York City – 1988
- Kretzer's Boat Yard, City island – 1989-1993
- Capri Marina and Yachting Center, Port Washington – 1993-1994
- Chelsea Piers, New York City – 2000-2014
- The Sagamore Resort, Bolton's Landing, Lake George – 2005-2006
- New York Maritime College, Ft. Schuyler – 2005-2008
- Pier 25, New York City – 2013- 2014
- North Cove Marina at Brookfield Place, New York City – 2015-2016

PUERTO RICO
- Palmas del Mar, Humacao – 1974-1975

RHODE ISLAND
- Treadway Inn, Newport – 1985-1987
- Admiral Fitzroy Inn, Newport – 1988
- Admiral Farragut Inn, Newport – 1994-2000
- Newport Harbor Hotel, Newport – 2001-2006

SOUTH CAROLINA
- Sea Pines Plantation, Hilton Head Island – 1972-1978
- Palmetto Dunes Resort, Hilton Head Island – 1979

ST. LUCIA
- The Moorings Club Mariner Resort, Marigot Bay – 1989
- Marigot Bay Resort, Marigot Bay – 1990-1996

TAHITI
- The Moorings, Raiatea – 1988-1989 (cruising only, no Learn to Sail)

TEXAS
- April Sound, Lake Conroe – 1975

VIRGINIA
- Tides Inn, Irvington – 1980-1982

WASHINGTON
- Anacortes Yacht Charters, Anacortes – 1994

WISCONSIN
- Leathem Smith Lodge, Sturgeon Bay – 1971-1972

Photo Credits

About the Author

An award-winning sailing journalist, and avid inshore and offshore cruising and racing sailor, Herb McCormick is the former editor-in-chief of *Cruising World* magazine and yachting correspondent for *The New York Times*. He's written five sailing books, including *As Long As It's Fun*, the biography of voyaging icons Lin and Larry Pardey, and *One Island, One Ocean*, a first-person account of the Around the Americas Expedition, a voyage around North and South America via the Northwest Passage and Cape Horn. A graduate of Williams College, where he captained the football team, he lives on the island where he was born and raised, in downtown Newport, Rhode Island.